THE THEATRE AUDITION BOOK 2

Playing monologues from contemporary, modern, period, Shakespearean and classical plays

edited by

GERALD LEE RATLIFF

MERIWETHER PUBLISHING LTD.
Colorado Springs, Colorado

Meriwether Publishing Ltd., Publisher
PO Box 7710
Colorado Springs, CO 80933-7710

www.meriwether.com

Editor: Arthur L. Zapel
Assistant editor: Amy Hammelev
Cover design: Jan Melvin

Library of Congress Cataloging-in-Publication Data

Ratliff, Gerald Lee.
   The theatre audition book 2 : playing monologues from contemporary, modern, period, Shakespearean, and classical plays / edited by Gerald Lee Ratliff. -- 1st ed.
      p. cm.
   ISBN 978-1-56608-165-8
   1. Monologues. 2. Acting--Auditions. 3. Drama. I. Title.
   PN2080.R39 2009
   808.82'45--dc22

                                        2009028883

            1   2   3   09   10   11

CONTENTS

Chapter Three
PLAYING THE CLASSICS 65

Chapter Four
PLAYING SHAKESPEARE 96

Chapter Six
PLAYING THE CONTEMPORARY 164

PREFACE

One of the basic principles at work in this theatre audition handbook is that both beginning and advanced actors need to design their own performance blueprint in order to spotlight individual talents. Although there is considerable discussion in Chapter One and Chapter Two that describes familiar audition expectations and practices, each actor must define an individual approach to a performance style that captures fresh, original character portraits that are honest and true to life. The performance guidelines suggested in the introductory chapters should help refine your individual audition technique and transform abstract stage figures into flesh-and-blood theatrical characters.

Monologues and duologues selected for audition or classroom performance are conveniently grouped in historical periods and include a brief summary of the historical period, basic approaches to analysis and interpretation of scripts, and performance styles. Chapter Three, for example, focuses on playing the "classical" Greek style, Chapter Four on playing Shakespeare, Chapter Five on playing selected theatre "period" styles, and Chapter Six on playing contemporary monologues. These chapters also explore the skills necessary to visualize the dramatic and theatrical elements in an audition monologue. Chapter seven is an introduction to acting in musical theatre and the medium — commercials, industrials, situation comedies, and soap operas — and includes a number of sample scripts and song lyrics for classroom study and performance.

There are a number of vocal and physical exercises included to promote ease of movement and distinctive vocal variety in an audition. The exercises feature sensory, emotional, and relaxation approaches to performance that may provide an attitude, gesture, mannerism, or voice to clearly define the monologue or character in a duologue, included in each chapter. There is minimal descriptive narrative or stage direction to introduce each character, so you will need to read the complete script whenever possible in order to "visualize" how your character will look and sound in an audition, and then be very selective in the integration of personal traits and mannerisms that might enrich your character portrait.

1

Honesty and simplicity are the keys to creative role-playing in an audition. Approach the suggested performance techniques in a manner that is appropriate and comfortable for your individual style of character development and dialogue delivery. Read the complete script when possible before concentrating on each sample monologue and duologue. In order to bring credibility and vitality to an audition, remember to avoid overly precise use of the voice, exaggerated movement, or theatrical posing.

Auditions — theatre, musical theatre, or medium — offer an intimate, fleeting glance at a character in a given moment in time. Focus on that significant moment with a simplicity and subtlety that suggests you are playing the character role for the first time. Concentrate on the "present tense" described in a monologue or duologue as you search for the most appropriate gesture, movement, and voice that will clearly visualize the character event or incident taking place during an audition performance. It may also be useful to chart a character's vocal and physical change or to integrate appropriate personal traits and mannerisms to reinforce the character portrait being drawn.

The organizing principle of this introduction to the audition process is a challenge for you to always strive to do better. It is not enough to simply prepare for the audition performance — attention must also be paid to an intensive rehearsal period. The rehearsal period is the place for you to constantly refresh skills in character development, line reading, and interpretation. The rehearsal period is also the time to tune voice, body, and mind to meet the expectations of any audition. Set aside a regular schedule of rehearsal to practice and polish the techniques explored in this theatre audition handbook and there will be a marked improvement in the poise and self-confidence needed to engage in competitive auditions.

Gerald Lee Ratliff
June 2009

CHAPTER ONE
AUDITION PREVIEW

"If you look for the truth outside yourself,
it gets farther and farther away."

— Tung-Shan, *Dialogues*

We have all been role-playing, more or less instinctively, from early childhood. Our youthful games of "let's pretend" and "make believe" are the basic ingredients we now need to recall in an audition. It is these imaginative stories, inspired deceptions, and intrigues — some of which continue far beyond childhood years — that have instilled in us a significant measure of persuasion in role-playing. It is these early role-playing games, however, that also help sustain believable character actions in an audition.

Think of an audition as a playdate between character (actor) and spectator (audience). Stage characters, of course, do not leap full-blown from the printed pages of a script. They emerge slowly, in subtle and frequently disguised clues that point the way to creative role-playing opportunities for the actor, if the actor can recognize the clues. That is why it is important in an audition to search for an honest and truthful character portrait using your own personal experiences, rather than looking "outside" yourself to fill in an author's tentative character sketch.

Audition expectations for theatre, musicals, commercials, or soap operas share a number of similar characteristics, although each may have different terms or techniques to describe the process. See Chapter Seven: Playing the Musical and the Medium for audition strategies appropriate to those genres. In a theatre audition, you will be asked to create a three-dimensional character portrait in a limited amount of time. The vocal and physical choices you make will suggest not only your potential acting skills, but also your stage personality. Some of the criteria used to evaluate your performance might include the following standards:

3

- Physical Appearance: Posture, height, weight, stage presence, movement. Does the actor "look the part," and make physical choices in gesture or movement that suggest the character?
- Vocal Expression: Diction, pitch, rate, projection, volume, vocal variety. Does the actor "voice the role" with clarity, exhibit standard American speech free from regional dialects, and deliver a nuanced vocal interpretation that defines the character?
- Concentration and Focus: Poised, intelligent, confident, flexible. Does the actor "relate to the role," and appear connected with the character's action, attitude, or mood?
- Performance Potential: Creative spirit, passion, risk taking, believable. Does the actor "understand the script" in terms of a character's spoken text or unspoken subtext, and effectively demonstrate an ability to engage or entertain an audience?

Don't be afraid to follow your basic childhood instincts in an audition, but make adult performance choices that highlight mature vocal and physical strengths. The choices you make should reflect your age, emotional range, and acting technique. The challenge is to cultivate a well-rounded performance that has simplicity as well as sincerity and is truly self-expressive.

THEATRE AUDITION PREVIEW

Preparing for a theatre audition involves more than selecting a random monologue and memorizing the character's dialogue. It is just as important to be aware of audition practices and be prepared for any unanticipated requests made by the director. There are as many approaches to conducting an audition as there are theatre directors, so you need to know in advance what kind of audition is being scheduled. Some directors use a *cold reading,* where the actor is given a prepared or set speech of a character and asked to perform the excerpt with little time for preparation. The cold reading gives the director an initial impression of an actor's skill in interpreting dialogue and suggesting vocal or physical characterization.

Other directors prefer the *prepared reading,* where an actor memorizes and then performs two brief, contrasting monologues from classical Greek, Shakespeare, period, or contemporary scripts. The prepared reading helps a director identify the level of potential talent available for possible callbacks and evaluate each actor's ability to distinguish different character attitudes or moods. Still other directors like auditions that are *open* to all interested actors or *closed* and only those who have been invited may attend.

A *general* audition, however, is the most common type and is used primarily to "screen" actors for more intensive review at a later, callback audition. Each type of audition may also include *improvisation* — a brief sequence of impromptu exercises or theatre games — or a *directed reading,* where the director gives actors specific instructions in vocal interpretation or physical movement before asking them to perform a prepared character speech. Improvisation exercises and directed readings are crucial elements in an audition. They allow the director to evaluate an actor's spontaneity, flexibility, and capability to follow direction — so be prepared for the unexpected!

Before proceeding immediately to a detailed discussion of what is involved in an audition, it is necessary to point out some basic assumptions you should consider as part of the "pre-audition" process. Much of the anxiety that accompanies auditions may be relieved if you follow the *3-P* approach in pre-audition preparation: purpose, passion, and product.

Purpose

The choice of monologues should exhibit an emotional or intellectual range that is compatible with your life experiences. Select characters whose emotional depth or intellectual curiosity you can immediately define and understand. Honest and simple — rather than slick and polished — are basic ingredients for all auditions. Approach the audition in a calm, relaxed manner. Strive to live moment-to-moment in your character's brief audition life. Explore monologue characters that exhibit variety in their emotions and overcome significant obstacles in their struggle.

Always read monologues *aloud* before making character choices. Do you *hear* the character's intellectual conflict, or is it just polite conversation? Do you *see* the character's physical struggle, or is it simply resignation to what has already happened? Do you *feel* the character's emotional anguish, or is it merely sympathetic identification with the circumstances? Do you *sense* the character's climactic resolution of conflict, or is there a noticeable change in attitude and mood?

5

A successful audition is more than just an exhibition in acting technique. There is an expectation that the actor has made a careful analysis of the script to discover potential performance clues — vocal and physical — needed to sketch a believable character portrait. It is also an expectation that an actor has read the entire script and that a specific monologue was selected because it promotes vocal variety, ease of movement, and emotional or intellectual honesty in the performance.

Passion

The choice of monologue characters should be made with a burning desire that excites you to want to perform and share your character portraits at an audition. Always play your characters as *I* and act in the *present tense* so actions and attitudes are fresh and spontaneous. It is important to be concise in both vocal delivery and physical movement to highlight, or give additional meaning, to a monologue character's intention or motivation.

It may be helpful to define a character's intention or motivation with active verbs that give vocal color and meaning to the dialogue. Choosing active verbs to define characters should help you visualize the conflict described in the monologue. Active verbs, of course, only surface after a detailed analysis of the character's attitude, mood, and word choice in the complete script. Examples of some active verbs to describe a character's intention or motivation might include: to seduce, to expose, to ridicule, to revenge, or to humiliate.

It is also a good performance idea to explore a character's *moment before* the monologue begins. The moment before is that recent emotional, physical, or verbal incident that propels the character — and you! — into the monologue. Being able to clearly identify an inciting incident should provide abundant clues to explore as you first react and then respond to the character's emotional or intellectual state described in the monologue.

Product

The final product of any audition is a well-crafted performance. You will need to give your performance an original flavor and a fresh character interpretation. Make it a daily routine to gain a wide range of experiences and examples — people, places, and things — from which to draw more complex character portraits. Jot down distinctive vocal and physical traits you observe in others as part of a *memory book*. Later, draw upon these critical observations to portray authentic character actions, postures, walks, or vocal patterns. These portraits, based on personal observation, should suggest a marked degree of believability when you later assume the role of fictitious monologue characters.

There are also opportunities to select personal traits such as comic flair, unique skills — a cappella singing, juggling, pantomime, rap, fencing, magic tricks — or styles of movement — jazz, hip-hop, tap — to give added dimension to monologue characters. The role of personal traits, however, should only become part of an audition if they complement your character portrait. To do that, they must be restrained and subtle traits that help you *complete* the character portrait. Personal traits should not distract or give any impression that you are displaying vocal gymnastics, stylized movements, or theatrical poses.

PREVIEW PRINCIPLES

The first step to take in a preview of potential audition monologues is to read and analyze the script. If you hope to create a believable character portrait, it is crucial that you know and understand a character's changing attitude and mood in the complete storyline rather than in just an independent monologue. Unless you become familiar with the complex incidents or issues that motivate a character's *action,* your audition interpretation and performance may fall flat because it lacks sustained continuity and depth.

When you read a script, paying special attention to what a character *says* and *does,* a fictional life history should emerge. This background information informs you *why* a character behaves or speaks in a certain manner. In some scripts, however, the author may include only a few brief phrases or key words to describe a character. The dramatic visualization of a theatre script then, like the musical interpretation of a printed score, depends on an actor's ability to imagine a performance based solely upon a character's words and actions.

Reading the complete script as a prelude to understanding the character's role in a monologue is one of the root ideas of script interpretation. Script interpretation is part of the literary criticism tradition and includes an analysis of the author's writing style, structure, language, and theme. These are the critical textual elements that provide invaluable insight and help an actor translate a character's behavior, habits, speech patterns, or even storyline events into concrete actions that inform performance possibilities.

Five Ws

In some ways, script interpretation is similar to the journalist's use of the 5 Ws to frame a news story. Like the inquiring journalist, the actor should ask — and be able to answer — the following questions about a character: *Who* am I? *What* am I doing? *Where* am I doing this? *When* am I doing this? *Why* am I doing this? Once these preliminary questions are answered, an actor can begin to make more informed character choices and determine the potential role that voice, body, and movement will play in an interpretation of the character.

In an audition, however, there is limited time to create a character, so you may need to be the character on the first line of dialogue in your monologue! If you have carefully examined the circumstances and identified all the relevant facts that help define a three-dimensional character — including statements made about the character by others — your audition performance should be marked by a degree of honesty and truthfulness that has been refined by a critical examination of the script.

SCRIPT ANALYSIS

Here is a brief summary of key principles to consider in reading a script for meaning. This brief summary should alert you to what to look for in searching for well-defined monologue characters that inhabit a specific place, exist in a certain time, and respond in explicit theatrical action. Reading a script for meaning should also enhance your performance choices as well.

Introduction or Preface

Familiarize yourself with any critical commentary that precedes the printed script. Of particular interest should be a discussion of the author's dramatic techniques, character hints, and any autobiographical or historical references identified in the script by the author. Use this information to create an imaginary biography of your character that answers some of the following questions: How old is the character? What does the character look like? What does the character sound like? How does the character dress? How does the character move? What peculiar behaviors or habits does the character exhibit?

Script Title

A title may suggest the author's point of view or indicate the theme of a script. Sometimes a title may foreshadow the obstacles characters may struggle with in the script. August Wilson's *Fences,* for example, suggests an image of barriers or restricted spaces that will have to be overcome by the characters in the script. Eugene O'Neill's *Desire Under the Elms,* on the other hand, suggests an image of craving or lust that will have to be satisfied by the characters in the script.

Character Names

Specific names may indicate a character's attitude and mood or reveal a special role they play in the script. The name Willy Loman, *low man,* in Arthur Miller's *Death of a Salesman* aptly describes the frustration and thwarted dreams that eventually culminate in the title character's apparent suicide. Arnold Powell's use of symbolic names like Everymom, Alldad, and Baby in *The Death of Everymom* may suggest that the author selected these specific names to indicate a searing parable or allegory related to the impending demise of a family unit.

Character Description

The author's description of a character — in either narrative, parenthetical remarks, or stage directions — may help you sketch an audition blueprint that reveals the consequences of certain character's actions or decisions. For example, Tom in Tennessee Williams' *The Glass Menagerie* is referred to as a loner and a dreamer. You should not be surprised to learn, then, that Tom's purpose in leaving home at the end of the script is to join the merchant marine and journey to all the exotic places he has visited in his dreams.

Character Actions

If you chart character actions from first entrance to final exit, you will be able to identify that character's changing attitude or mood in each scene of the script. For example, Nora's first entrance in Henrik

Ibsen's *A Doll's House* introduces her as a timid, bird-like creature incapable of forceful movement. Later in the script, however, Nora assumes a more assertive self-identity and her actions become more aggressive until she finally exits the stage in a flourish, abandoning both her husband and children to seek her own destiny in the world.

Character Imagery

The author's use of imagery — metaphors and similes in particular — to define a character provides an added dimension of insight to pursue in an audition. A vivid example of character imagery is Tennessee Williams' description of Blanche DuBois in *A Streetcar Named Desire* as a genteel, Southern lady who is like "a gentle soul burning with passion for a lost love." Similarly, Paula Vogel's image of Myrna, the "good" twin in *The Mineola Twins,* who "danced and danced a happy ending" after her prodigal twin sister died suggests a celebratory ending to the strained relationship of two sisters.

Character Moments

Reading for meaning should also isolate significant character moments that are revealed in individual scenes of a script. Identifying the ebb and flow of dramatic moments in character conflicts, circumstances, or situations should help your performance build to a more memorable climax in the audition. Always be precise, however, in defining individual moments with direct, simple vocal delivery and physical movement to emphasize character words and actions.

The Times

In some instances, it may be helpful to briefly research the life and historical times of an author. An understanding of Eugene O'Neill's treatment of family would be significantly more perceptive with prior knowledge of his hostile and combative relationship with a domineering father, alcoholic brother, and morphine-addicted mother. Similarly, prior knowledge of the political and social views of authors Bertolt Brecht, Anna Deavere Smith, Athol Fugard, David Mamet, or Ntozake Shange would be invaluable in understanding their fiercely independent and rebellious character portraits.

ADDITIONAL DIMENSIONS

Read a script as you might read a novel or short story by sorting out the characters and the storyline. Chart the build to the climax and focus on character relationships caught up in the action. Pay particular attention to a description of the setting and any suggestion of potential wardrobe pieces or hand props that might later give additional meaning to your character in an audition.

Always reread the script a second or third time, looking for nuances of meaning that may have surfaced since your initial analysis of the character. Rethink and reconsider your interpretation if there are noticeable changes in the character's circumstances that may need to be addressed in a refined interpretation. When you have a concise character portrait firmly in mind, it will be time to amplify your interpretation in the rehearsal period, described later in this chapter.

Understanding the basic principles of script interpretation will give you the analytical skills necessary to read individual monologues with a discerning eye. Being able to capture and then catalog a flurry of vivid images should also provide the imagination needed to portray memorable character moments in an audition. The more knowledge you have about a script, the more likely an informed interpretation and inspired three-dimensional character portrait will emerge in an audition.

CAUTION

As you gain more experience in reading a script for meaning through repeated practice, your interpretation skills will gain a measure of maturity. Similarly, as your ability to respond to character clues — inherent or implied in a script — increases, your audition skills will gain a measure of spontaneity. There are, however, initial roadblocks to anticipate on your audition journey. Here are some caution signs to avoid unnecessary missteps along the way.

Identify only those potential monologue characters that represent your age range — usually within six to eight years of your own age — and physical type. Avoid monologues you may have performed in recent stage productions, unless you are prepared to offer a fresh interpretation of the roles. Satisfy the specific requirements that are advertised in the audition call notice, especially the number of monologues to perform and the stated time requirement.

Select monologues that engage you on an emotional or intellectual level, but avoid those monologues that use crude or sexually explicit language. An actor who curses, screams, and yells during an audition is not a welcome sight! As a general rule of thumb, avoid monologues filled with excessive past tense narration or background exposition. Simply telling a story without specific character actions to suggest a build to a climax is essentially an exercise in reading aloud or oral interpretation of literature.

Finally, avoid stand-up comedy routines and film or television materials, particularly those that call for an accent or dialect. Familiar comedy skits and current film or television scripts are usually identified with a popular actor or comedian, and you may be viewed as a mimic when compared to the original. These popular culture snapshots rarely meet standard audition expectations for a monologue that captures a character's desire and passion to overcome an obstacle or resolve a conflict.

REHEARSAL PERIOD

The rehearsal period is like an experimental laboratory and should stimulate you to explore new performance insights. It is a risk-free opportunity to rethink your interpretation, refresh the character portrait, and refine any action described in the monologue. It is also a time to fill in those blank spaces that may have been left unanswered in the complete script, especially any unresolved questions about character intention or motivation.

Although the rehearsal period is primarily focused on fine-tuning a character's habits, mannerisms, gestures, movements, and vocal qualities, it is also a time to discard inhibitions. Some actors use rehearsal to search for a creative *metaphor* — an implied comparison between the character and something inventive — that might give added luster to the character portrait. Other actors use rehearsal time to engage in *word play* with images, phrases, or individual lines of dialogue to orally punctuate a character's spoken language. A few actors use the rehearsal to *visualize* action in the script, and then translate that action into character behaviors or movement patterns.

One of the fundamental principles of the rehearsal period is *marking* your monologues. The first marking should chart character intention or motivation suggested in an analysis of the script. You may also wish to mark the rhythm or tempo of character action to chart the apparent build to a climax in a monologue. The second marking should chart vocal and physical responses of the character. For example, you may choose to underline in different colors operative words or phrases that indicate subtle word play or potential character gesture and movement.

The first two markings should be used exclusively in the rehearsal period. However, if subsequent rehearsals reveal new character insights, don't hesitate to revise or adjust your initial markings. At the conclusion of the rehearsal period, you should have in hand a final blueprint for voice and body to polish the audition performance. Regardless of the approach you take in the rehearsal period, use the time wisely and don't forget to include vocal and physical exercises.

A regular routine that tunes the voice and tones the body should also help you combat the initial anxiety associated with an audition. A consistent schedule of exercise is essential to condition the voice and body to respond to the vocal or physical demands of an audition, but should help you discover expressive vocal qualities and movement styles that give vitality to character portraits.

Here is a brief checklist of familiar techniques a number of actors rely on to uncover additional layers of character meaning in rehearsal. See if you can apply the terms listed below to an interpretation of the monologue models that are included at the end of this chapter. Later, of course, you may discover that all of the terms are appropriate to explore in the rehearsal period as you begin to define a character's *inner and outer* action and reaction.

- Objective Memory: Stanislavski's technique that asks an actor to recall the stimuli present during a past emotional incident, and then to *re-experience* the stimuli in an interpretation of a similar experience described in a script.
- Beats: Break down a script into a series of character intentions called *beats*. A beat begins when a character's intention begins and ends with its completion.
- Inner Monologue: What the actor is thinking as the character is speaking. The inner monologue is similar to *subtext*, the hidden meaning of a character's language.

• Transfer: The actor uses a specific reference person from a recent life experience and projects that person's personality onto the character described in a script.

FINAL WORDS

There is no simple formula to predict the degree of success an actor will achieve in an audition. Long before actual auditions are posted for a call, the theatre director may have already begun to imagine the production and to *see* and *hear* the characters in the script. It is only when an actor, with an indescribable aura and a life spirit, performs a monologue with an honest and natural flavor that a director suddenly awakens and begins to consider alternatives for an imagined *dream cast*.

As you begin to review the following models, look for *me* monologues that speak directly to your own dreams, fears, or simple pleasures. Visualize how these fictitious characters look, feel, speak, and move. Finally, if you are to capture the heart and soul of the monologue characters, you must first form a bond of mutual compassion and understanding that speaks to similar experiences or circumstances in your own life.

MONOLOGUE MODELS

These models are original monologues, not excerpts from full-length scripts, written to initially challenge you in script interpretation and classroom performance. They should serve as excellent models for study as you start to design your own audition blueprint. Begin with a close reading of each monologue to identify those that best suit your age range, vocal quality, and physical type. Then determine which monologues express your own views on the issues or themes being addressed.

Following preliminary choices, give some thought to what you have learned in this chapter and from a discussion of the audition preview and reading a script for meaning. Apply as many of the basic principles you have learned to an interpretation and classroom performance of the monologues you have selected. Although analysis of original monologues may at first glance appear to limit character choices and analysis skills, it is still an excellent model to learn

14

firsthand how to isolate and identify potential performance clues for an audition. The lessons learned in this introductory exercise will be useful tools to polish and sharpen your understanding of reading for meaning as we explore the audition process in more detail in Chapter Two.

The Piano Tuner
by Dwight Watson

Tony, a young man in his early twenties, makes his way cautiously to the edge of the stage with toolbox in hand. He has just finished his job tuning the piano, but is reluctant to leave the empty theatre. His recently deceased sister, Theresa, was an actress and Tony's presence in the theatre makes him feel close to her. In this conversation with the technical director, Tony finds an opportunity to share his sister's memory and the respect he continues to have for her art.

TONY: *(Directing his voice to the top of the theatre.)* The piano is tuned. Hey, did ya hear me? I tuned that piano. It's ready. *(He listens.)* Anyone out there? Hey, can you hear me? Umm, Newt, you up there on the catwalk? You up there? *(Squinting to see beyond the stage lights.)* Yeah, you're there, ain't ya? I can hardly see ya under these stage lights. They're too bright. Wave your hand or something. What've you got in your mouth? Is that a rope? A cable? Or what? You focusing lights? *(Nodding.)* For the auditions this afternoon? *(Shaking his head.)*

I could never perform up here, Newt. On the stage. Under these lights. Under these conditions. *(Placing his toolbox on the stage.)* I don't know how they do it. I mean, it makes me nervous just standing here talking to you. I could never audition for people. Honest to God, it makes my stomach bounce just saying the word "audition." But my sister, Theresa, she was a triple threat … though … I mean she could sing, dance, act … she did it all. Honest to God. I don't know why some Broadway agent didn't scoop her up. I mean, she was an artist … a real triple threat. *(Changing the subject.)*

Okay, the piano is ready, Newt. If they move it too much, I should have to tune it again. And I … ahh … located the reason for that vibration. We call it ... ahh ... "sympathetic rattle" in the tuning profession. She ain't cracked, thank God, or split, or anything like that. It was a piece ... of ... candy ... or a wad of bubble gum ... under the soundboard. Can you believe that, Newt? *(Reaching into his toolbox.)* And I got the candy out with this piece of hickory stick. Honest to God, I don't understand why anyone would treat a work of art ... this instrument of the gods ... like that ... by throwing a wad of disgusting gum garbage in it! *(With growing irritation.)* To me, it's like someone defacing the face of Mona Lisa or carving his initials in the Vietnam Veterans Memorial. They don't deserve to touch it or even be near it. What is it with these people? Don't they know, Newt, that art is rare ... like the best of our dreams ... Newt, like my sister, Theresa, the triple threat, who would have loved to audition here ... but ... is ... no longer. Honest to God, Newt, if we are ever to know heaven here on earth, we must take care of the artist and ... and ... her instrument. *(He pauses.)*

I'm sorry, Newt. I didn't mean to preach to you. I know it's not your fault. I ... ahh ... guess ... I'm feeling a little ... ahh ... I don't know ... emotional ... today. On this stage. *(Nodding his head.)* Well, yeah, I guess auditions start soon ... uh ... so ... ahh ... you light them well, Newt. You make their faces shine bright. And I hope all these kids auditioning here this afternoon find work. I hope they all get to sing and act and dance. And I'd consider it a privilege to tune their pianos on Broadway ... some day ... or even next door at the little theatre. *(Collecting his tools.)*

So, anyway, you tell 'em that that piano has great action, she's in first-class condition. I've ... ahh ... set the temperament ... and ... ahh ... if they treat her well, she will play. And ... about ... my sister, Theresa. I hope ... I just hope, Newt, that some of those characters ... you know ... from *Cats, Rent, Little Shop of Horrors, Jesus Christ Superstar,* and all those Rodgers and Hammerstein musicals ... well ... I just hope they are in heaven. Otherwise, honest to God, my sister, Theresa, is not very happy. *(He starts to leave.)* Oh, yeah, I left the bill on the piano. They need to pay it in ten days.

Burying Mom
by Matthew Fotis

Paul, a compassionate young man, recalls buying a funeral casket for his mother, who died on September 11, and the grief counseling that has followed. The unusual circumstances of his mother's death are like a time bomb ticking in the back of his head, and a sudden explosion might expose the veiled secret that he has been complicit in mingling his mother's accidental death on September 11 with the horrific national tragedy that occurred on the same day.

PAUL: Anyway, it's like, okay, she died six years ago — On 9/11. Yeah, no, she fell down the stairs. Talk about a tough break. I mean, oh, hey, three thousand people just died and my mother fell down the basement stairs. That's the thing. It isn't a tragedy. I feel like this total jerk, because I'm like trying to mourn my mom, but I feel bad about it.

Right after it happened I started going to grief counseling. I don't know why I didn't put two and two together. At the first meeting we all went around the room to tell our stories. The first woman to speak was this twenty-five year old widow. *Twenty-five.* Her husband had been called out to Boston on some last minute business — did I mention that they were on their honeymoon? — and he was flying back home, on United Flight 93. The next guy tells this story about his wife who worked in the north tower on one of the top floors — she's trapped in the building. She calls him to say goodbye but he doesn't pick up, he's too afraid to answer the phone; he just sits there with the phone in his hand staring at her number, just fixated on the number, totally frozen in time. He never picks up. And now all he has is a voice mail. It haunts him. Devastates him. He'll never escape it. This goes on for two hours, story after story. The whole room is in tears. I'm getting into it — everyone is hugging everyone, you can feel the communal grief; but you can also feel this underlying surge of hope and power and community. It's this totally beautiful moment.

And then it's my turn. I have to tell these people that my mother fell down the stairs. Oh, your husband was on Flight 93, your brother was in the Twin Towers, well my mom fell down the basement stairs getting some extra canned peas. I was this close to making up some tragic 9/11 story, like, oh I mean my mom fell down the stairs at the Pentagon saving babies, but I don't even know if the Pentagon has stairs let alone babies. I'm sitting in this room filled with people whose lives have been irrevocably altered and I'm trying to figure out a way to make my story more tragic? Is that wrong? I just want it to be done.

Numbers
by Mary E. Weems

In this intriguing tale, 4413, a "dead soul" held hostage to the anguish and bitter memories of early, troubled years, slowly enters with a sense of urgency holding a bouquet of white roses. She moves center stage to stand in front of a barren gravesite, and then slowly turns to face the audience to recall the crushing intrusion of her sudden death. It is a tale that will not let you escape the pulverizing truth of vanishing souls unable to free themselves from the purifying fires of eternal guilt and retribution.

4413: At first I cried buckets — Mama put me here — everything in my mind coming out in sharp knives, sucker punches to her face, her hate-words not helping, the oatmeal in the attic always cold, lumpy. *(Pause)* No visitors for weeks at a time. She told everyone I was dead long before I was — kept me hidden like a locked diary. *(Pause)* Spit on me for being alive — fed me enough to keep me from going to Hell — she was a true believer in Christ — used to make me carry a heavy cross up and down the attic stairs until my hands bled, my feet had blisters. *(Pause)* One night when I was about I don't know how old — old enough to figure how to push the skeleton key out of the lock — I got to her room *(Pause)* where she was sleeping — set her bed on fire. *(Pause)* She didn't die. Brought me here after that — never came to visit.

I never knew my name. People here called me 4413 — all the others had numbers too — I memorized the names of the nurses that kept us — the doctors — the people who came to clean the place where we slept like dead on the medicine that kept us from losing anything else, that kept us from dreaming. *(Pause)* D-I-E the first word I learned to spell because every few days someone did. *(Pause)* I didn't stay here long. A rope left outside the bathroom — long enough to make a knot let me out of this place. *(Pause)* They buried me with my mouth open — a scream in my throat caught when I dropped from the ceiling calling out God — asking Him for my name.

(Character walks back to her grave, kneels to brush away the dust with one hand, then carefully places the roses on it with the other. She exits humming "Amazing Grace.")

Sally Does Stand-Up
by Shirley King

Sally, a chic woman whose meteoric political ascent has inadvertently raised conservative eyebrows — as well as gales of unintentional laughter — is accepting her party's nomination for president of … "whatever." Sally's acceptance speech is a wild, thrilling ride across the political landscape, laced with a whimsical glimpse of what the future may hold. Any resemblance to current politicians is purely intentional!

SALLY: *(Drum roll as Sally enters.)* Greetings, Mr. Chairman, delegates, and fellow citizens. I am honored to be considered for the nomination of … whatever. I've got a lovely room and bath in the hotel here. My room is so small, the mice are hunchbacked. Bah-dah-boom. If you didn't get that one, don't worry. I've got more. My room is so small when I put the key in, I broke the window! But seriously, folks —
   Gettin' on a plane, I told the ticket agent, "Send one of my bags to Minnesota, one to Los Angeles and one to Miami." She said, "We can't do that!" I told her, "You did it last week!" No, seriously. I accept the challenge of a tough fight in this election against inexperienced opponents. Like, c'mon, senators? Hello!
   A writer observed: "We grow good people in our small towns, with honesty, sincerity, and dignity." Well, I grew up with those people there in those towns. They did some of the hardest work in America before their jobs got outsourced because that's how capitalism works best in this great country so let's hear a shout-out for those fine folks.

Ladies and gentlemen, we need to help our homeless become self-sufficient. Reminds me of a story. Homeless guy comes up, asks for ten dollars till payday. "When's payday?" I ask. He goes, "I don't know, you're the one who's workin'!" Homeless guy says he hasn't eaten in two days. I go, "You should force yourself!" One more? Don't stop me now, I'm on a roll. Homeless guy tells me he hasn't tasted food all week. "Don't worry," I tell him, "it still tastes the same!" Bah-dah-boom!

Speakin' of our young — and we were, weren't we? I was just your average hockey mom signin' up for the PTA cuz I wanted better education for our young. I told those teachers, you make my kids learn or I'll be over there gettin' in your face big time. And that's exactly what I'll do there when it comes to callin' out terrorists, you betcha.

When a hurricane strikes the Gulf of Mexico, this country should not be so dependent on imported oil that we are forced to draw from our Strategic Petroleum Reserve ... whatever that might be. No, what we need to do is Drill, Baby, Drill! Drill in all the forty-eight till we get gushers spoutin' all over this great land — what? It's fifty? Fifty states? Well, yes, if you want to count Hawaii. Alaska? Oh, right. We do need to count Alaska.

In conclusion, a vote for me is a vote for ... whatever. Thank you all and may God bless America!

Don't Walk in My Head
With Your Dirty Feet
by Mary Depner

Here is a thoughtful portrait that raises issues very much of the moment. The nameless character appears to know that proverbs often speak truths of the common place, and resonate with a sense of the unspoken word. Drawn from Native American lore, this proverb puts forth simple values and virtues with such warmth and wisdom that it also becomes a moral lesson as well.

YOUNG GIRL: There's an old Native American proverb that goes, "Don't walk in my head with your dirty feet."
Do you know what that means?

I didn't think so.
You see, what it means is, don't go trying to put your
negative or hateful thoughts in my mind.
I like to keep my mind focused on the positive.
I like to stay upbeat.
And I'm getting a little tired of having to constantly tune out
your negativity.
I'm usually able to tune it out, but I have to admit, lately,
you're really starting to get to me.
Believe me, if I wanted to sit around and whine, I could
probably think of a million things to complain about.
But I choose not to.
And I don't need to start every day hearing you whine and
complain.
It's starting to rub off.
And what starts out to be a good day, suddenly turns sour.
So, please, please, please, either wash your feet, or don't
walk in my head!!

Freedom High
by Adam Kraar

*Henry, an independent and industrious African-American veteran
of the 1960's Civil Rights Movement, has been training white student
volunteers on a college campus in Ohio to travel to Mississippi and
help African-Americans register to vote. In this speech, Henry recounts
a disturbing incident to Jessica, a white student volunteer from
Maryland with whom he has become involved.*

HENRY: You don't! Just shut up. You don't understand … See …
before they got to my brother, they had me. I was canvassing some
farmers outside town, and took a shortcut through the woods. Suddenly
I was surrounded by the … reddest of rednecks I ever seen. They were
pink with anger, 'cause they heard some Freedom Riders were talkin'
to their colored folk. Five of 'em, with bicycle chains and a big pipe.
One of 'em had this big wad of pink bubble gum he kept poppin'.
(Pause.)

21

So you know what I did, Jessica? I pretended like I was somebody's cousin, like I was just some sharecropper, payin' a visit from the next county. Started sayin' all this bull jive like … "No, suh, I, I, I don't want to get involved in no politics. My family's a good family, we works for Mr. Reed over in Florence. Mr. Reed good to us, we never want no trouble, no suh!" I'm bowin' and movin' my head around like a wooden puppet, and cryin' … *(Pause.)*

I'd been beaten before, shot at, jailed in the night. But somethin' happened that day … Suddenly, didn't wanna die, not like that. They bought my story, and let me go, with just a kick to my pants. But later, those crackers find out who I really am, and come after me. They come to Mabley, and grab my brother off the street. Friend of the family saw it. "We know who you are, boy. You takin' a ride with us." Thought he was me!

Sticker Shock
by Chris Shaw Swanson

Jenna, an inspiring substitute teacher at the dreary inner-city Hawthorne Elementary, wages a courageous battle each day to provide her special needs students a quality education. She is an inexhaustible source of encouragement and energy to the students drawn into her celestial orbit. In this plaintive monologue, Jenna shares one of her classroom lesson plans with us and we learn a great deal more about the rich texture of her life's mission.

JENNA: It's a long day, when I substitute at Hawthorne Elementary. It takes a good half hour or more to get the kids on their twenty buses at 3:30 p.m. None of the Hawthorne students live within walking distance of the school — which is surrounded by shoddy abandoned commercial buildings — so I have to wait for each bus to arrive and each child of mine to depart. Then I return to the classroom and write up my substitute teaching report, easy but often time-consuming due to the many special needs kids at Hawthorne, after which there's that forty minute guilt-ridden commute back up here, to my cushy suburban home, imagining as I drive my little darlin's-for-a-day crammed into generic ghetto apartments — shadowy places where gangs rule and illegal immigrants hide and where homework and dreams are all too often ... lost in the rubble. The truth is, I could substitute up here in the suburbs. I'd be guilt-free and home in no time flat. But given the choice ... I did sub around the corner once — at ever-so-elite Mark Twain Elementary. Kindergarten. Like always, I brought with me my shiny *good job* book. *(Shows book.)* I told the kids if they behaved, they'd be invited to sign their names in this book at the end of the day and pick out one of these fabulous stickers. *(Shows sticker bag.)* A red-freckled boy blurted out, "I hate stickers." Then this rather pouty blond, all aglow dressed in pink right down to her diamond-studded princess tennis shoes said, "Our real teacher gives us real candy not lame stickers." Of course that prompted Huck Finn's evil twin to pipe in, "Is that the best you can give us? Don't you have something better?"

I subbed for a Hawthorne Kindergarten teacher one day last week. I went through the same drill, explaining how my shiny *good job* book works and flaunting my lame bag of stickers. It was a lousy day, cold and rainy. When it was time to get ready to leave, I lined the kids up single file and one by one, helped them button and zip their jackets. When I reached the end of the line, I stepped back and discovered that every single child had undone what I had just done. I didn't understand it because these kids had worked darn hard for me all day, each earning the singular honor of signing the book. "Why did you undo your jackets?" I asked, beginning once again to go down the line and fasten them up. Gently, so gently, this tiny speck of a Mexican girl touched my hand and said, "No. I want to see my *good job* sticker on the bus home. Por favor?" Maria, like all of her classmates, had put the sticker on her faded shirt. And Maria, like all of her classmates, wanted it to show.

I do not delude myself into thinking that as a substitute, I can make a significant difference in these kids' lives. But maybe, just maybe I can make a difference in their day. "Is that the best you can give us? Don't you have something better?" The kids at Hawthorne Elementary never ask me that, for which I am grateful. And humbled.

Feather

by Claudia Barnett

This dark character portrait stretches the mind with its maze of self-doubt and guilt. It is a perplexing story that explores the parallel life of sisters — one living and the other strangled to death at birth by her twin sister's umbilical cord. Natalie, the survivor, wistfully reflects on her love for, and jealousy of, her twin sister Destiny. We are only left to wonder if Natalie would know any more about herself if she were able to go back in time and deal with her unanswered questions.

NATALIE: My twin sister was Destiny, but my parents were always so mysterious when they mentioned her, I never realized that was her name. I thought it was a euphemism for her condition — which was dead. My first act in this lifetime was murder, my twin sister strangled by my umbilical cord.

My parents named her just in time for the funeral, two days after her death, our birth. They chose the name to comfort themselves, to relieve the burden of responsibility that had descended upon them. Her middle name was Faith. Because I never knew her, I imagined her, and at first she was exactly like me: she looked like me, dressed like me, and like me she hated her hair. I called her by my own name, Natalie.

Later, she was clumsy and ineffectual, scrawny, with stringy hair, and she wore the ugly old clothes from the back of the closet, the ones I couldn't stand. And I blamed her for the things I broke and thought of her as Gnat, spelled with a G. But finally she became a fairy tale princess: the prettiest and the best loved. And I was the ugly stepsister. When my mother looked at me, she saw Destiny. She saw the void where my sister should have been, and she always looked so sad. I wondered if she blamed me, and I knew I was never enough.

I felt guilty for not loving my sister, so I would try to appease her. I'd never wear my prettiest dress because I considered it hers. I saved her the cupcake with the thickest frosting, on a china plate, until it got stale. Then in high school, I stopped thinking about Destiny all the time. I stopped believing in fairy tales.

Until recently. Until around the time I got married. Fairy tales are okay if you're the ugly duckling, but not if you're the ugly stepsister.

Then you don't turn into a swan; you just end up trying to squeeze your foot into a shoe that doesn't fit.

Last Night at the Owl Bar
by Mark Scharf

Jonathan, a straightforward theatre director, is having trouble acting out his own life so he confronts a recent marital mishap in this sunny but somber stand-up comedy routine. There is a surface shimmer to it all, and a shared awareness that life for all its disorder and untidiness is meant to be lived ... for richer or poorer. Jonathan clings to the idea that each of us has a be'shert, that perfect soul mate created by God who could be anywhere on earth and must be found.

JONATHAN: *(Addressing the audience.)* Good evening, Ladies and Gentlemen. Good to see you all. Thanks for coming out tonight. I'm sure some of you guys don't really want to be here. Admit it — you're here because your wives wanted to come. Don't worry about it. There are only two times when a man doesn't understand a woman: Before marriage and after marriage. I mean, nobody has an ideal marriage. Well, maybe Adam and Eve had an ideal marriage. He didn't have to hear about all the men she could have married, and she didn't have to hear about the way his mother cooked. *(Sound of canned applause. Rebecca holds up sign that reads "Not Funny.")*
Yeah — you married people know what I'm talking about. Marriage is a three-ring circus: engagement ring, wedding ring — and suffering. I guess that's why half of all marriages end in divorce. But that's not as bad as it sounds — the other half ends in death. *(Sound of canned applause. Rebecca holds up sign that reads "Still Not Funny.")*
There is only one thing that divorce proves — whose mother was right in the first place. *(Sound of canned applause.)* Now *my* wife wants a divorce for religious reasons: she worships money, and I don't have any! *(Sound of canned applause.)* Thank you! Thank you very much! You've been a wonderful audience. You're beautiful! Every single one of you! Thank you and good night!
(Sound of applause fades away. Small pause, as the spotlight is turned off and the lights rise on stage. The back screen projection is

switched off. Jonathan pulls the lawsuit papers from his pocket.)
  'Guess you thought I'd forgot about these. Hard to forget about being served with your final divorce papers. *(He unfolds and looks.)* Okay! This is the end of the first act. Who knows? Maybe I'll find my be'shert in the second act. You wouldn't want to miss that, would you? *(He exits the stage as lights fade to black.)*

Past Curfew
by Arthur M. Jolly

Kirstie, a crisply funny sixteen-year-old, is on her first date — against her mother's wishes. In her coming of age act of rebellion lurks an undercurrent of strongly held beliefs. Kirstie is both sage and sensitive, and underneath her bubbling banter is an unexpected maturity laced with a dash of realism. Here, she good-naturedly recites her mother's "favorite story," and we are left to wonder if Kirstie is just now beginning to view life as a grown-up.

KIRSTIE: She's there, with her parents, and there's this guy standing next to them, watching the tigers. And the tigers aren't moving. They're like a rug, so this guy takes his cigarette, and he flicks it at them. Lit cigarette, bounces off the Momma tiger — and she like shrugs, gets up and walks away. The cigarette lands in this — like a clump of dried grass, which catches fire. There's a little fire, burning inside the tiger pit. And the baby tiger comes over. And he's never seen fire before. Completely fascinated. He pats at it, and swipes at it. Like a cat playing. Mom says their paws must be real thick, because he keeps batting, and playing with this burning grass. And finally he pounces, and tries to bite the flames. And that's when he gets burned. He leaps straight up in the air, yowling and screaming ... and goes running off to his mother. My Mom loves that story, because he goes running back to his Momma. That's her go-to "I told you so" story ...
  (A beat — a moment of discovery for Kirstie.)
  It's stupid — the whole thing. The tiger should've jumped in the moat. There was water right there. He ran the wrong way. All this time, my Mom missed the whole point of the story. What's your Mom gonna do if you're on fire? Just get in the water.

26

The Birthday Present

by Ginger Rankin

Danny, a likeable young man with depth of feeling, has tender memories of growing up as an only child of a single mom. There is whimsical humor in his recollection of those bygone days and, at times, a longing for those good old times. Here, he is unpacking a suitcase and holds up a framed picture as he reflects on that very special birthday present that changed his life.

DANNY: It's ten years ago now. We're living in an apartment on Fourth Street, Mom and I, near where the bus turns around. I remember one morning so clear. It's my birthday. I am turning fourteen. My mom puts five dollars on the kitchen table before she leaves for work this morning. I'm thinking — it wouldn't kill her to say "Happy Birthday" or "Have a Great Day" or something. But my mom isn't like that. She just puts the five dollars on the table under the salt shaker, like some big wind was going to come in the kitchen and blow it out the window or something.

I know the money's for my birthday so I take it and after school I stop at Wal-Mart and buy some hair dye. Yeah, hair dye. It's supposed to be "Ash Blond" … but something goes wrong. Maybe I leave it on too long. Anyway, there's nothing I can do about it, and so the next day I go to school with orange hair. That's bad. I mean really bad — just what I need. We just moved to Renton the end of September, I hardly know anyone at school, nobody talks to me anyway. So I just get some weird looks. But it's like I can hear what they're *thinking*. Stupid.

When I get home from school there is a can of spaghetti on the table, and a Mars Bar. I throw my junk on the table and eat the Mars Bar. I'll get to the spaghetti later. I watch a little Scooby Doo and some Samurai Jack and fall asleep on the couch. She must have gotten home really late because I wake up in my own bed. I don't know what time it is or how I got there. Anyway I can't sleep so I start staring at that old guitar on the wall. I'd got it for Christmas the year before. She told me it was my dad's … when he was … around. I remember I was pretty excited to have it. And I was determined to learn to play it. But I couldn't figure it out and the strings kept popping and everything. I finally hung it on the wall, like a picture. I don't know, I really thought it would be easy to learn to play a guitar. Later that night I can hear music and voices coming from the living room. Mom is out there with her friends. This is Thursday, but they all work together up at Benny's and they like to party when they can. I get a towel and stuff it under the door to keep the noise and the smoke from creeping in. And finally I fall asleep. The next day, Friday, I get off the bus, run upstairs and when I open the door I hear the TV already on. Geez … I'm thinking, maybe somebody broke in or … so I sneak real slow past the living room and see my bedroom door is open. *Now* I'm scared. Then I see her. There she is, standing in the middle of my bed trying to keep her balance holding onto the light bulb up there and … she's sticking stars to my ceiling! They're those little plastic stars you can buy at Wal-Mart. You've seen them. She must be at it for a while because there are a ton of them up there already.

When she sees me she gives a little laugh and grabs my shoulder to steady herself as she gets down off the bed. We both look up. Stars all over. Then she tells me that she'll be working second shift now. She says there's a sandwich on the table, gives me a quick hug and leaves. I guess I look stupid with my mouth hanging open but I can't honestly think of anything to say!

Later that night I'm lying in my bed looking up. My eyes are trying to focus and all of a sudden I see them — hundreds of them — hundreds of little bluish stars glowing up on the ceiling. They aren't in any particular shape or anything — just all over. Some of them even look like they are twinkling. After a while they begin to fade. I know they have to. But for a while they are *really something! (Pause.)* I think about that birthday a lot. I think of my mom in her blue starched uniform and black apron from Benny's … her little nametag. She has her hair pulled back with a black ribbon. She's holding a package of stars. Then she looks at me and gives a little laugh.

And that's the moment that I realize … she understands.

I Keep Walking
by Jonathan Bernstein

This monologue is a perfect allegory for human frailty and the loneliness of those on life's long distance journey to discover the truth about themselves, and they may not be that unfamiliar in these abruptly changing times. Here, an unnamed victim of a sidewalk confrontation and, later, insulting taunts chooses to "keep walking" toward an even more uncertain future in search of some sense of self-fulfillment.

YOUNG GIRL: Couldn't have been for more than a second. I'm walking down the street. People all around me, in stores, doorways, I catch this man's eye, innocent, on the street, a second, at the most.

Now, I'm not sending any signals, here, you see, I don't mean anything by it but I do, I catch his eye, this man's eye, by chance, and he starts walking, starts following me, I know he's following me, down the street.

I keep walking.

I'm at a red light, at a "Don't Walk," he taps me on the shoulder. Taps me and I turn around, and he says, and I'll never forget, and wish I could, he says, "I could have you."

He's looking right through me. To the real me. Or thinks he is. "I could have..."

Then he walks off, just like that, just that, back, back down the street.

"Don't Walk" turns to "Walk," I keep walking.

I pass about a half dozen construction workers, sitting there, on lunch, to my right, as I walk.

The whistling starts.

I hear "Thass it, thass right, walk it like that for me, shake that." I hear "Hey mama, mamacita. Shake that. Over here, right here" to my right. Right there.

"Whyoanchu smile for me?," one of them says. "Whyoanchu go 'head, gimme a smile, lemme see it?" — I don't look. I'm not going to give them the satisfac — "Whassamatter, baby? C'mon baby, doantchu got no smile for me?" and I don't. I don't have anything for them. Should I?

I just keep walking.

Never stop walking, never start looking. Chin up, eyes down, keep walking.

I want — I want what anyone wants: I want to believe. I want to believe I can find someone. I want love. I want to love. I want to trust, be trusted, I want to give over.

I want to feel what that's like, that moment, that split second of abandon. I want to know that moment and have that moment for the rest of my life.

I want faith.

I want to come out of hiding.

I don't want him to have me.

I want to smile but I don't want to have to smile.

I just want to believe. That's all.

I've walked so far, I want to believe I can find my way back.

I want to stop walking.

Living Dolls
by Elaine Romero

Sofia, a teenage Latina with a soulful look, sits quietly next to a stained window in a twenty-four hour café, gazing at the raindrops that fall gently outside. She is a runaway suffering from the terrible insecurity of youth and the equally frightening fear of being alone in a world that has no meaning for her. Here, Sofia contemplates the next step in her journey of self-discovery.

SOFIA: "Me and the Rain." I've been sitting here in this twenty-four hour café for three days now. I've established myself at a certain table. I leave my stuff here when I go to the bathroom, or get up to stretch. My table's next to the window. *(She looks out the window.)* I'm safe here. 'Cause the people who are looking for me, they don't look very hard. *(Beat.)* The owner, he's been real nice. Sometimes, I think

I'm here just so I can be close to him. He cleans up after the people when they leave. He's always shoving little bits of paper into his back pocket. He makes you feel good. The way he takes control. Not like home. Where the people scream until their throats bleed. Just 'cause it makes 'em feel better. To be bleeding. 'Cause blood makes you feel real. The way it pours straight out of your veins. *(She sighs.)* The owner smiles when I catch his eye. I think he likes having me here. Especially during the rough times. When nobody else's here. He's the kind of person who needs people. You can tell. He lights up like a match when they come in. And it's not just a money thing 'cause sometimes they just want to use the phone or the toilet, and he always lets them. *(Beat.)* He called me behind the counter today for a little conversation. At first I was sort of scared 'cause I thought he was gonna send me away. Turns out, he noticed I was down to my last two dollars. He asked me if I'd start working in exchange for coffee. I think he's really trying to help, but I don't know if he wants something else. *(Avoiding the thought, she looks out the window.)*

(Beat.) It's been raining these last two days. Rain makes you feel safe 'cause it covers you. The whole you. Rain has a way of slipping down inside the openings of your clothes. Or touching you even when it never hits your skin. I love the rain. 'Cause it's okay to cry. Outside in the rain. See, everybody thinks it's just the rain in your eyes. The rain blends with your tears and you can't tell what came first. Your tears or the rain.

Scrambled
by Paula Stone

This delightfully absurd comic duologue probes the amusing predicament of Henrietta — would-be chicken actress — who feels trapped in a nest of routine boredom, and seeks to escape in celebrity fantasies from the dreary barnyard scene. She is at a crucial crossroad in her life, and has pecked out a plan to place a singles advertisement in the Chicken Gazette. *Roxanne, her sweet tempered, realistic sidekick insists that Henrietta shouldn't complicate her life by trying to become something she is not. The verbal banter that follows is proof enough that the more things change, the more they really stay the same.*

(Daytime in a hen house, with minimal props and egg cartons to suggest a coop, where chickens are continually laying eggs.)

HENRIETTE: Number Ninety-Eight. *(Lays egg.)* Number Ninety-Nine. *(Lays egg.)* Number One Hundred! *(Lays egg.)* That's it. I'm finished. I'm flying this coop.

ROXANNE: Yeah, right, Henrietta. May I remind you — you said the same thing after you laid Number Twenty-Five, after Number Fifty, and after Number Seventy-Five, too.

HENRIETTE: Well, I mean it this time. Life's too short. I wasn't born to be a chicken.

ROXANNE: Oh really? Then what were you born to be? Cluck, cluck.

HENRIETTE: Rich and famous. And I will be, too. Just look at this ad — I'm going to sign up with Hen House Agents, they'll put me in a movie, and I'll become a great star.

ROXANNE: And so how much will you have to pay these agents, huh?

HENRIETTE: Me, pay? Really? It says … all my "rations of corn for a year." What!? Okay, okay. So I won't be a star. But what if I was born to be an adoring wife — yes! — live in a huge mansion, raise a big family. Here, see? I already put a personal ad in the *Chicken Gazette:* "In search of true love. I'm one plump, tender chick and yours. Signed, Ready For A Change." And I got a response from the most wonderful rooster.

ROXANNE: Oh, you did, did you? So who is this rooster? What do you know about this rooster? How do you even know he is a rooster?

HENRIETTE: But he sent me a letter, his photo, even a résumé. You mean, he lied?

ROXANNE: What do I know? Go to your rooster. But I'd watch my neck if I were you.

HENRIETTE: Look, I don't care what you think. I'm not wasting my life like this, only to wind up in some stew pot — I know! I'll become an explorer, travel the world, write chicken travel guides. And I've heard great things about the Catskills — I'll start there.

ROXANNE: Where the cats kill? Are you crazy? Look, Henrietta, like it or not, you're a chicken. You were born a chicken. And you're going to die a chicken.

HENRIETTE: You're wrong, Roxanne. You'll see. Because I've got a plan —.

ROXANNE: Yah, to go get yourself killed! You'll need a better plan than that. And you'll be a goner here, too, if you don't start laying eggs again. So keep on counting, my fine feathered friend, at least until Number One Hundred Twenty-Five.

CHAPTER TWO
AUDITION PROCESS

"The actor should not play a part. Like the Aeolian harp that used to hang in the trees to be played only by the breeze, the actor should be an instrument played upon by the character ... "
— Nazimova Alla

It has often been said that the best approach an actor can take to an audition is not to think too much. Although there may be a kernel of truth in that suggestion, an actor would be foolish to seriously approach an audition without some familiarity with its customs, traditions, and even manners. An actor must exhibit self-control and self-discipline at an audition, and that implies an orderly system of preparation and rehearsal. An actor must exhibit mature acting techniques, and that translates as an audition that is spontaneous and true-to-life.

Beginning actors sometimes stumble at auditions when they select monologues that are well-known, without regard to the limits or the range of their own vocal and physical talents. As you learned in Chapter One, the solid foundation for building a successful audition is:

• Careful analysis of the script to identify potential performance clues
• Rehearsal exploration to flesh-out or refine character interpretations
• Practical experience gained in classroom performances

You will now need to design an audition blueprint that complements your performance skills and reflects an understanding of audition expectations. A good starting point is to make sure you have selected monologues that have a: noticeable build to a climactic moment, series of striking turning points, conflict — internal or external — that leads characters to make difficult choices. Monologues should also have a simple sequence of character actions that have a beginning, middle, and end that are ultimately resolved in a concluding incident of some intensity.

At the same time, when you know that the audition playing space may be restricted in size, it may be necessary to exclude monologues that rely on elaborate set pieces or scenic devices. Remember that audition monologues should be simple and direct so the focus is on character *actions*. Finally, there should not be multiple references to other characters in a monologue — just the character speaking — unless it is essential to understanding the circumstances being described in the dialogue.

STAGE FRIGHT

Before a discussion of customs, traditions, or manners, it is important to address an inevitable audition phantom: stage fright! Stage fright is not difficult to describe because we have all experienced the gnawing symptoms in public speaking or oral presentation situations. It generally manifests itself in acute attacks of anxiety that strangle the voice and tighten the body. It is that puzzling fear that leads us to doubt our ability to speak or even to move at times. With more experience, however, we all learn how to combat the sweaty palms, knocking knees, and pounding heart that are associated with stage fright.

The place to begin to combat performance anxiety is to conduct an inventory of personal behavior under stress and strain. What are those peculiar facial expressions, bodily actions, or forced gestures that surface when you feel nervous? What are those dreadful habits that leap forward when you are insecure? Do you mumble, perspire, take deep breaths, or simply stand in a corner and shiver? Once you become aware of your automatic physical responses to public presentations, you should be better prepared to deal more calmly with an audition.

Remember that all performers — actors, singers, dancers, musicians, teachers, and politicians — may experience similar reactions in periods of stress. Just knowing what to expect can be a significant step forward in learning to harness the positive energy of audition anxiety. In order to address both vocal and physical anxiety, concentrate on exercises that free the voice from stress or strain and relieve the body of tension. Here are two brief exercises designed to address initial vocal stress and physical tension that should become part of your audition routine.

Vocal Fine-Tuning

The primary goal of the vocal fine-tuning exercise is to cultivate an awareness of the role that *phonation* — the vibration of the vocal folds to produce variety in vocal tone — plays in relaxing the *larynx*, voice box, to produce variations of vocal color in a character's dialogue. This is also a good exercise for a later discussion of the vocal qualities needed to voice the rhythm of Shakespeare's verse that follows in Chapter Four.

Begin the exercise by standing at ease in a small, open space. Slowly drop your head forward and allow the lower jaw to sag. Yawn several times and allow your head to gently sway from left to right, and right to left. Repeat this part of the exercise five times. Now return to an upright position and sound each of the vowels softly and slowly. Breathe quietly, using a relaxed tone as you repeat each of the vowel sounds another *five* times. Then extend each individual vowel sound for five seconds.

Now repeat the vowel sounds *five* more times using a slightly louder tone and then a softer tone. The five minute exercise continues as you repeat the vowel sounds in a lower and then higher pitch until you are producing the lowest and highest pitch possible without vocal strain. Conclude your vocal fine-tuning by repeating the vowel sounds in increments of five seconds to explore meaningful changes in pitch, rate, and volume. Repeating this exercise at regular intervals in the rehearsal period should help you achieve the tonal quality needed to lend vocal color to audition monologues.

Movin' and Groovin'

The primary goal of this exercise is to promote awareness of the role that individual parts of the body play in relieving tension that may inhibit expressive movement. Begin the exercise in a large, open space and slowly walk in a wide circle, keeping head and shoulders erect while the chest is up. Walk for a count of twenty-five and then relax the shoulders slightly, but keep head and chest erect. Then, *jog* in a circle for a count of twenty-five. Relax the chest slightly, keeping your head erect, and quickly *run* in a circle for a count of twenty-five.

Now relax head, shoulders, and chest as you begin to conclude the five minute exercise with a slow *skip* around the circle for a count of twenty-five. While *relaxed,* make sure the head and shoulders remain erect with the chest up. This brief warm-up and cool-down exercise may be extended to include other parts of the body as well. While walking, jogging, or skipping in a circle you may "shake" tension from fingers or rotate wrists in smaller circles. You may also rotate shoulders in larger circles for a count of five, first to the left and then right. Rotate your arms in still larger circles for a count of five, first to the right and then left. Relax, and "twist" away any residual tension that remains in the upper body.

Next, focus on relaxing the lower part of your body. Lift the left leg and rotate it in small circles for a count of five, first to the left and then right. Then lift the right leg and rotate it in small circles for a count of five, first to the right and then left. Conclude the exercise by standing at ease and slowly rotate the toes of the left foot in small circles for a count of five, and then slowly rotate the toes of the right foot in small circles for a count of five. Now relax and "shake" or "twist" away any residual tension that remains in the lower part of your body.

AUDITION BLUEPRINT

Auditions are similar to job interviews, only in a theatre audition you are performing answers to questions that a director may not ask out loud. Was the actor sufficiently prepared? Did the actor understand the audition instructions? Was the actor dressed appropriately? Did the actor warm-up vocally and physically? Was the actor courteous? Did the actor follow posted audition directions? Was the actor an early or late arrival? Would I want to work with this actor?

There is an audition etiquette that you should be aware of as your blueprint unfolds. Theatre auditions are generally limited to two or three minutes of *performance* time for two *contrasting* monologues. You may need to edit longer monologues to meet the time limit. Auditions that call for a classical selection usually mean a monologue written in verse rather than prose. In order to become more familiar with the basic principles of audition etiquette, please review the guidelines listed below. Think of these as best practices to introduce yourself as a more experienced actor than first impressions might suggest. Although you will discover some of your own best practices through actual audition trial and error, the following guidelines may give you a more competitive edge.

Accents

Use character accents or dialects *only* if they can be voiced with accuracy. Include a catalog of standard audition accents — British, Cockney, German, Italian, Oriental, Gypsy, New York/Brooklyn, Southern American, Spanish, and Midwestern — in your audition arsenal. It may be useful to purchase accent tapes or learn the phonetic alphabet in order to cultivate dialect authenticity.

Audience

It is not a good idea to use specific audience members to represent a character you may be addressing in a monologue. The role of *off-stage focus,* however, is a very effective tool in placing characters or incidents "out" of the playing space in a straight or angled line slightly above the heads of the audience. Off-stage focus also places the actor in a full-front position to direct subtle facial expressions toward the audience.

Stage Business

The traditional role of stage business to advance the storyline or provide clues to character interpretation is limited in an audition. The most frequent use of stage business calls attention to character behavior or habits and involves handling small props — newspaper, fountain pen, book, wallet, mirror. Exhibiting peculiar or repetitive mannerisms — stammering, cracking knuckles, fidgeting, and yawning — to punctuate a character's point of view or state of mind may also be effective stage business.

Callbacks

If you are called back for final casting consideration, re-read the entire script to review character relationships and interpretations. Do not prepare reactions in advance, and do not anticipate the character or the dialogue you may be asked to perform. You should, however, be prepared to perform a cold reading, directed reading, improvisation, or engage in theatre games.

Makeup

Light street makeup is appropriate for women and a warm bronzer for men. The role of makeup in an audition is simply to accent facial expressions with a hint of color. Women sometimes wear their hair up or pulled to the side for classical monologues, and men may grow mustaches, beards, or sideburns for period monologues, but the hair is always nicely shaped and trimmed to suggest the historical style. Do not rely on elaborate accessories like false hair, padding, masks, wigs, hair extensions, or prosthetic devices that appear unnatural. You would not, for example, wear white clown face makeup to audition for the master of ceremonies role in *Cabaret* or a distorted half-mask to audition for the title character in *Phantom of the Opera*.

Movement

Movement in an audition is always relative to the playing space available. Although movement plays a significant role in fleshing out character actions in full-length scripts, it is less likely to have a meaningful impact on a monologue. It may be helpful to explore more subtle variations in stance, posture, or gesture to suggest a sense of character movement. The best approach is to maintain a healthy balance between movement that underlines a character's action, and movement that accentuates the tempo or rhythm of your audition.

Portfolio

Begin to build a portfolio of monologues that represent different historical periods and styles. The portfolio should include six to eight monologues, each of which has a performance time of two or three minutes. The monologues should represent a good mixture of comic and dramatic character portraits drawn from classical Greek, Shakespeare, period, and contemporary scripts.

Select monologues that are appropriate for your age, vocal range, physical type, and script being cast. For example, if you audition for the classical role of the rebellious heroine in Sophocles' *Antigone*, don't use a Peppermint Patty monologue from the musical *You're a Good Man, Charlie Brown*. Likewise, if you audition for the title character in the musical *Jesus Christ Superstar*, don't use the Shakespeare monologue of the drunken Porter in *Macbeth*.

Your portfolio should also include monologues that have an obvious contrast in character attitude, mood, and point of view. Arrange your monologues in an order that is not only comfortable for you — comic before dramatic or emotional before serious-minded — but that also builds your audition performance to a recognizable climax.

Props

Hand props should be limited to objects indicated in the script and small enough to handle easily without distraction — letter, watch, glasses, cigarette lighter, and handkerchief. Do not litter the playing space with an assortment of hand props that become part of your performance some time later in the audition. An audition is never about props or other theatrical accessories. An audition is always about how *you* fill an empty stage using yourself as a prop!

Résumé

When asked to submit a résumé at an audition, include a professional photograph and a summary of roles performed. The photograph is a current black-and-white 8"x10" head shot in an informal, natural pose. Avoid a photograph that is highly theatrical or artificially posed. Wear subtle makeup, light-colored shirt or blouse with modest open-neck exposure, and avoid accessories like ear or nose rings, body piercing, and flamboyant costume jewelry.

A performance résumé is also 8"x10" and should be stapled or attached with rubber cement to the backside of the photograph. The résumé — printed on white paper — is a thumbnail sketch of basic information related to name, address, height, weight, and color of eyes and hair. The résumé also lists current performance credits — character name, script title, date, director, and location — and may include brief categories related to an actor's special skills and professional training.

Space

Try to rehearse in the designated location before the audition date to explore vocal and physical demands of the playing space. Pay special attention to stage dimensions, entrance and exit doorways, seating arrangement, and acoustics. Being familiar with the playing space should help you combat the anxiety associated with auditioning in an unfamiliar environment. If you are unable to gain access to the scheduled playing space, rehearse in a number of different locations to anticipate those later auditions that might be held in a classroom, dance studio, cafeteria, rehearsal hall, or lounge rather than on a traditional stage.

Staging

Anticipate a limited number of audition set pieces — perhaps a single chair, stool, and small table. Do not consider monologues that require elaborate set decoration, special effects, ramps, or platforms. Stage *blocking* — directed movement in the playing space — should also be limited to focus attention on character intention or motivation in the monologue. The most important element in staging is *placement* in the playing space. Set up the space to face the audience, and be careful not to deliver your monologue in profile.

Recall the earlier discussion of off-stage focus, and place imaginary characters in the audience or at a smart angle downstage center. Do not look down at the stage floor or off-stage while performing. Do not back up, turn around, or move upstage unless the script suggests such movement. Perform monologues in the center of the playing space, and move downstage right or downstage left as appropriate to highlight character actions, attitudes, or moods.

Time

Anticipate arriving early for an audition, and never arrive late! If there should be an unexpected emergency that will delay you, it is a professional responsibility to call the theatre and inform the staff of the problem. Use your time wisely while waiting to audition. Review your monologue, warm-up vocally and physically, or practice relaxation exercises until your name is called.

Show common courtesy for fellow actors by keeping cell phone calls, loud conversations, music, and noise to a minimum. Time also refers to the minutes allocated for an individual audition performance. Use a wristwatch with a second hand to time monologues. Don't forget to allow time for a brief introduction of each monologue, pauses, transitions, and the build to a climax. Respect the time limit set for you, or there may be a rude awakening when you hear a voice in the audience shouting, "Time!" or "Cut!"

Wardrobe

An audition wardrobe is simple and reflects the attitude or mood of monologue characters. The wardrobe should be carefully selected in terms of color, cut, or style with a focus on traditional designer principles of line, texture, and modest ornament. Warm and soft colors that complement the eyes and skin tone are particularly effective. *Under no circumstances* should you wear a theatrical costume! When you audition two contrasting monologues, dress in neutral colors and let performance choices suggest subtle differences in the character portraits.

Tight jeans, short skirts, jogging suits, cut-offs, hats, excessive jewelry, tank tops, sweatshirts, and plunging necklines are inappropriate for an audition. You should also avoid platform shoes, flip-flops, sneakers, or high heels that tend to make stage movement awkward and unnatural. A carefully selected wardrobe can also suggest a monologue character's idiosyncrasy or lifestyle. If called back for a second audition, wear the same wardrobe again to subtly remind the director of your initial performance.

Warm-Up

Arrive at an audition at least thirty minutes in advance to warm-up your voice and body. Regular vocal and physical relaxation exercises are essential to promote an expressive voice and flexible body. If you have discovered a number of your own relaxation exercises in the rehearsal period, use them as part of an audition warm-up routine. You may also choose to use the Vocal Fine-Tuning or Movin' and Groovin' exercises described earlier in this chapter.

ADDITIONAL DIMENSIONS

If your monologues have a recent history of stage production, make sure that you secure the *acting edition* of the script. The acting edition is a chronicle of the script's production history. It may include character interpretation clues, stage directions, or performance hints that emerged in rehearsal or in the public production of the script. Acting editions are relatively inexpensive and may be purchased directly from well-known script publishers like Dramatists Play Service, Playscripts, Inc., Samuel French, or the Theatre Communications Group.

Think of your monologue introductions as another performance moment that is marked with a personal signature of self-confidence. Spoken introductions should be brief and memorized. A sample audition introduction might simply say, "Hello. My name is Richard West. I'll be performing Tom's "fire escape" speech from Tennessee

Williams' *The Glass Menagerie* and the prologue of the "chorus figure" in Jean Anouilh's *The Lark*." Don't forget to pause at the end of an introduction and at the beginning and end of each transition that sets the scene for your monologues.

Use brief transitions to move easily from one monologue to another. Transition statements are also brief and memorized. They generally include remarks that identify the character and set the scene. A sample transition for Edward Albee's *A Delicate Balance,* for example, might include this description: "Claire, bored with her humdrum life, is talking to her brother-in-law and his daughter and takes special delight in sharing her recent misadventure in search of a topless bathing suit."

Audition entrances and exits are also potential performance moments. As soon as you enter, seize the space! Walk with an air of self-confidence and make direct eye contact with the audience. If you need to move a chair or table to set the scene, do so quickly and quietly. Then go directly center stage to introduce yourself and the monologues. At the end of an audition, pause to help frame the final climactic moment or concluding line of dialogue. Then cordially say, "Thank you," and start to exit with the same self-confidence that marked your entrance. Do not comment on your performance, offer no apologies, and make no excuses for any part of the audition. Be prepared, however, should the director ask you to remain behind for a cold reading or to engage in an improvisation.

NON-DRAMATIC RESOURCES

Non-dramatic audition monologues usually include excerpts from novels, essays, song lyrics, short stories, narrative poems, memoirs, diaries, or historical biographies. Non-dramatic materials frequently provide fresh and intriguing character portraits, particularly when compared to some of the shopworn monologues that strut the stage in today's auditions. There is a caution, however, because some auditions may explicitly state that monologues must come from theatre scripts.

Adapting non-dramatic materials for an audition involves ruthless editing to isolate memorable character moments. It also includes carefully crafted transitions that condense the dramatic action to meet audition time limits. Audition adaptations from non-dramatic sources should be structured to:

- Focus on a single character's point of view
- Identify a significant conflict
- Provide memorable character actions
- Promote vocal and physical performance opportunities
- Build to a climax
- Allow the actor to place a personal signature on the character portrait

Novels, narrative poems, memoirs, and short stories are particularly popular adaptations for theatre auditions because of the *thread of action* that appears to give these genres their basic structure and unity. For example, each individual adventure or episode of both the primary and secondary character(s) may be easily extracted for theatrical treatment without compromising the author's form, style, theme, or meaning. A number of non-dramatic monologue adaptations have been included in Chapter Three, Playing the Classics and Chapter Five, Playing the Period for use in classroom exercises. Just remember, however, that whatever is *descriptive* in non-dramatic literature must become *active* in an audition.

FINAL WORDS

Now that you have an understanding of the demands of an audition, it is a good time to remind you not to be concerned about *going up,* or forgetting your lines, during performance. If you should momentarily stumble, however, just do what every other actor has learned to do: Go on! You should be prepared through a rigorous rehearsal period to either paraphrase character dialogue or improvise character action.

Remember, you are the only person with a copy of the audition monologue, so learn to be flexible and don't skip a beat! Hesitate briefly, and then go on as if any momentary pause is an integral part of your character portrait. *Never* ask permission to begin an audition performance again. Of course, you can significantly reduce the possibility of mental lapses if you also schedule regular line reading rehearsals that focus on good memorization and retention skills as part of your audition blueprint.

AUDITION MONOLOGUES

The following monologues are appropriate for classroom performance or competitive contests that call for a solo performance. Begin, as you did with the monologue models in Chapter One, with a close reading of each excerpt to identify those that best suit your age range, vocal quality, and physical type. In these monologues, however, focus on a more three-dimensional approach to performance. It may be useful to consider the role of stage business, like handling small props, to more clearly define each character. Then look for subtle physical actions, mannerisms, or gestures suggested in the monologues to help flesh out your character portraits.

Give some thought to a simple way to convey potential character clues by speaking in a conversational tone and moving in a natural, relaxed manner. Finally, recall your own recent catalog of personal experiences or observations and see if you can apply any of the performance theories you discovered in Chapter One — objective memory, beats, inner monologue, or transfer — to uncover additional layers of character meaning in the monologues that follow.

Another Way to Dance
by Mary E. Weems

Marjorie, a mature and graceful African-American woman, appears regally on-stage dressed in the loose fitting clothes of a free-spirited dancer. Her movement is fluid, with a tantalizing rhythm that captures the heart and soul of the monologue's vivid prose. Marjorie's warmth and majesty is infectious, but her dance is the symbolic portrayal of a woman whose unquenchable desire offers new hope to light the way out of darkness and despair.

MARJORIE: I invented another way to dance. Part of the future of my father, a buffalo soldier — I was born learning how to fight. But in order to win any battle, you have to have a chance to begin with. I was born a day late and a dollar short for dancin' dreams — at least I couldn't dance for a living — sure I could do all the dancin' I wanted to at home, at a neighbor's party, in the streets. *(Pause.)* When it came

45

to being a professional — chances were few, far between, and without money — nonexistent. Even as a little girl in Wyoming, I knew I was different. Maybe that's why I found the words. See for me, before the first body-beat hits the floor — you need the words — the poetry in motion that tells the body what to do and why. I think that God put us here to do some things together — and dancin's one of them. So, my dances are made up of more-than-ones. You know, more than one word, more than one spirit, more than one body, more than one movement. It's a group experience, a special connection, and the total groove is music. I've lived long and remember my whole life — lots of lessons learned during a life that passed like tears — hot, one at a time, and differently.

Sometimes you cry for sad so bad it don't stop until you run out of water. Sometimes you cry for happy so sparkly each tear is another sun — it relights your face. Sometimes you cry and don't know why — life is like that. *(Pause.)* When well put together words make my mind and body move together — I begin to create a mental group — starting a circle of women in synch with me, and themselves, and ourselves. When we finish the air around us is changed for a time and the rhythm touches everybody. When I realized my dancin' shoes would always be too small to fit my dreams — it hurt like lye left on the head too long, but like my grandfather and every one of my people who lived before me, I kept going on — loving the dance, working my groups. To be a success you have to last.

Getting Home
by Anton Dudley

Jan, an "invisible" young African-American girl, stands frozen center stage holding a flashlight in her hand and staring coldly at the audience as she spins a sardonic tale of someone who hungers for personal dignity and recognition. Set against the ominous backdrop of a zoo's reptile house, Jan's silent plea is quite moving but also full of biting humor. Here is a compassionate wake-up call for those who cry out for human kindness and sympathy in the face of unspeakable ridicule and rejection.

JAN: I am invisible.

I know you're thinking "she's a black girl standing in the darkness, of course she's invisible." But that's not what I mean. People don't really notice me. Which is hard, because I'm never one to make the first move. I always think, if a man really loves me, he'll just walk right up and tell me so. And he'll be the one worth having, because he was the one who took the risk. That hasn't happened yet. Probably because I'm invisible. It's one of the reasons I got this job. I was a zoology major in college. When I applied for a job at the zoo, they told me I'd be perfect for the reptile house. Unlike the penguins and monkeys and sea lions, the reptiles don't like to interact with their handlers. Unlike the friendly fur backs, the sealy ones just want their food to magically appear and to not really notice their vital signs are being checked. My boss was quite up front in saying that actually what they needed in the reptile house was a well-trained handler who could also be invisible! So though I do enjoy my job, it hasn't exactly done wonders for my self-esteem. Neither, of course, has my stepmother. But when you combine the two, it's just devastating. As my stepmother loves to say to me, "Jan. Being ignored by men is one thing. Being dissed by a tree frog is just plain pathetic."

The 1st Annual Achadamee Awards
by Alan Haehnel

Norman, a hopeless misfit, is shrouded in a perpetual cloak of anonymity at Achadamee High School and has reconciled himself to an eternal life of teenage angst. Norman has been nominated for the best male actor — liar — at the high school and this excerpt showcases his innate ability at duo acting — playing both roles — in an imagined confrontation with a bully ... and, like all good actors, he knows how to make a dramatic exit!

NORMAN: I ain't afraid of you, man. No way I'm afraid of you. You want to fight me? I'll fight you. Don't you even think I won't fight you, man. Bring it on — any time! Right now? Uh, now's not actually a good time for me. A chicken? Me? You calling me a chicken? Is that what you're saying? Oh, man, you're not going to get away with that.

Nobody calls me a chicken. Nobody. It don't matter to me that you're taller by five inches or that you outweigh me by a hundred pounds. Don't even think it bothers me that you're three times Golden Glove champion and that you've been invited as a guest commentator for the Ultimate Fighting League. So what? That's nothing! If you get me mad — and let me tell you, you're getting close! — then you just better watch out! I don't care if you're Superman. Or the Amazing Hulk. Or any of those 'cause I'll take you on just the same. I ain't afraid of you; I ain't afraid of nobody! Nobody! You hearing me? So you just better back off. Right now! Just back away and you won't have to get trounced! I'm telling you, you take one more step and I will not be responsible for what I do! *(He watches, as if his adversary has stepped closer. He looks up.)* Oh, yeah! I ain't afraid of you, and if my mother didn't need me home right now, you'd be dead meat. *(He runs away.)*

Dancin' to Calliope
by Jack Gilhooley

Shaunelle, "The Carnival Queen," has a blithe exterior that conceals an underlying earnestness. Here, she is reflecting on the sorry state of affairs in a dying entertainment business and is embittered and resentful. In spite of her bittersweet situation, however, Shaunelle weaves a charming love story of "The Three-Eyed Man and The Bearded Lady," for whom she has unequivocal reverence for teaching her how to celebrate the authentic power of love.

SHAUNELLE: Triclops and The Bearded Lady are legendary ... like saints. Maybe not to you. But to true carnies. *(She animates this with the histrionics of a movie star wannabe.)* When I was just a li'l bitty tadpole, my folks were with Adamo Brothers Starlight International Show. Momma had a jam store, Poppa ran a hanky-pank. One day, Triclops an' Lucy arrived. They got stranded when American Variety went belly-up. Well, I figgered like you do now, that they were just a couple of God's shortchanged people. No big deal. Most people are, one way or another. Triclops caused a li'l bit of a stir 'cause of the third eye in the middle of his forehead. Even the veterans — who thought they'd seen everythin' in the way of freaks — well, they were even taken aback. Bearded Ladies are pretty easy t'come by. But three-eyers ... well, they ain't exactly found on every street corner. Anyway, everybody adjusted t'them an' they settled in. After awhile, I became attracted t'them. First thing I noticed was they never went anywheres without each other. Even when they went to the ten-in-one. He'd walk her to her booth an' then proceed t'his own. They'd do their exhibitions then they'd head back to their trailer, hand-in-hand. Just the way they do today. They didn't smoke or drink or curse. An' they had those same little flower boxes in alla the windows. They kept the trailer neat as a pin. Never fought — never raised their voices. That's rare in carny life, as we well know. An' it's unheard of in the straight world, from what I hear.

Anyways, after awhile they started t'ask me t'run errands. So I'd go inta the various towns for 'em cause they didn't wanna leave the grounds. You can imagine how the marks woulda reacted iffn the Three-Eyed Man and The Bearded Lady strolled through K-Mart. When I'd return with their stuff, I'd come to their front door and peer in. And quite often, I'd see 'em standin' stark still in each other's arms. Right inna middle of their cheery little livin' room. An' they had this look on their faces ... a look that had nothin' to do with the deformity of their faces. The look had to do with ... well ... with ecstasy, I guess. Yeah, ecstasy was what it was. I didn't really know at the time what that feelin' was with two people. 'Cept from the movies. All I knew was the opposite. I could only draw on my own experience. An' whatever the opposite of ecstasy was, my parents had it in spades. I'd knock onna door an' they'd bring me in. They'd show me their pictures of their daughter. She was beautiful ... truly lovely. No third eye. No beard. Just this gorgeous face. They tole me she had run away at an early age 'causa the embarrassment. That made me feel sad. But they weren't bitter ... not even hurt, it seemed. They said it was best for the girl. Can ya imagine that? They said it was God's will, that they were happy just to have had 'er.

I thought it was funny when they spoke of God. I knew they didn't go to church. I guess they had deeper feelin's. I do remember that day ... real early in the mornin' ... before the townies woke up, they'd stroll off alone together, hand-in-hand, like always. Towards some secluded spot. An' one time, I set out t' follow 'em. The sun hadn't even come up yet. But they had no trouble seein'. Then they'd raise their hands an' offer up these prayers to God. The sun musta been God to them cause it was just risin'. They went for a good twenty minutes with these prayers I never heard at any Pentecostal Baptist church. An' every last prayer was of thanksgivin'. Can you imagine that? A prayer of thanksgivin' for God's bestowed graces!!!

Amazin'! Then as they finished up with a long, loud "Amen!," they turned and kissed the longest kiss I ever seen. Not a soul kiss, y' understand. It was clean an' neat an' warm. Then like nothin' at all had happened, they turned and headed back. An' I knew beyond a shadow of a doubt, my life would never be quite the same again. Never again the same.

Dogface
by Kellie Powell

"Dogface," a young woman who was brutally attacked as a young child by a vicious dog, has been cruelly ostracized from society because of her scarred face. Although her family provides emotional support, the young woman still struggles to reestablish her life ... and her self-identity. Dogface talks about the traumatic event that changed her life forever, as she wavers between remembering the event and reliving it. One minute she is twenty-three, the next she is seven-years-old.

DOGFACE: This is how it happens: One minute, you're just another awkward second-grader. And then your mom takes you and your brother to her friend's house, out in the country. You get out of the car, and there's a big yellow dog wagging his tail at you. And your mom and your brother go to ring the doorbell, and you get down on your knees in front of this friendly dog, and you're petting him ...

And then, suddenly, the dog snaps his jaws. And your life as you know it ... ends. It happens so fast ... You're not even sure what happened. It feels like a very sharp pinch, and then it's spreading, fast through your whole face. There's blood. There's a lot of blood. You yell for your mom, you run towards her. She turns, and when she sees you, she gasps in horror and she covers your brother's eyes, and she screams, "Don't look!"

That's how these things happen, I guess. Anyway, that's how it happened to me. The dog never barked, never growled. He followed after me, still friendly and playful. Blood pouring from the holes in my face ... and he's looking at me, wagging his tail.

My mother grabbed my jacket from the car. It was green. She pressed it against my face. I was crying. I was so panicked I felt like I was choking. When we got to the hospital, she called my father. They had been divorced for maybe two years at this point. The fact that they weren't fighting with each other made me realize how worried they were about me. Nurses were coming in, mopping up blood and asking questions and trying to establish how much of my face was still there, whether the nerve endings were alive. My face felt puffy and I was light-headed. The nurses were friendly, they wanted me to trust them.

And I did. I believed them when they said that doctors would be able to fix me. My father didn't — he couldn't — look directly at me. He kept staring at a space on the wall above me. He kept saying, "You're being very brave." I didn't feel brave. I was still crying, but quietly. I was pressing cotton against my face, just wanting it to be over. I just wanted to go home.

And then, I was lying on a table, squinting into a bright light above me. The doctor was coating my face in something cold and blue, telling me that this was going to numb my face so that I wouldn't be able to feel the stitches. At the first stab, I wailed. I swore that I could feel the needle going in. They didn't seem to believe me, but they waited a few minutes, then tried again. Now I can't feel it. If I look out of the corner of my right eye, I can see it, the silver needle, moving up and down. So I don't look. They keep talking to me. Half the time I don't know what they're saying, the other half of the time, they're telling me how brave I am, but that's only because they don't know how afraid I feel. You're not allowed to cry or they might mess up your stitches. You can't move at all. They keep saying, "It will all be over soon."

They lied. I was conscious the entire time. I was awake while they sewed my face back together. What I remember most is the bright light, and the strangely disembodied voices of my parents and the doctors, trying to keep the patient calm. When they finally let me see myself, when they gave me a mirror, I had prepared myself for a Halloween mask, for a horror movie, for a nightmare. But the blood had been cleaned away. It was just neat rows of stitches. I was actually relieved. But two weeks later, I went back to school. And then the real trauma began.

Girls, Stop the Hatin'
by Stella Alexander

This non-dramatic piece is a plaintive call for reconciliation, and evokes the potential power of young women to bond as sisters as they embrace one another's differences rather than being competitive or jealous. There is a call-to-arms here to stake a personal claim on life and to show compassion for those who, although different, cry out just as loudly for understanding in the face of unspeakable rejection that erodes the heart and the soul.

GIRL: Hey there sister friend looking down on me
Why are you hatin'; what could it be?
What's on your mind; what do you see?
Are you judging my surface features?
My long golden hair bleached by the sun's rays?
Or, is it my eyes the color of emeralds found in Australia?
Could it be my skin the color of the sand in the Sahara Desert?
I am not my outer features
I am my inner soul
I'm looking back at you
And, this is what I see:
Beautiful smooth skin the color of the rich soil at the banks
of the Amazon,
Eyes sparkling like the finest quality diamonds mined in South Africa,
Your hair thick and coarse like the foliage of a Brazilian rain forest.
Let's stop hatin'
Let's choose to give support on the journey to our
ordained destinies.
Hey there sister friend stop looking down on me
Let's stop the hatin' and help each other live free

Dog of War

by Todd Caster

Roland, a retired Army Sergeant, finds himself in a relentless personal war since the inexorable passage of time he served in Vietnam. In a session with his therapist, Roland recalls the profound sense of alienation he felt on the return trip home and an explosive incident with Paula, his first wife. This poignant odyssey explores the yet unresolved impact war has on a man's humanity.

ROLAND: How long was I in the Nam? Thirty-two months total. I finished my second tour in '69. Then they shipped me back here. Let me tell you, it was like rising from the bottom of the ocean without decompressing. There wasn't anything about me that was ready for civilization. And the worst of the deal is I didn't have anyone to help me get through it. Not unless you count my first wife, Paula. *(Beat.) (Pause.)* I'm home about a week and we're sitting at the dinner table and she's talking to me … 'cept I ain't there. Pretty soon, she catches on … asks me what I'm thinking about. "A penny for your thoughts," she says. I tell her, "No. You don't wanna know." But she insists. She wants to *understand* what's going on with me. So I give in. I tell her what I was thinking about. *(Beat.)* I tell her about a drill we used to do when we captured a village. If the enemy returned fire before we moved in to take final control, we'd have what was known as a "mad minute." For one minute we'd cut loose everything — tanks, machine guns … *everything* into the village. If it moved, it died. *(Beat.)* I turn and see Paula and she's about three shades of pale. I'm looking at her and she's lookin' at me like I'm some kinda monster or somethin'. I hear her voice … it's a whisper. "And the women and children?" she asks. *(Beat.)* Like the rounds that I'm firin' have a conscience. "If it moved, it died! What part of that sentence don't you understand? What do you think I've been doing over there … playing golf? What do you think we toss at the enemy … water balloons? You wanna know what my job is, Paula? Do you? It's to spill every drop of Vietnamese blood that I can! Until the rivers run with it! Until it seeps up from the ground! I ain't no Boy Scout, Paula!" *(Pause. Sits.)* She moved out that night. Three days later I get some papers from her attorney. Apparently she couldn't live with me any more. *(Beat.)* I can't say that I blame her. I have a hard time living with me myself.

Windstorm

by Leigh Podorski

Eva, a valiant young girl recently stricken with leukemia, interviews with a writer from Life *magazine and Dr. Elisabeth Kubler-Ross at the University of Chicago in 1969, where Dr. Ross has been conducting her renowned death and dying seminars. Although Eva's interview is a touching chronicle of individual heroism, lurking just beneath the surface is the tragic overtone and stark reality of her impending death.*

EVA: I have some really great friends. I used to have more. But they don't come anymore. *(Beat.)* They can't. I understand. They're afraid. I know. And yet — it makes me feel so bad. *(Her eyes well with tears.)* Like my boyfriend? I mean, I know he loves me. We're getting married. We're going to have children. But ... he hasn't been to the hospital to see me. I haven't even heard from him since I've been here. That's two weeks now. *(Beat.)* He's afraid. I know. I mean, when they first diagnosed me he refused to believe there was anything wrong with me. He was convinced they had just made a big mistake. But now, he knows that's not true, and I know he's thinking, I mean, what if we do get married and have children right away and then she dies. *(She looks directly at Elisabeth.)*

But I know what I'm going to have to do, I have a plan. *(Beat.)* I'm going to call him. The dunderhead. And I'm going to tell him, "Look, I know how you feel. You're worried about kids. So? We weren't planning on having kids right away, anyway. I mean that isn't real smart no matter who you're marrying! So look. Let's just get married. After five years or so, then we can talk about starting a family." *(Beat.)* I mean, after all, we both still need to graduate from college first anyway. My parents would not be very happy with me if I had a baby before I graduated from college. *(Beat.)*

And my parents? My parents are really terrific. They're from Europe. My father is this big guy, strong and stout, like a bear, but he's so gentle and kind. And my mother — she's little — and so beautiful. You know they come to see me every day. And they stay as long as the hospital lets them. We laugh and talk and sing together.

(Eva begins singing "Edelweiss." After a moment she suddenly stops.) Sometimes, when they come to my room, we don't laugh or sing. Sometimes, we don't even talk. Sometimes, we just sit there, all three of us, quietly, and hold hands. *(Beat.)* It's so hard. *(Beat.)* And there's nothing I can do to stop their pain.

Be Ye Glad
by Alison I. English

Mary Lou Dobbs, a mature woman gently clutching her Bible, sits quietly on a park bench at the courthouse square in a small Southern town. Although Mary Lou doesn't have a formal education, she possesses that rare gift of practical wisdom gleaned from her study of scripture. Here, the flinty Mary Lou cheerfully greets newcomers and passersby with a charming smile as she shares her homespun wisdom.

MARY LOU: Howdy! Welcome to Pine Bluff! Haven't seen you here before. You new around town? Me … I've been living here my whole life. Five generations of Dobbs are buried up on that hill behind you!

Oh! I didn't introduce myself? I'm Mary Lou Dobbs, and I live just up the road a piece. I come here 'bout every day in good weather, just to sit under this pecan tree to think about things. Used to climb it when I was younger, but now I sit here and just visit with the folks who got business in the courthouse and end up sitting on my bench under the pecan tree …

Well now, if there's one thing I do real well other than thinking — it's talking! I do love to talk! And I do pretty good at listening, too. You know if you sit and listen, you learn a lot of things. Why, I was listening the other day to my niece, Rachel. She was home from the University and was talking about this psychology class she was taking. Said the teacher was talking about laughter and how good it is for you. Imagine that!

Did you know that they're finding out that laughter is scientifically and medically good for you? It seems that some high falutin' scientist has been studying the subject. In fact, they've even got Laughter Clubs springing up all over the world now ... Teaching people how to belly laugh ... Ain't that somethin'? They say it sets off en-dor-phins — or some such thing. Well now, I've done me some thinking on that en-dor-phins idea and laughter.

You know what I think? I think that science has caught up with Scripture! Yes, I believe it has. It appears to me that Old King Solomon had a handle on that information 'bout 3000 years ago ... Now, the book of *Proverbs* in Chapter 17 and verse 22 says, "A merry heart doeth good like a medicine, but a broken spirit drieth the bones." Well now, I don't know about you, but I don't want no dry bones. And something else ... it seems to me that verse tells me what'll happen to a person who isn't laughing. You can have something good going on inside of you, or you can just dry up! You want to dry up? Me-e-e neither!

So maybe we've got to start thinking about laughter as a source o'life for the body ... if it's good like a medicine, then it must be good for what ails you. In fact, the more I think on it, it looks to me like that verse says I got a choice about living a happy life or living a dead one. Now that's food for thought, ain't it? That reminds me. When I was a little girl, I read a book about an orphan girl who went to live with her unhappy aunt. Her aunt was rich in money, but poor in spirit. Now, the girl's name was Pollyanna and her daddy had been a preacher and had died suddenly — he and his daughter had been poor in material things, but they was rich in spirit.

Well, her daddy had taught her to think different from most other folks. He taught her to play The Glad Game ... He told her that there was more than 700 "glad texts" in the Bible ... You know, the ones that say: "Be joyful!" "Be ye glad!" "Rejoice!" He said if God had bothered to write so many, then it must be important to think about the good things and to look for the good in other people, too. Well, that little girl, Pollyanna, she changed a whole town, 'cause of her joyful attitude. She helped a lot of folks get well, 'cause they'd been thinking wrong — There was even one old lady that'd been sick for 30 years — she was so danged negative that she'd made herself sick.

So, I been thinking about that preacher's admonition — Be Ye Glad! And I thought maybe I ought to be dwelling on some of those "glad texts" from the Scripture. I been doing that for a while, now, and doggone ... I think my arthritis has done got better! Now, I'm not against doctors. No siree! They do some fine work ... but seems to me that how you think can have a whole lot to do with how you feel.

Now, my niece Rachel, well, she tells me that's true. Take anger and fear, for instance. It seems like these same psychology folks have figured out that those two things are different sides of the same coin ... and they cause all kinds of problems — stomachaches, headaches, and some even think it has an effect on arthritis. So, I thought, maybe if I exchange my anger and my fear for joy and a bit more laughter, then I might just get over my arthritis — or at least move a little faster than I do now! My niece Rachel says that's what the psychologists call the ther-a-peu-tic use of humor.

Shucks! All that means is: Our choices make us what we are.

Welcome to Our Festival
by Leon H. Kalayjian

Kurt, a devilishly funny young man, stands alone on-stage feigning a slightly lopsided smile as he patiently waits for a hush to fall over the audience. He is dressed casually and is upbeat, with a fast-talking stand-up delivery of some riotous and rueful announcements on theatre safety that should have you walking — if not running — for the nearest exit.

KURT: Hello, my name is Kurt and welcome to our festival of very funny ten-minute plays we got without paying the playwrights. The best things in life are free, right? I have a few announcements before the plays begin.

First, if you have a cell phone, please turn it off ... 'cause they cause cancer. *(Laughs.)* I don't know why I'm laughing. They really do. It's sad actually, tragic. A lot of the companies have buy-one get-one free deals, and it's like *(As if handing a cell phone to someone)* here's a bout of chemo for you *(Handing to another)* and another one for you.

Next, if you need to smoke, there are smoking facilities … in your house. Or in your car. Try and sell one of those babies that reek of cigarettes, good luck. And remember, for every two packs you smoke I smoke one, so please refrain. My grandfather didn't smoke but my grandmother did. And when he died, they did an autopsy. Yeah, his lungs were like wet kelp. *(Grimacing.)* Disgusting, kind of like the baby with a mouth on the side of his head. *(Demonstrates.)*

And let's see … fire exits … there's the doors from which you came in. And if there is a fire, I suggest you run, don't walk, to the exits. 'Cause I think only the first few will get out okay. And given the size of this crowd and the pandemonium that would ensue in a fire, I would think a great deal of you would be trampled underfoot in the frenzy for survival. Yes, yes, it's terrible but the young athletic ones always push from behind. They push and push, knock the weak ones to the ground … just like in high school. Then you fall and your torso becomes like a piñata getting beaten by a group of starving children. For the elderly and the disabled, I would just remain in your seats. Slow asphyxiation is a much more humane form of death than having a group of flamenco dancers doing a number on your back. *(As if he hears a voice from offstage)*

Oh yes, there is one other exit I forgot about, yes. If you can make your way up the stage and to the right, there is a hallway. You go down the hallway, make a right, go down a second hallway to the third door, make a left, go down another set of stairs, make a right, go down a hallway, then through a cave. And then there's a door marked "House of Pain" on the right. Go through the "House of Pain." You will be in no pain. *(Pause.)* No pain if you move quickly through and avoid the funny little man. Then there's the dressing rooms. And then a left and a slide and the funhouse mirror and exit.

Of course if the fire originates in the boiler room, then scratch all that. There are pull boxes and fire extinguishers located in … in … *(Looks offstage for prodding.)* Okay, if you have a large blanket … or maybe a coat, and one that's made out of naugahyde or suede is best — 'cause they're ugly and if you burn one, you'd be doing us all a really big favor. So that would be a good thing. You may have a singed lung, but there can be a bright side. As for bathrooms *(Shakes his head.)* I would say only in life and death emergencies. The bathrooms have not been cleaned since 2005. And I'm sure they're almost as dirty as that taco place they closed down with all the mice. As for toilet paper, I'd bring my own. Sinks, they don't work so *(Shrugs)* it's a staph infection waiting to happen is what I'm saying. I would just hold it till I got out on the street. But if you're still interested, they are located in the lobby and up the stairs. And I shouldn't be telling you this but the liability policy on the theatre has lapsed. So if you slip on a wet stair and fall headfirst down and hit your head and black out, there is no insurance. Right, none. If you sued the theatre, and won, the theatre owners would gladly, and I mean gladly, let you have — all of this. So if there is a member of your family that is not gainfully employed, who sits around the house and plays Wii or Gameboy, here is a chance to take a bullet for the team. Here's a golden opportunity to gain entry into the world of drama. How do you get to Carnegie Hall? Practice, right? But how do you get to own Carnegie Hall? Icy steps, buckling carpets, and unscrupulous lawyers. And last, just to remind everyone, next month, we will be reading monologues from those that survived near death experiences involving coronary thrombosis. We hope you can attend our production of "The Angina Monologues." Thank you.

Imani
by Heidi Decker

Imani, a confident bi-racial young girl, is confronted at her new school by a group of insensitive and inquisitive classmates who are puzzled to learn "what" she is. Imani's response is a timeless testament to the persistence of the individual human spirit in the battle against ignorance and prejudice. In Imani we see a strength of character not so much lost as waiting once more to be found.

IMANI: What? You don't know me. You don't get to say. What kind of question is that? That's not okay. I am not half black or half white. Those are COLORS. You can't be HALF of a COLOR. Unless, of course, you are one of those delicious cookies. Do I look like a cookie to you?

What I am is a blend. I'm a hundred different shades from a thousand different people. You can't look at me and decide what I am. You know why? Because my grandmother told me that she and her grandma and her grandma's grandma all got looked at and judged and told what they were enough that I don't have to.

So *you* don't *get* to.

She said there was a time when you had to have a color, then people got to decide what that color meant. There were good colors and bad colors and it made no sense. But if people said it made no sense, they got hurt, bad. So you had to be careful. If your color was bad, you had to pay somehow. Everybody's blood was red, but that didn't matter. My grandmother said, "Darlin', we paid that price long in advance so you wouldn't have to."

So YOU don't GET to.

And you know what else? You don't get to decide if I'm pretty, or if my butt is too big, or if I'm good enough for you. You don't get to call me Cutie or Ugly or Cookie or Sweet Thing or anything other than the name my Mama gave me. You don't get to look at me and make me feel bad because I don't look like you. You don't get to decide how I feel, or what I think, or where I belong or what I know I can be. You know why?

Because my Grandmother said *you* don't *get* to. She said she paved my way. PAID my way, already. She said she paid. They all paid. For me. One day I asked her, "Grandma, how much did it cost?" She said it doesn't matter. What matters is who I am. What matters is that I always remember WHAT I am.

You know what I am?

I'm the receipt.

(Pause.)

Mmm hmm. That's right. You just keep walking.

The League of the Unexpected
by George Sauer

This duologue is about two teenagers lurking silently beside a railroad track as the sound of a speeding train is heard in the distance. Mike, methodical and serious, is bent over pulling up his pants and buttoning his shirt. Tim, nervous and a little awkward, stands naked except for his running shoes and a large, floral beach towel wrapped around his waist, his clothes in a pile at his feet. This is a cautionary — but cunning — tale of a young man's coming of age and the sometimes perilous misadventures young men pursue to capture the spirit of bravery that they believe defines them as adults.

TIM: That was awesome! Totally awesome! You are indeed a master!

MIKE: *(Continues to dress.)* Ah, I've been better. My timing was way off.

TIM: Didn't look that way to me. But, of course, I am still a novice in the League.

MIKE: We were all novices once. The point is to move beyond that level to full membership. Now are you sure you want to do this? I don't want to pressure you —

TIM: No. I'm here to participate. That's what it's all about isn't it?

MIKE: That is exactly what it's all about.

TIM: Unless you don't want me to.

MIKE: I told you about it didn't I?

TIM: Yes, but maybe it's your "thing." Maybe you don't want someone else being part of the action. That's okay, ya know. I'm cool with that. We could just end it right here —

MIKE: Listen. It's not like a vocation. It's not a career choice. You just strip and run alongside the commuter train as it's taking off from the station.

TIM: God, I bet the passengers go nuts!

MIKE: Especially the first time they see you. Most of 'em are half asleep, so they do this double take like they're not sure if they're dreaming. And then they whip around to see if someone else has seen it too. Like they're afraid it's an apparition.

61

TIM: And you can see all this?

MIKE: Oh, yes. For a while you're running at the same speed as the train. So you make eye contact with the passengers.

TIM: And no one's stopped the train yet?

MIKE: You mean yell, "Stop this train!" — like in a film noir?

TIM: I mean can't they pull a cord or somethin'?

MIKE: But you're missing the point. The commuters look forward to this. It's the highpoint of their day. It's a jolt of pleasure. It's the unexpected!

TIM: Ah, yes. The unexpected! *(They high-five.)*

MIKE: But now they need some variety in their lives. That's why you're here. Imagine what they'll think when this nude guy running next to their train, who has become part of their daily routine, is replaced by someone else. Totally different. Imagine how that will get their creative juices flowing!

TIM: They'll wonder, has nude guy, in fact, been replaced? Or is nude guy sick and called an agency for a nude guy temp.

MIKE: Or are they on the wrong train?

TIM: Or are they imagining it all in some sort of elaborate erotic dream?

MIKE: And then once you become the routine, the unexpected again! We could say ... run together!

TIM: Or on different sides of the train to reach a wider audience.

MIKE: Or towards one another from opposite directions.

TIM: So they wouldn't know which way to look.

MIKE: Yes. Perfect!

MIKE and TIM: The unexpected! *(They high-five.)*

MIKE: Now another thing I need to discuss with you is the wave. You see you can keep up with the train for awhile but as it accelerates, and leaves you behind, I usually flash a cheesy smile ... *(Mike smiles)* and then wave. *(Mike waves.)* My point is ... I think we should be consistent.

TIM: Absolutely.

MIKE: To review. Cheesy smile. Try it. *(Tim smiles.)* Good. I usually then give a version of the Royal Wave. *(Demonstrates.)* Very discreet. Very respectful. Try it.

TIM: How's this? *(Tim waves.)*

MIKE: Perhaps a little more enthusiasm. Like one of the younger Royals. *(Tim waves.)* That's it. All in the wrist. Excellent. Well, I think we've covered everything. Any questions?

TIM: Just, when do I get my big break?

MIKE: *(Checks watch.)* Let's see. The next train should be arriving any minute.

TIM: Really? Commuter trains run that often?

MIKE: Well, no. You see, there is one thing I haven't told you. The next train is not actually a commuter train. It's an Amtrak train from New York.

TIM: From the Big Apple!

MIKE: So you will be playing to a more sophisticated audience. I don't want you to be disheartened by your reception.

TIM: Oh, jeeze! Can't I wait for a commuter train? Maybe even wait 'till tomorrow?

MIKE: No. I think it's better to start off like this to build your confidence early.

TIM: But I wish I brought better running shoes. With these I don't think I can keep up. Especially since I twisted my ankle a little the other day. See, it's swollen, don't ya think? And these shoes don't give me any support. Maybe I should wait.

MIKE: *(Sternly)* It's too late for that! Why don't you use this time to get centered. *(They stand, heads bowed. After a moment, Mike begins the pledge. Tim joins in but makes mistakes.)*

MIKE and TIM: We don't create harm. We create the unexpected.
We cause the heart to beat faster and the head to clear.
We cause the adrenalin rush and the sudden smile.
We fight the routine. We are anti-routine.
Go a different route. Get lost.
Peddle backwards. Do the funny walk
Act out! Act! Act! Act!
Ah, yes! The unexpected! *(They high-five.)*

TIM: Did you change the pledge a little?

MIKE: It is never the same.

TIM: Ah yes, the unexpected! *(Tim tries to high-five. Mike ignores him.)*

MIKE: I might suggest some lower body stretching now. You do need to accelerate quite quickly to keep up with the train.

TIM: Oh, good idea. *(Tim starts to stretch.)*

MIKE: I should tell you that there has been some concern of late about your enthusiasm or the lack thereof for the League of the Unexpected. That you may have some doubts about continuing. I only bring this up to let you know that it's out there. This feeling. This opinion. This rumor.

TIM: But I —

MIKE: Keep stretching. There is no need to defend yourself. After all, it's a voluntary league. Either you are a fit or not a fit. In a sense it's all up to you. You are judged by your actions ... And in the past, I believe you have celebrated actions. However, our concern is your recent lack of action. Your last minute reluctance. Your last minute change of heart.

TIM: Can you be more specific?

MIKE: Sadly, rumors of conformity.

TIM: No!

MIKE: Yes, I'm afraid so.

TIM: I'm shattered. *(Afraid to ask.)* Is it already too late?

MIKE: Even that I cannot reveal.

TIM: Yes, I see.

MIKE: You do know the method of expulsion from the League?

TIM: Yes. Public humiliation

MIKE: Yes, public humiliation. *(Sound of train approaching.)* Ah, I can hear the train coming now. And on schedule! That's a good omen. And a bit strange for Amtrak. Are you sure you are ready?

TIM: Ready! I just want to thank you for giving me this chance to redeem myself. And one other thing —

MIKE: Yes? Hurry!

TIM: Please feel free to criticize my performance. And be brutal! *(Train sound increases.)*

MIKE: Well, it's magic time! On your mark. Get set. Go! *(Tim dashes off-stage. Mike yells.)* Tim, your towel! *(The towel is thrown onstage. Mike watches, detached. The train sound continues and then fades. After a moment ...)* Ah yes, the unexpected! *(Mike gathers up Tim's clothes and the towel and runs off-stage in the opposite direction.)*

CHAPTER THREE
PLAYING THE CLASSICS

"The mask which an actor wears is apt to become his face ..."

— Plato

The number of scripts that fall under the heading of ancient Greek classics is scarce — only eighteen complete scripts survive — but there is an abundance of intriguing characters to actively engage an actor's dramatic imagination. Auditions that require a classic excerpt are speaking of a monologue written in verse, and the most traditional are those from Greece written during the fourth and fifth century BC. The most familiar authors of the period are Aeschylus, Sophocles, Euripides, and Aristophanes.

There is less information available on the acting style of the period than any other era in theatre history. What is known, however, may inform your understanding of the classical "style." There were rarely more than three actors — all male — on-stage at a single time, and they wore thick, padded clothing, ornamental robes, and elevated shoes with thick soles. The seating capacity of the auditorium — ranging in size from a few thousand at Oropus to more than 15,000 at Epidarius — suggests that actors had to exaggerate height and project voice to be seen and heard by the spectators.

While large, grotesque masks were used to indicate a character's attitude or mood, paintings and sculptures of the period suggest that actors relied on choreographed gestures, statuesque poses, and highly stylized movement to depict character portraits. Classical actors also cultivated resonant voices similar to Greek orators, whose dramatic and oratorical speaking style was most striking in public declamations and debate contests. The emphasis on articulation and enunciation of verse was crucial to voice the lyrical qualities an actor needed to sing choral odes or chant recitatives, which were written as solo or duet accompaniment to a character's spoken dialogue.

HISTORICAL VIEWS

Aristotle, the ancient philosopher, defined the acting style of the period in his text the *Poetics* as he recalled that actors had to learn " ... the proper use of the voice as a musical instrument to express several emotions." This definition, of course, still continues to define an actor's ability to voice a classical monologue in today's audition: Is there vibrant resonance? Is there precise articulation? Is there appropriate variety in inflection, pitch, and rate? Is there adequate volume? Is there a musical quality to the voice? Did the actor use the vocal instrument to its fullest potential to give the verse added nuance?

PERIOD STYLE

The period style of acting appears to have encouraged *song-speech,* or short, alternating lines of dialogue spoken and sung in a rhythmic pattern of intonation that established character attitude or mood. Since actors of the period played more than one role in a script, they had to cultivate a versatile range of tone in both speaking and singing to clearly distinguish the intellectual and emotional state of each individual character role. Although we today might think that the classical acting style was artificial and contrived, in its historical context the audience found the style to be an accurate reflection of period customs and manners.

There are, however, some notable historical accounts of actors who appear to have broken with tradition and sketched inspirational portraits of the tragic figures they portrayed. The Roman grammarian Aulus Gellius recounts an incident in which the Greek actor Polus actually used the ashes of his own dead son — caressing the urn holding his cremated remains in a scene where the tragic heroine Electra tearfully mourns the death of her brother.

Perhaps the most revealing commentary on the acting style of the classical period is Plato's account in *The Dialogues.* Plato was fascinated by an actor's ability to completely assume a role that revealed an "inner" self behind the ornate theatrical mask. He was also puzzled about the actor's ability to separate passion from reason in a performance. In the following excerpt, he has the Sophocles character question the actor Ion on the role that inspiration plays in his acting style.

> **SOCRATES:** I wish you would frankly tell me, Ion, what I am going to ask you: When you produce the greatest effect upon the audience in the recitation of some striking passage, are you in your right mind? Are you not carried out of yourself, and does not your soul in an ecstasy seem to be among the persons or the places of which you are speaking?
>
> **ION:** I must confess that at the tale of pity my eyes are filled with tears, and when I speak of horrors, my hair stands on end and my heart throbs.

Perhaps that is why Greek audiences appear to have held actors like Polus and Ion in such high esteem. It was not unusual for popular actors like Thespis — the first recorded actor, or thespian — to attract sizeable audiences at the City Dionysia, an annual festival to celebrate the harvest, for his interpretation of tragic roles. It was also common practice to loudly ridicule actors whose character portraits were not similarly inspired. It is widely reported in chronicles of the period that the actor Aeschines performed so poorly that he was actually "stoned" out of the business.

What emerges from these isolated historical documents is the image of a disciplined, inventive, and well-trained classical actor. At the same time, there was significant emphasis on the musicality of the voice and efficiency in acting style that featured a dignified, formal, and symbolic tone of delivery. Although the classical acting style appears larger than life in scope — mythical characters, cosmic themes, grotesque masks — there were apparently moments of intimacy and simplicity that spoke directly to the audience.

MODERN APPROACHES

It is important to approach Greek monologues with sensitivity and avoid the temptation to punctuate an audition performance with exaggerated poses, stiff posture, stylized movement, or sculpted gestures suggested in ancient vase paintings and statues. Make no attempt to document the historical period with character masks, elaborate props, robes, elevated shoes, or padding. It is essential, however, to tune your vocal instrument to crisply pronounce full, round sounds and syllables and to voice the poetic lines of classical verse with subtle layers of color and shading.

One of the best ways to cultivate dynamic vocal color and shading is to *sing* lines of dialogue in rehearsal. The value of singing — even if you are not a singer — is that it enables the voice to experience different inflections or variations in pitch, rate, and volume. If you are to be vocally fit for a verse audition, singing lines of dialogue in rehearsal will promote the rhythm, tonality, and phrasing needed to express the lyrical thoughts of classical characters.

In the following Musical Verse exercise, focus on the tone of your voice to convey a character's dialogue through variety in tempo, inflection, and duration of sound produced. Become aware of your ability to convey a wide range of pitch, from low to medium to high, and the distinct speeds of the voice from slow to medium to fast. If you concentrate on the musical nature of the voice while avoiding a sing-song pattern, your vocal tone will exhibit a more colorful and expressive quality in an audition.

Begin the exercise with a brief warm-up of the jaw and throat. To relax your jaw, allow the head to fall slowly toward the chest. Rotate the head up and down, keeping the jaw relaxed. Slowly roll the head toward the right and then left, slowly making a semicircle with head motions. Relax and place hands on the cheekbones as the head is slowly lifted upward, keeping the jaw relaxed and motionless. When the head is finally lifted, the jaw should be open and relaxed. Now, repeat the following phrases using the musical scale: *do-do-do-do, re-re-re-re, me-me-me-me, fa-fa-fa-fa, so-so-so-so, la-la-la-la, te-te-te-te, do-do-do-do*. Continue to use the musical scale as you repeat the exercise ten times, or until the jaw begins to tense.

To relax the throat, yawn deeply and take slow, sustained breaths for a count of ten. Then slowly exhale, and repeat the following phrases as you relax the jaw and open the throat to give voice to vowels that are rounded and full: *da-da-da-da, de-de-de-de, da-da-da-damp, de-de-de-deep, le-le-le-le, la-la-la-la, le-le-le-leap, la-la-la-lamp*. Repeat the vowel sounds ten times as you explore vocal variety in pitch, rate, and volume with each repetition. When you have completed these vocal gymnastics, the jaw and throat should be free of tension. Now "sing" the following classical monologue from Euripides' tragedy *Hippolytus*.

This is the story of the youthful Hippolytus, who has taken a vow to abstain from physical love and devote his life to the worship of the chaste goddess Artemis. In this excerpt, a revengeful Aphrodite, the goddess of love, tempts Hippolytus' stepmother, Hippolyta, to seduce her stepson. Here, Hippolyta reveals her growing attraction and conflicted desire for Hippolytus. As you sing the verse, pay attention to the way your mouth changes shape to form the lyrical sounds. During the rehearsal period, you may wish to record classical music or an operatic aria to play softly in the background to set an appropriate mood for the exercise.

> This is the truth I saw then, and see still;
> Nor is there any magic that can stain
> That white truth for me, or make me blind again.
> Come, I will show thee how my spirit hath moved.
> When the first stab came, and I knew I loved,
> I cast about how best to face mine ill.
> And the first thought that came, was to be still
> And hide that sickness. For no trust there is
> In man's tongue, that so well admonishes
> And counsels and betrays, and waxes fat
> With grief's of its own gathering! And that
> I would my madness bravely bear, and try
> To conquer by mine own heart's purity.

ADDITIONAL DIMENSIONS

You are not trying to recreate the historical period vocally or physically at an audition. The classical character portrait is simply a subtle *reflection* of period mannerisms, gestures, movements, and vocal qualities. Play the character role with your own voice, move naturally, and avoid excessive theatricality. Your performance goal is to suggest a believable and realistic vocal and physical interpretation of the character. Physical actions should appear to be fluid, natural, and spontaneous. Exploring dance movement or pantomime in the early rehearsal period may help to promote good poise, posture, and well executed gestures that give a more here-and-now audition performance.

Classical monologues demand an emphatic identification with the character to lend believability to an interpretation. The rehearsal period is the time to clearly define *who* the character is, *what* the character is doing, *where* the character is doing it, *when* the character is doing it, and *why* the character is doing it. The rehearsal period is also the time to pursue a performance *metaphor* that may have surfaced in an analysis of the monologue. For example, a striking performance metaphor for the character Medea — included in the monologues in this chapter — might suggest a "lady of sorrows" or the "gentle hand of death" and inspire a truly imaginative audition.

AUDITION MONOLOGUES

Honesty and simplicity are the keys to role-playing monologues from the classical period. Approach each monologue with a keen sense of purpose that suggests focus, concentration, and energy. Playing the role in a classical monologue is much more than simply saying the words and doing the actions. Look for the *spirit* of the character, especially those character sensibilities and sensitivities that help to clearly define your interpretation. Don't forget to *tune* your voice and practice relaxation exercises before the audition so that both the voice and body are free from tension.

The following monologues are freely adapted or translated from classical originals to encourage a more realistic performance approach whenever possible. There are also a number of non-dramatic excerpts from classical literature that may suit your audition needs as well. Although you should approach each monologue with an appreciation of the historical period, your audition performance should place emphasis on universal *human nature* rather than ancient history.

The Knights (424 BC)
by Aristophanes

Aristophanes' script is one of the most scathing satires in classical drama. The author attacks Cleon, leading spirit of the Athenian democratic party since the death of Pericles, and directs his merciless wit on the bribery, corruption, and miseries of war that have ravaged Athens under Cleon's reign. It is the impudent and unscrupulous Sausage-Seller who speaks for Aristophanes as he describes how Cleon is finally disgraced and humiliated by his own tricks-of-the-trade.

SAUSAGE-SELLER: The story is worth hearing. Listen! From here I rushed straight to the Senate, right in the track of this man; he was already letting loose the storm, unchaining the lightning, crushing the Knights beneath huge mountains of calumnies heaped together and having all the air of truth; he called you conspirators and his lies caught root like weeds in every mind; dark were the looks on every side and brows were knitted. When I saw the Senate listened to him favourably and was being tricked by his imposture I said to myself, "Come, gods of rascals and braggarts, gods of all fools, toad-eaters and braggarts and thou, market-place, where I was bred from my earliest days, give me unbridled audacity, an untiring chatter and a shameless voice."

No sooner had I ended this prayer than a lewd man broke wind on my right. "Hah! 'tis a good omen," said I, and prostrated myself; then I burst open the door by a vigorous push with my back, and, opening my mouth to the utmost, shouted, "Senators, I wanted you to be the first to hear the good news; since the War broke out, I have never seen anchovies at a lower price!" All faces brightened at once and I was voted a chaplet for my good tidings; and I added, "With a couple of words I will reveal to you, how you can have quantities of anchovies for an obol; 'tis to seize on all the dishes the merchants have." With mouths gaping with admiration, they applauded me. However, the Paphlagonian winded the matter and, well knowing the sort of language which pleases the Senate best, said, "Friends, I am resolved to offer one hundred oxen to the goddess in recognition of this happy event."

The Senate at once veered to his side. So when I saw myself defeated by this ox filth, I outbade the fellow, crying, "Two hundred!" And beyond this I moved, that a vow made to Diana of a thousand goats if the next day anchovies should only be worth an obol a hundred. And the Senate looked towards me again. The other, stunned with the blow, grew delirious in his speech, and at last the guards dragged him out. The Senators then stood talking noisily about the anchovies. Cleon, however, begged them to listen to the Lacedaemonian envoy, who had come to make proposals of peace; but all with one accord, cried, "'Tis certainly the moment to think of peace now! If anchovies are so cheap, what need we of peace? Let the war take its course!" And with loud shouts they demanded that the Prytanes should close the sitting and then leapt over the rails in all directions. As for me, I slipped away to buy all the coriander seed and leeks there were on the market and gave it to them gratis as seasoning for their anchovies. 'Twas marvelous! They loaded me with praises and caresses; thus I conquered the Senate with an obol's worth of leeks, and here I am.

The Self-Tormentor (160 BC)
by Terence

Here is a curious study of a father and son relationship from the perspective of Roman playwright Terence. Although the monologue bears little resemblance to similar topics treated by the classical Greeks, there is much here that strikes a familiar, almost contemporary, note. A perplexed father, Chremes, just doesn't understand his younger son's love escapades and intrigues. The son, Clitipho, wrestles with his own identity as he tries to make sense of what he thinks is his father's nonsense.

CLITIPHO: Fathers are so unjust! They don't understand young people at all! They think we ought to start being old men the minute we stop being boys. They don't think we ought to be involved at all in the things that come naturally to young fellows. They set up the rules by the way they feel *now,* not by the way they used to feel when they were our age. Believe me, if ever I have a son, he'll have a father that understands, yes, sir! If he gets into trouble, he'll feel free to tell me about it; he'll know I can forgive and forget. I won't be like my own father — using somebody else to let me know how he feels. Ye gods! When he's had a couple of drinks too many, the tale he tells of what he used to do! But now he says, "Learn a worthwhile lesson from other people's examples!" Ve-e-ery smart! Hah! He has no idea how little I heard of his lecture. I'm about as discouraged as you can be. Look at Clinia, now. He's pretty much fed up with the way things are going, but just the same he has a nice girl; well brought-up, completely respectable, and innocent. That girl of mine is a real dictator, has a terrible tongue, a regular duchess, expensive tastes, and what a reputation! Then when she names her price, I say, "All right!" — because I don't have the nerve to tell her I have no money. I've never been in a mess like this before, and my father still doesn't know anything about it!

Antigone (442 BC)
by Sophocles

The classical heroine Antigone has acted bravely in pursuing a course of action that she knows will bring her inevitable suffering and death: She refuses to obey the law of her uncle and King, Creon, and attempts to bury her brother Polynices in a ceremonial ritual. Polynices had attempted to overthrow his uncle, and Creon has now declared that Polynices' body will not be buried in a ceremony that would allow his spirit to ascend to the gods. In the first monologue, Antigone challenges Creon's divine right to pass judgment on her attempts to provide a proper burial for her brother. In the second monologue, Antigone has now been led away to be walled up in a vaulted tomb, sealed forever from the light of day.

ANTIGONE: Your edict, King, was strong, but all your strength is weakness itself against the immortal unrecorded laws of God. They are not merely now: they were, and shall be, operative for ever, beyond man utterly. I knew I must die, even without your decree: I am only mortal. And if I must die now, before it is my time to die surely this is no hardship: can anyone living, as I live, with evil all about me, think Death less than a friend? This death of mine is of no importance; but if I had left my brother lying in death unburied, I should have suffered. Now I do not. You smile at me. Ah, Creon, think me a fool, if you like; but it may well be that a fool convicts me of folly.

. . . .

ANTIGONE: Tomb, my bridal-chamber, eternal prison in the caverned rock, when I come to you I shall find mine own, those many who have perished, who have seen Persephone. Last of all I take that way, and fare most miserably of all, my days so few! But I cherish good hope that my coming will be welcome to my father, and pleasant to my own mother, and to you, my brother, pleasing too; for each of you in death I washed with my own hands, and dressed for your graves; and I poured drink-offerings over you. And you too, Polynices; for you also in death I tended, and for that I win such recompense as this. Yet he just will say I did rightly in paying you these honors. Not for my children, if I had been a mother, nor for my husband, if his dead body were rotting before me, would I have chosen to suffer like this in violent defiance of the citizens.

For the sake of what law do I say this? If my husband had died, there would have been another man for me; I could have had a child from another husband if I had lost my first child. But even with my mother and father both hidden away in Hades, no other brother could ever have come into being for me. For it was thus I saw the higher law; but Creon calls me guilty, brother, and leads me captive on the way to death. No bridal bed, no bridal song have been mine, no joy of marriage, no children at my side; and thus forlorn and friendless I go living to the grave.

Antigone (442 BC)

by Sophocles

Creon's denial of Polynices' funeral rites — a fate reserved for the worst of criminals — provokes eternal sorrow and tragedy for the king as the momentum of Antigone's defiance reaches a stage of horror. Here, the traditional role of the Messenger to deliver fateful news is used to reveal what has now befallen the heroic Antigone and Creon's son, Haemon, in the cold nuptial chamber they now share as spiritual lovers.

MESSENGER: I will tell you what I saw, I will hide nothing of the truth. I would gladly tell you a happier tale, but it would soon be found out false. Truth is the only way. I guided your lord the King to the furthest part of the plain, where the body of Polynices, torn by dogs, still lay unpitied. There we prayed to the goddess of the roads, and to Pluto, in mercy to restrain their wrath. We washed the dead with holy rites, and all that was left of the mortal man we burned with fresh-plucked branches; and over the ashes at last we raised a mound of his native earth. That done, we turned our steps toward those fearsome caves where in a cold nuptial chamber, with couch of stone, that maiden had been given as a bride of Death. But from afar off, one of us heard a voice wailing aloud, and turned to tell our master.

And as the King drew nearer, the sharp anguish of broken cries came to his ears. Then he groaned and said like one in pain, "Can my sudden fear be true? Am I on the saddest road I ever went? That voice is my son's! Hurry, my servants, to the tomb, and through the gap where the stones have been torn out, look into the cell — tell me if it is Haemon's voice I hear, or if my wits are tortured by the gods." At these words from our stricken master, we went to make that search; and in the dim furthest part of the tomb we saw Antigone hanging by the neck, her scarf of fine linen twisted into a cruel noose. And there, too, we saw Haemon — his arms about her waist, while he cried out upon the loss of his bride, and his father's deed, and his ill-starred love.

But now the King approached, and saw him, and cried out with horror, and went in and called with piteous voice, "Unhappy boy what a deed have you done, breaking into this tomb! What purpose have you? Has grief stolen your reason? Come forth, my son! I pray you — I implore!" The boy answered no word, but glared at him with fierce eyes, spat in his face, and drew his cross-hilted sword. His father turned and fled, and the blow missed its mark. Then that maddened boy, torn between grief and rage and penitence, straightway leaned upon his sword, and drove it half its length into his side; and in the little moment before death, he clasped the maiden in his arms, and her pale cheek was red where his blood gushed forth. Corpse enfolding corpse they lie; he has won his bride, poor lad, not here but in the halls of Death; to all of us he has left a terrible witness that man's worst error is to reject good counsel.

Agamemnon (458 BC)
by Aeschylus

The classic story of Agamemnon revolves around his spiteful wife, the queen Clytemnestra, who has grown disenchanted with the king and also been unfaithful. In this monologue, Cassandra — a captive princess and concubine to Agamemnon — who is also a prophet and able to unravel cosmic mysteries, foretells her own death and that of Agamemnon at the bloodied hands of Clytemnestra. The intense pathos of Cassandra's prophecy offers a candid portrait of the diabolical scheme that awaits the intended victims.

CASSANDRA: Oh, misery, misery! Again comes on me the terrible labor of true prophecy, dizzying prelude. Do you see these who sit before the house, children, like the shapes of dreams? Children, who seem to have been killed by their kinsfolk, filling their hands with meat, flesh of themselves, guts and entrails, handfuls of lament — clear what they hold — the same their father tasted for this I declare someone is plotting vengeance — a lion? Lion but coward, that lurks in bed. Good watchdog truly against the lord's return — my lord, for I must bear the yoke of serfdom. A daring criminal! Female murders male. It is Agamemnon's death that you shall witness!
What a fire it is! It comes upon me. It is the two-foot lioness who beds beside a wolf, the noble lion away, it is she will kill me! Brewing

a poisoned cup she will my punishment while sharpening the dagger for her husband; to pay back murder for my being brought here. Destruction! They call me crazy, like a fortune-teller, a poor starved beggar-woman — and I bore it! And now the prophet undoing the prophetess has brought me to this final darkness. Instead of my father's altar the executioner's block waits me the victim, red with my hot blood. I will go in and have the courage to die. Look, these gates are the gates of Death. I greet them, and pray that I may meet a deft and mortal stroke so that I may close my eyes as my blood ebbs in an easy death.

The Thesmophoriazusae (411 BC)
by Aristophanes

The women of Athens are in riot gear because the playwright Euripides continues to portray female characters as mad, murderous, depraved predators. They plan to have their revenge at the annual Thesmophoria Festival, the venue of women's secret rites and a fertility celebration dedicated to Demeter. Here, the First Woman voices her grievances against Euripides in a sharp and biting tongue as he is sliced, diced, and served well done to the ravenous crowd.

FIRST WOMAN: If I have asked to speak, may the goddess bear me witness, it was not for sake of ostentation. But I have long been pained to see us women insulted by this Euripides, this son of the grocer-woman, who loads us with every kind of indignity. Has he not hit us enough, calumniated us sufficiently, wherever there are spectators, tragedians, and a chorus? Does he not style us lecherous, drunken, traitorous, boastful? Does he not repeat that we are all vice, that we are the curse of our husbands? So that, directly they come back from the theatre, they look at us doubtfully and go searching every nook, fearing there may be some hidden lover. We can do nothing as we used to, so many are the false ideas which he has instilled into our husbands. Is a woman weaving a garland for herself? 'Tis because she is in love. Does she let some vase drop while going or returning to the house? Her husband asks her in whose honour she has broken it, "It can only be for that Corinthian stranger." Is a maiden unwell? Straightway her brother says, "That is a colour that does not please me." And if a childless woman wishes to substitute one, the deceit can no longer be a secret, for the neighbors will insist on being present at her delivery. Formerly the old men married young girls, but they have been so calumniated that none think of them now, thanks to the verse: "A woman is the tyrant of the old man who marries her." Again, it is because of Euripides that we are incessantly watched, that we are shut up behind bolts and bars, and that dogs are kept to frighten off the gallants. Let that pass; but formerly it was we who had the care of the food, who fetched the flour from the storeroom, the oil and the wine; we can do it no more. Our husbands now carry little Spartan keys on their persons, made with three notches and full of malice and spite. Formerly it sufficed to purchase a ring marked with the same sign for three obols, to open the most securely sealed-up door; but now this pestilent Euripides has taught men to hang seals of worm-eaten woods about their necks. My opinion, therefore, is that we should rid ourselves of our enemy by poison or by any other means, provided he dies. That is what I announce publicly; as to certain points, which I wish to keep secret, I propose to record them in the secretary's minutes.

Electra (410 BC)
by Sophocles

The ancient myth of Electra is a triumph of justice and divine retribution when Orestes, the son, and Electra, the daughter, avenge the murder of their father by plotting to kill their adulterous mother, Clytemnestra, and her lover, Aegisthus. Early in the play Electra and her mother exchange angry words as they blame each other for the misery that fate has inflicted on their tortured relationship. Later in the play, Electra seeks her revenge for those who had conspired to slay Agamemnon, a father and king who was beloved by all who knew him.

CLYTEMNESTRA: What? You got out again? Aegisthus isn't here, or you'd be kept locked in so you couldn't slip past the gates, embarrassing everyone who loves you. No, now he's gone, you ignore me, and you gossip about me, calling me a tyrant, pushing roughly past the law, taunting me and mine. No insolence in me — catcalls from you, and so many that when I hear one now, I throw it back. Your father, yes. You use that pretext always — yes, killed, and by me. I know that all too well. Why deny it? Justice struck him down — not just my arm. If you had been fair, you could have helped justice. This father you're always weeping for was the one Greek who dared kill your sister as a sacrifice to the gods. He had not suffered to bring her into life; he was only the father.

Why did he sacrifice her? Did he do that to help Greece? What did they have to kill my daughter for? Did he kill my child for his brother's sake? Menelaus? And shouldn't he have to pay? Menelaus had two children — they should have died first. After all, their parents were the reason so many Greeks first set out for Troy. Did Hades want to eat my children, rather than hers? Did that cursed father feel paternal love for Menelaus' children, but not for you and her? Thoughtless, and stupid: that's what I think of him, no matter what you say. The dead girl would agree with me if she could talk. I am indifferent to what happened. If you think I am bad, check your own mind before you blame mine.

.   .   .   .

ELECTRA: This time, at least, you can't say I brought this attack on myself — but now, if you allow, I will lay out the truth, for the sake of a father and a sister, both defenseless and dead. You say you killed my father. Just or not, that act should swamp you with shame. And I will take my stand: Not justice, but the seduction of a rotten male, led you to murder. Ask Artemis, the virgin hunter, why she clamped up the winds at Aulis that day. No, I'll tell you. She'd never tell you. What I've heard is this: My father was hunting inside the goddess' own grove; a stag, dappled, with horns, jumped up. He shot it and, having killed it, shouted out some boast. The goddess heard, and her anger stopped the Greeks from going, until my father gave up his daughter for the deer's life. So she was sacrificed.

Nothing else could free the fleet to go home or to Troy; he resisted, he dodged, but at last he killed. Not for Menelaus, as you suggest, why should he have to die at your hand? Is that law? If you make that law for men, you may be making a noose for yourself. If we go on killing whoever has killed, you would be first to die by that justice. Isn't that all just an excuse? Tell me, if you can, why are you now indulging in such a foul life — you act like a wife to the man who helped you kill my father; he's guilty of blood, and you have children by him, and you drive us out, the honest children of an honorable marriage. Is this worth praise? Is this, too, some retribution for your child? If you say so, shame makes you beg. Marrying a killer, just for your daughter! Ha! Indecent. But how could you consider my advice? You tell me I can't attack my mother. But you are not my mother; you are my boss. You and your man make my life miserable. The other has just barely escaped your knife — poor Orestes, exhausting himself in years of exile. How often you say I brought him up to be your executioner. I wish I had. I would have, you can be sure. Go ahead and announce in public that I am a traitor, a liar. If I am, I'll know I'm really your child.

Odi Et Amo (55 BC)
by Catullus

The non-dramatic lyrical character sketches of the Roman poet Catullus offer a sensitive view of life in the period. A number of the sketches are self-portraits in which the poet reveals himself as artist, simple man, and frustrated lover. The following self-portrait — "I Hate" (her) and "I Love"(her) — reveals a disillusioned man suffering from the pangs of despair and rejection over lost, or temporarily misplaced, love.

CATULLUS: If there is any pleasure for a man remembering favors past,
When he feels he has kept all faith and formed no bond
Betraying gods to lie to men: then many years are yours,
Catullus, for this empty and thankless love. For, favors men
May say or do for men have been both said and done by you.
But all was lost in trust to a thankless soul. Why suffer more
Self-torture now? Why not resolve upon retreat from that?
The gods say no. Quit courting grief and look at life anew.
It's hard to drop at once a lasting love; it's hard, but do it.

This is your only hope. You've got to do it, impossible or not.
Dear gods, if you know pity or bring help to souls who feel
The pain of death, look on my pain, and, if my life's been
Clean, take this destructive blight from my soul and sight!
My god, this pain crawls through all my limbs and drains my
Heart of happiness. I don't ask for requited love or for what
Cannot be, her decency. I want to lay aside this foul disease.
Dear gods, restore me through my everlasting faith!

The Pot of Gold (195 BC)
by Plautus

The Greek "old comedy" style of bawdy, slap-stick characters survived as Plautus, a Roman writer of farce, adapted a number of Aristophanes' comedies and invented a host of new stock characters to delight his audience. Euclio, a miserly man who hoards his gold in a buried pot, is overcome with paranoia at the thought his hidden treasure might be discovered. Plautus' storyline later provided the inspiration for a similar treatment of the greedy title character in Moliere's seventeenth century comedy The Miser.

EUCLIO: Now I'll go and see if all my gold is still untouched as I have hid it; for it keeps me racked with utter misery with every moment. I take pains to hide my wealth from men, lest they know, but they seem to know, in my despite; and all salute me with a greater deference than they have shown me before. They notice me, they stop me, take my hand, inquire about my state of health, my business and what I am about. *(Removes the lid of the pot.)* I'm lost! I'm ruined! I'm slain! Where shall I run? Where not run? Catch him, catch him! Whom, or who? I know naught, see naught, walk with blinded eyes. Know not where I go, nor where I am, or who know I for certain. *(To the audience.)* Pray you, lend me your aid. I crave, entreat you, point me out the man who's filched it. *(To one of the spectators.)* What say *you*? I'm quite dispos'd to trust you, since you have an honest face. *(To the audience as a whole.)* What is it? Why do you laugh?

I know you — men who hide themselves with whitened clothes and sit like honest folk. What? None of them has got it? You've been the death of me! But tell me, then, who *is it* has got it? You don't know? Alas! What misery is mine! In utter woe I perish utterly. In sorry guise I go, so much of grief this day has brought; so much of groaning and misery. Yea, poverty and hunger. None in all the world is more acquainted with grief than I am. For what avails my life, when I have lost so much of gold I'd been at pains to guard? Now others lick their chops at this my loss and my distress — 'Tis more than I can bear! *(Runs about the stage, crying and wringing his hands.)*

The Brothers Menaechmus (188 BC)
by Plautus

In his most famous comedy — the major source for Shakespeare's The Comedy of Errors *and the Rodgers and Hart musical* The Boys from Syracuse — *Plautus weaves a complicated tale about mistaken identity involving a set of twins. Moschus, a merchant of Syracuse, had taken one of his sons, Menaechmus, on a business trip to Tarentum, at which point the child is abducted and taken to Epidamnus, where in the course of time he marries a wealthy wife. The other twin brother, Sosicles — renamed Menaechmus in remembrance of the lost twin — has spent most of his adult life searching for his brother. At last, Menaechmus of Syracuse arrives in Epidamnus and the comic mishaps escalate as the twins dash from one mistaken identity episode to another. Here, "real" Menaechmus is pilfering his wife's clothes and jewels to present to the courtesan Erotium at their next rendezvous when he is abruptly confronted by his wife.*

MENAECHMUS: If you weren't mean, if you weren't stupid, if you weren't a violent virago, what you see displeases your husband would be displeasing to you, too. Now mark my words, if you act like this toward me after today, you shall hie yourself home to your father as a divorcee. Why, whenever I want to go out, you catch hold of me, call me back, cross-question me as to where I'm going, what I'm doing, what business I have in hand, what I'm after, what I've got, what I did when I was out. I've married a custom-house officer, judging from the way everything — all I've done and am doing — must be declared. I've pampered you too much; now then, I'll state my future policy.

Inasmuch as I keep you well provided with maids, food, woolen cloth, jewelry, coverlets, purple dresses, and you lack for nothing, you will look out for trouble if you're wise, and cease spying on your husband.

(Lowers voice as wife goes back inside.) And, furthermore, that you may not watch me for nothing, I'll reward your diligence by taking a wench to dinner and inviting myself out somewhere. Hurrah! By Jove! At last my lecture has driven her away! *(Looks around.)* Where are your married gallants? Why don't they all hurry up with gifts and congratulations for my valiant fight? *(Reveals a woman's mantle worn beneath his cloak.)* This mantle I just now stole from my wife inside there, *(Gleefully.)* and it's going to a wench! This is the way to do — to cheat a cunning jailer in such clever style! I have taken booty from the enemy without loss to my allies!

Hippolytus (428 BC)
by Euripides

The youthful Hippolytus, illegitimate son of Theseus, King of Athens, has vowed to abstain from physical love and devote himself to the worship of the chaste goddess Artemis. Aphrodite — the goddess of love — curses Hippolytus and tempts Hippolyta, his mother, to desire her stepson. Later, Hippolyta confesses secret feelings for her son just before she hangs herself. She leaves behind a message for her husband that Hippolytus has violated her, and an innocent Hippolytus is then exiled in spite of his sincere denial of the accusation.

HIPPOLYTUS:
Father, the hot strained fury of thy heart
Is terrible. I have no skill before a crowd to tell
My thoughts. 'Twere best with few, that know me well
Nay, that is natural; tongues that sound but rude
In wise men's ears, speak to the multitude with music.
None the less, since there is come
This stroke upon me, I must not be dumb,
But speak perforce, and there will I begin
Where thou beganst, as though to strip my sin
Naked, and I not speak a word!

83

I make a jest of no man; I am truly honest.
No woman's flesh hath ever this body touched.
My life of innocence moves thee not; so be it.
O, had I here some witness in my need,
As I was witness! Could she hear me plead,
Face me and face the sunlight; well I know,
Our deeds would search us out for thee, and
Show who lies! I never touched this woman that
Was thine! No words could win me to it, nor incline
My heart to dream it. May God strike me down now
Nameless and fameless, without home or town;
An outcast and a wanderer of the world. May
My dead bones never rest, but be hurled
From sea to land, from land to angry sea,
If evil is in my heart and false to thee!
If it was some fear that made her cast away
Her life … I know not. More I must not say.
Right hath she done when in her was no right.
And right I follow to my own despair!
O, ye walls, will you not speak? Bear witness
If I be so vile, so false! Alas! Would I could
Stand and watch this thing, and see my face,
And weep for the very pity of my life!

The Clouds (423 BC)

by Aristophanes

This sharply drawn comedy about the financial headaches of an eccentric father and his "at-risk" son makes hilarious observations about a dysfunctional father and son relationship. Strepsiades — loosely translated as scheming or deceptive — is tossing in bed thinking about his mounting debts and extravagant son, who is addicted to horse racing. In a panic, he jumps up and stumbles forward in a stupor to share his tale of woe. It all began when he abandoned the solitude of a pastoral life in the countryside and married a stylish city woman.

STREPSIADES: Great gods! Will these nights never end? Will daylight never come? I heard the cock crow long ago and my servants are snoring still! Ah! 'twas not so formerly. Curses on the War! Has it not done me ills enough? Now I may not even chastise my own servants — they never wake the whole long night, but wrapped in five coverlets, cut wind to their hearts content. Come! Let me nestle in well and snore too, if it be possible ... oh! Misery, 'tis vain to think of sleep with all these expenses, this stable, these debts, which are devouring me, thanks to this fine cavalier, my own son, who only knows how to look after his long locks, to show himself off in his chariot and to dream of horses! And I, I am nearly dead, and my liability falling due ... Servant! Light the lamp and bring me my tablets.

Who are all my creditors? Let me see and reckon up the interest. What is it I owe? ... Twelve minae to Pasias ... What! Twelve minae to Pasias? ... Why did I borrow these? Ah! I know! 'Twas to buy that thoroughbred, which cost me so dear. Oh! Curses on the go — between who made me marry your mother! I lived so happily in the country, a fine commonplace, everyday life, but a good and easy one — had not a trouble, not a care, was rich in bees, in sheep and in olives. Then forsooth I must marry the niece of Megacles, the son of Megacles; I belonged to the country, she was from the town; she was a haughty, extravagant woman, a true Coesyra. On the nuptial day, when I lay beside her, I was reeking of the dregs of the wine-cup, of cheese and of wool; she was redolent with essences, saffron, tender kisses, the love of spending, of good cheer and of wanton delights.

I will not say she did nothing; no, she worked hard ... to ruin me. Later, when we had this boy, what was to be his name? 'Twas the cause of much quarrelling with my loving wife. She insisted on having some reference to a horse in his name. I wanted to name him after his grandfather. She used to fondle and coax him, saying, "Oh! What a joy it will be to me when you have grown up, to see you, like my father, Megacles, clothed in purple and standing up straight in your chariot driving your steeds toward the town." And I would say to him, "When, like your father, you will go, dressed in a skin, to fetch back your goats from Phellus." Alas! he never listened to me and his madness for horses has shattered my fortune.

Alcestis (438 BC)
by Euripides

This classical version of a modern "problem play" treats contentious ethical and moral issues. The Fates have granted King Admetus an unusual gift: he may live past the allotted time of his death … if he can persuade someone else to take his place when Death comes to claim him. The time of Admetus' death has now arrived and his devoted wife Alcestis — who is close to death as the play begins — reluctantly agrees to be taken in her husband's place if he, in return, agrees never to forget her or to remarry. An angry and irascible Admetus now mourns the death of Alcestis and is forced to deal with his own demons.

ADMETUS: My friends, I deem the fortune of my wife happier than mine, though otherwise it seems; for never more shall sorrow touch her breast, and she with glory rests from various ills. But I, who ought not live, my destined hour o'erpassing, shall drag on a mournful life, late taught what sorrow is. How shall I bear to enter here? To whom shall I address my speech? Whose greeting renders my return delightful? Which way shall I turn? Within lonely sorrow shall I waste away, as widowed of my wife I see my couch, the seats deserted where she sat, the rooms wanting her elegance. Around my knees my children hang, and weep their mother lost: these too lament their mistress now no more. This is the scene of misery in my house: Abroad, the nuptials of Thessalia's youth and the bright circles of assembled dames will but augment my grief: ne'er shall I bear to see the loved companions of my wife. And if one hates me, he will say, "Behold the man, who basely lives, who dared not to die, but, giving through the meanness of his soul his wife, avoided death, yet would be deemed a man: he hates his parents, yet himself had not the spirit to die." These ill reports cleave to me: why then wish for longer life, on evil tongues thus fallen, and evil days?

Casina (185/184 BC)
by Plautus

The salty comedies of Plautus are rich in their Roman flavor of innuendo and satire. His rustic characters delight in zany antics that poke fun at polite society and traditional values of the period. Olympio, a simple and admittedly naïve servant, works on a large, rural farm and has grown tired of the pretentious airs of city servants who visit from time to time. Here, he pleads his case of having discovered true love to Chalinus — a rival servant from the city — who is much more mature and sophisticated in matters like these.

OLYMPIO: I haven't forgotten my responsibilities, Chalinus. I put someone in charge of the farm who'll take good care while I'm away. I came to the city to ask if I could marry that fellow slave of yours, the cutey beauty Casina; the girl you're so madly in love with. And if I do, once I take her off to the farm with me, I'll stay put in my headquarters as still as a hen hatching an egg. The things I'm going to do to you at my wedding! As sure as I'm alive, I'll make you miserable! I'll start off by having you carry the torch for my new bride. Next, I'll hand you one single jug; and point out eight casks, a copper basin, and one single path to one single fountain. And if that basin and those casks aren't full to the brim every minute of the day, I'll fill that hide of yours full of welts! You'll have such a beautiful crook in your spine from hauling water we'll be able to use you for a yoke. Then, once we're out at the farm, if you ask for something to eat, either you'll chomp hay or you'll eat dirt like the worms — because, if you don't, I'll have you hungrier than the patron saint of starvation on a fast day!

Last of all, when you're all tired out and famished, I'll see to it you get the rest you deserve during the night. I'll wedge you in the window where you can hear me kiss her and hear her say, *(Switching to a falsetto voice)* "Olympio, my darling, my honey pot, my joy, my life — sweetheart, let me kiss those sweet little eyes! Oh, you're so lovely, let me love you to death; light of my life, dickey-bird, turtledove, bunny-kins!" And, all the time she's talking like this, you — damn you! — will be stuck in the middle of the wall like a rat in its hole. *(Turning away)* And now, to keep you from getting ideas about answering me back, I'm going inside. I'm sick and tired of your talk!

Medea (431 BC)
by Euripides

This horrific tragedy depicts the heartless revenge that Medea unleashes on her husband, Jason, who has betrayed her for a younger woman. Jason brought the barbarian Medea to Corinth after his adventures of the Golden Fleece, but has now deserted her to marry a royal princess, Glauce — although he hopes to retain Medea as his mistress. An enraged Medea scorns his overtures and plots to murder her children. On the verge of near hysteria, Medea struggles to confront a profound sense of guilt and loss for the heinous act she is about to commit.

MEDEA: O, do not do this deed! Let the children go.
Unhappy one, spare the babes! For if they live, they
Will cheer thee in our exile there. Nay, by the friends of
Hell's abyss, never will I hand my children over to their
Foes to mock and flout. Die they must in any case, and
Since 'tis so, why I, the mother who bore them, will give
The fatal blow. O my babes, my babes, let your Mother kiss
Your hands. Ah! Hands I love so well. O lips most dear to me!
O the sweet embrace, the soft young cheek, the fragrant
Breath!
My children! Go, leave me! I cannot bear to look longer upon
You; my sorrow wins the day. At last, I understand the awful
Deed I am to do; But passion, that cause of direct woes to
Mortal man, hath triumphed o'er my sober thoughts.

My friends, I am resolved upon the deed; at once will
I slay my children and then leave this land, without delaying
Long enough to hand them over to some more savage
hand to
Butcher. Needs must they die in any case; and since they must,

I will slay them — I, the mother who bore them, O heart
of mine,
Steel thyself! Come, take the sword, thou wretched hand
of mine!
Away with cowardice! This one brief day forget thy
children
Dear, and after that lament; for though thou wilt slay them yet
They were thy darlings still, and I am lady of sorrows.
(Medea slowly moves toward the house with sword held high.)

Lysistrata (411 BC)
by Aristophanes

*In this adaptation, the classical feminist Lysistrata has assembled
all Athenian women in the public square to stage a "sex strike" to end
the perpetual Peloponnesian War. She is aided in her sensual strategy
by the temptress Voluptia, "fair-peach of Athens," who is preparing to
lay the battle plan for a frontal attack as she instructs the new recruits
in the art of women's warfare.*

VOLUPTIA: Women of Greece, if you would end the war and
secure the peace for which you lay awake each night, you must wipe
all decency from your face! Steady, sisters! A dose of hellbore to give
you a brainwash, that's what you need! And not the common stuff the
apothecaries peddle in the marketplace either, but the special brand
from Antigua. Eyes emphasized with kohl and false hair, painted lips
and lined brows! Wax and Tarentine wraps, and earrings. Snake-
winding bracelets, anklets, chains and lockets. Steady, sisters! But no
roses! O, by Pluto, no roses! When they lose their fragrance both men
and gods stay away, for the odor has a marvelous capacity to drive
away all repose.

What you don't possess by Nature you may acquire by imitation,
and a little padding! And don't forget that a woman cannot possibly be
loved without perfume. So put it here and there and everywhere. And
when you walk spring forward with a light step. See, walk as I do and
men will gaze at you with wonder, their heads erect and their faces

beaming with delight at the sight. And don't forget to let your hands interlace, as though you were praying with each step! And, O, face without chalk. Remember, my dainties, for a woman redness of face is the shining flower of charm. To rouge, my sweets, to rouge! But do not be harsh or frightening, and do not seal your beauty away in scarf or veil. O, sisters, throw off those nets that sore beset you, and reveal your loveliness!

There's not a part of you but snares men to their doom. Love beckons in your eyes, your mouths are songs of grace, your hands are scions of strength and flowers blossom in your checks. If you do not believe my craft, take up your mirror and see how your face has changed. O, receive them with scented hair, in fragrant delicto at the half moon! O, my sweets, what a noble work of art is Woman! And don't forget to imitate the twelve postures of Cyrone.

Agamemnon (458 BC)
by Aeschylus

A solitary Watchman stands in silhouette against the stark and foreboding sky, looking for the distant beacon fires that signal the fall of Troy. He has been vigilant for a year and is now anxious to unload a wearisome burden almost too heavy to bear. The Watchman's resolute spirit surfaces as he reflects on the unending war and the turmoil that has wreaked havoc on his beloved land.

WATCHMAN: The gods it is I ask to release me from this watch
A year's length now, spending my nights like a dog,
Watching on my elbow on the roof of the sons of Atreus
So that I have come to know the assembly of the mighty stars
Those which bring storm and those which bring summer to men,
The shining Masters riveted in the sky —
I know the decline and rising of those stars.
And now I am waiting for the sign of the beacon,
The flame of fire that will carry the report from Troy,
News of her taking. Which task has been assigned to me
By a woman of sanguine heart but a man's mind.
Yet when I take my restless rest in the soaking dew,

My night not visited with dreams —
For fear stands by me in the place of sleep
That I cannot firmly close my eyes in sleep —
Whenever I think to sing or hum to myself
As an antidote to sleep, then every time I groan
And fall to weeping for the fortunes of this house
Where not as before are things well ordered now.
But now may a good chance fall, escape from pain,
The good news visible in the midnight fire.

Period Epigrams (Third Century BC)

Period epigrams — *short poems with a satirical point of view —
offer candid snapshots of classical figures that express themselves
anonymously in simple language. Epigrams provide intimate glimpses
of the daily lives of ordinary Athenian citizens and well-known public
figures, and frequently have a bittersweet or sardonic tone. The
following epigrams reflect on the perils of life and death — but there is
an ironic detachment in the poems that hints of a more universal
tragedy.*

Antiphilus of Cyzicus

When I was dead, they gave me a burial.
Now my bones bleach like a yellow wheat.
Once I was laid out with due funeral;
Now the iron share ploughs me below.
Stranger, who said that death ended pain,
Even when the tomb yields me again?
A vine climbs over me, who once
As many leaves and clusters fed.
Look at me, all —
In earth's narrow bed I lie,
Sorrow of strangers' eyes.

91

Poseidippus

Which way of life should suit a man?
The market sweats him all it can.
Home gives anxieties to bear;
The land is work, the sea is fear;
To travel rich risks loss of all;
To travel poor is unbearable.
Married men have too much care:
But lonely is the bachelor man.
Children make life a mess,
Yet crippled is he childless.
The young are fools; the old weak.
So only two choices to speak:
Either don't be born at all; or
Breathe your last at first bawl!

The Haunted House (181 BC)
by Plautus

The stock character role of the impulsive and sharp-witted servant is one of the comic inventions of Roman comedy. Phaniscus, a boisterous and bumbling schemer, serves a rather dull-witted, inept master who is unable to exert any semblance of order in his household. Here, the amusing rascal Phaniscus offers a comic portrait of both his master and himself engaged in a perpetual struggle for domination at any price.

PHANISCUS: *(Smugly)* Slaves that stand in awe of a thrashing, even while they're free from fault, they're the ones that are apt to be useful to their masters. For when those that stand in awe of nothing have once earned a thrashing, the course they take is idiotic. They train for racing. But when they're caught they earn and save more welts from whips than they ever could earn and save from tips. Their income grows from almost nothing till they become regular rawhide kings. But personally, my plan is to be aware of welts before my back begins to pain me. I feel it desirable to keep a whole skin, as I have hitherto, and avoid drubbings. *(Looks at his pilfering left hand.)* If I could only control this article, I'll keep well-roofed; and when it's raining welts on the rest of them, I won't get soaked.

For a master's generally what his slaves choose to make him. If they're good, he's good; if they're bad, he gets bad. Now you see we've got a houseful of slaves as bad as bad can be, that blow all their savings on their backs. When they're called on to fetch their master home, it's: "I'm not going, don't bother me!" I know what your hurry is — itching to be out some-where! Oh, yes, you mule, now you want to be off to pasture! That's all the thanks I got from them for being dutiful. I left them. Here I am, the only one of the whole gang to see master home. Tomorrow, when he finds it out, he'll give them a morning dose of cattle hide. Oh well, I consider their backs of less consequence than mine. They'll go in for tanning long before I do for roping!

Andromache (425 BC)
by Euripides

The murderous passion and remorse of a childless woman who fears that a young rival may win the affection of her husband echoes the self-sacrifice voiced by Medea. Here it is Hermione — driven by humiliation and rejection when her husband, Neoptolemus, abandons her in favor of Andromache — who seeks justice and retribution. The Nurse serves as the "ideal spectator" and prepares the audience for Hermione's fateful entrance.

NURSE: O dearest Women, how this day has brought to us
Evil on evil, followed one by one in turn!
My mistress in the house, I mean Hermione,
Bereft of father, and in consciousness as well
Of what she did, to try to kill Andromache
And her small boy, now wishes to die herself,
Fearing her husband, lest in payment for her deeds
She should be sent disgracefully away from home,
Or killed for trying to kill those she should help instead,

She wants to hang herself; the servants find it hard
Preventing her; they snatch the sword from her hand.
So greatly does she grieve, and what she did before
She knows was not done well, and I can hardly keep
My mistress from her suicide, dear friends of mine.
But you go in, go in to the house and set her free
From death, for new friends can persuade more than the old.

   ·   ·   ·   ·   ·   ·   ·   ·   ·   ·   ·   ·

(Enter Hermione)

HERMIONE: He'll kill me justly. Need I tell you that?
How did you make this error? Some one might inquire.
The visits of evil women it was that ruined me.
They puffed me up with vanity; they said these words:
"Will you endure to have that rotten slave girl here
To share your husband's bed, with you still in the house?
But Hera queen, she wouldn't look upon daylight
One moment in my home or wallow in my bed!"
I leant a willing ear to all these Siren songs,
Inflated by my folly and blinded by the troublemakers
For what need had I to keep an eye on him?
I might have borne him children in the course of time,
While hers, unlawful, would have been half-slaves to mine.
But never, never — I shall say it many times —
Should men who have sound sense, who have a wife besides,
Allow the frequent visits coming in and out
Of women; for they teach her only wickedness.
One woman, paid to do it, will corrupt the wife,
Another wants for her the same disgrace she has,
And many from sheer love of sin … and thus the homes
Of men grow sick. Be on your guard against such tricks.
Shut up the house and lock it tight with bolts and bars.
There's nothing healthy in this running in and out
That women do, but many evils do come from it.

Philoctetes (409 BC)

by Sophocles

Philoctetes, a Greek "Robinson Crusoe," is bitten by a poisonous snake and left to die on a deserted island by his comrades as they depart for the battle of Troy. Nine years have elapsed and the Greeks now need Philoctetes' magic bow to help them win the battle of Troy. Neoptolemus, the youngest son of Achilles, is sent to the island to persuade Philoctetes to rejoin the band of warriors, or at least yield up his magic bow. A crippled and caustic Philoctetes lashes out in anger as he feeds off bitter memories.

PHILOCTETES: How terrible I must be! The gods must hate me, to keep the news of me and my suffering from going back to my home or to any home in Greece! So the men who cast me out have kept quiet, laughing to themselves at their crime. They took off, leaving me rags, enough food for a beggar — heaven give them the same. And my sickness gets worse, spreads out. No one was left on this island, no one to help, no one to hold my elbow when the sickness shook me. All I owned was rage and agony — I had plenty of that. Time limped, summer, winter, summer. In my hut I had to be servant and master for myself. This bow brought down doves to eat, and then I had to crawl to get them, tugging my foot — this cursed hoof. Or if I needed water, or if a freeze set in, then, to get wood, I would crawl past my own misery to get it. This island, nobody sails here on purpose; you can't anchor here; there's no port, or market, or welcome. Sane men never make a voyage to this isle. Nine full years of hurt and anger, I've given myself over to decay, food for my disease. This much, boy, is what the two Atrides and that haughty Odysseus have done to me. May the divinities in heaven make them ache my aches, wince for every pain I've felt!

CHAPTER FOUR
PLAYING SHAKESPEARE

"The poet's eye, in a fine frenzy rolling,
Doth glance from heaven to earth, from earth to heaven,
And, as imagination bodies forth the forms of things unknown,
The poet's pen turns them to shapes, and gives to airy nothing
A local habitation and a name."

— A Midsummer Night's Dream, Act V, Scene i

In contrast to the classical period of mythic heroes and rebellious heroines, the Elizabethan period (1558-1603) of Shakespeare offers a more complex array of character portraits. Painting on a more expansive emotional and intellectual canvas than the classicists, Elizabethan playwrights sketch their characters in finer detail and with multiple layers of shading. Typically, the serious dramas of the period depict a host of tormented men and women driven by unseen — or supernatural — forces they can neither confront nor conquer.

It is these forces which compel characters to take drastic actions that ultimately result in self-deception, despair, or death. Shakespeare alone, however, appears to treat his characters as human beings rather than shadowy stage figures. He also makes greater performance demands on the actor by placing characters in situations that call for vocal power, physical agility, and emotional intensity that at times soars to the heavens and then, just as quickly, plummets back to earth. Discarding the heroic cardboard figures that flourished on the classical stage, Shakespeare appears to be more interested in revealing interior motives or psychological maladies. His characters are susceptible to fits of rage, exhibit symptoms of severe neurosis, rant and rave at the slightest provocation, and plot mischief or revenge with cheerful glee. In other words, they are flesh-and-blood characters that perform un-heroic deeds, engage in comic blunders, exhibit both courage and cowardice, and display the basic urges of all human beings. It is their tragic actions or comic antics, however, that arouse our self-identification as we watch them march off to battle injustice, slip into comic pratfalls, pursue foolish misadventures, or avenge imagined wrongs.

96

THE TIMES

Elizabethan actors — all male — were professional or under the patronage of royalty and Shakespeare's troupe — the King's Men — in particular appears to have been well-trained in music, dancing, fencing, gymnastics, stage combat, and even wrestling. Elizabethan scripts were generally staged in noisy outdoor playhouses that encouraged raucous audience participation. Period actors, of course, would have needed ample volume just to be heard, but would also have needed a flexible voice to give subtle expression to Shakespeare's poetic dialogue.

Shakespeare's theatre, the *Globe,* is thought to have held no more than 3,000 spectators, and the audience to have been a mixture of lords and ladies as well as rogues and ruffians. Titled lords and their ladies were seated in a series of boxed galleries surrounding a raised stage. Tradesmen, apprentices, servants, and other locals stood on ground level in the *pit,* a flat area surrounding an open or thrust stage. These *groundlings,* who remained standing throughout a production — two hours without an intermission! — often punctuated their critical reviews with apple-eating, nut-cracking, or ale-drinking that apparently went on throughout the afternoon.

A study of Shakespeare's scripts reveals how flexible the *Globe* stage had to be in order to accommodate the many scene changes indicated in a script. For example, when the actor playing Hamlet leaves the stage locale representing Gertrude's closet, that scene has ended, and a new scene has to be imagined as Hamlet moves to a different stage area to represent the graveyard locale. This *transition* approach to staging — like contemporary fade-and-dissolve film techniques — leads to simultaneous action on a number of stage levels, and requires that actors be agile as well as athletic in their movement.

PERIOD STYLE

Most historians agree that the Elizabethan acting style was more *natural* and had more character development than the classical period. It must have been more spirited as well, and demanded more stamina to hold the attention of such a boisterous audience. There are a number of persuasive arguments to suggest that the acting style was also more subtle and intimate than the classical period. Modern reconstruction theories of the *Globe* by theatre scholars C. Walter Hodges and John Cranford Adams suggest that Shakespeare's playhouse could be lowered into the auditorium of almost any modern theatre and still not touch the stage.

The intimacy of a smaller playhouse would have reduced the need for actors to project their voices in order to be clearly understood, and may have encouraged a more conversational approach to acting. A smaller playhouse may also have had an impact on the need for heroic characters to be portrayed solely by more robust actors. Although Shakespeare makes frequent reference to the physical stature of his tragic heroes in sword duels, hand-to-hand combat, and mortal battles, there is no historical evidence that his actors were more athletic than other performers of the period. Indeed, such an imposing physical figure in close proximity to the audience may have appeared as distorted and exaggerated as we imagine the ancient Greek actors must have appeared up close in their stylized masks, flowing robes, and elevated thick-soled boots.

HISTORICAL VIEWS

One of the curious features of the period was the public adulation of the *boy-player*. Although female roles were played by young men, boy-players apparently enjoyed a privileged position in an acting company. However, there does not appear to have been any attempt at female impersonation by these youthful Juliets, and their simple character portraits may have appealed more to angelic beauty than vocal or physical disguises. Most likely, cherub-faced young boys playing innocent young girls was a pleasing aesthetic for Elizabethans and reinforced their own period views on childish innocence and beauty.

It is also just as likely that the mature adult female roles were reserved for the more experienced male performers in the acting company. Scholars assume that the basic approach of adult male actors playing mature female characters would have been similar to playing a male character. This simplistic approach would have avoided excessive physical or vocal exaggeration, and may have relied more heavily on subtlety in voice and economy in movement when playing female roles.

The most notable accounts of the Elizabethan acting style surface in comments made by period authors, who were also actors, or from characters in period scripts. The role of gesture and movement must have played a major role in Elizabethan acting style. For example,

Thomas Heywood, period actor and playwright, urges his fellow performers " ... not to use any impudent or forced motion in any part of the body, no rough or other violent gesture; nor on the contrary to stand like a stiff, starched man."

Of course, it remains for Shakespeare to give us the most detailed account of acting style in the period. In his own historical time, it is believed that period scripts were staged in a presentational, or audience-centered style with little effort made to suggest an illusion of reality. Shakespeare, however, appears to have encouraged his actors to interact with the audience and to perform more believable character actions. Perhaps that is the acting style Shakespeare has in mind in Hamlet's famous advice to the players speech (Act III, Scene ii):

> Speak the speech, I pray you, as I pronounced it to you, trippingly on the tongue; but it you mouth it, as many of your players do, I had as lief the town-crier spoke my lines. Nor do not saw the air too much with your hand, thus; but use all gently: for in the very torrent, tempest, and as I may say the whirlwind of passion, you must acquire and beget a temperance, that may give it smoothness.

> . . . .

> Be not too tame neither, but let your own discretion be your tutor. Suit the action to the word, the word to the action; with this special observation, that you o'erstep not the modesty of nature; for anything so o'erdone is from the purpose of playing, whose end, both at the first and now, was and is to hold, as 'twere, the mirror up to nature; to show virtue her own features, scorn her own image, and the very age and body of the time his form and pressure.

For Shakespeare, the actor was expected to be an intelligent, well-rounded performer trained in physical and vocal techniques that could express the deep reservoir of emotion and motivation of the character. Graceful and fluid coordination of all parts of the body was especially desirable. The actor was also expected to be a flexible and versatile performer, capable of playing both comic and tragic as well as female roles.

The ability to effectively portray women in a believable manner is the highest tribute that can be paid to Shakespeare's actors. It offers strong testimony to the role that sensitivity and versatility can play in *any* period of theatre history. This will be an important lesson for you to keep in mind when playing the monologues that follow at the end of this chapter. After all, Shakespeare's characters are not historic relics and the significant moments in their lives need to be retold with passion and persuasion.

MODERN APPROACHES

Contemporary approaches to the Elizabethan style of acting should avoid the obvious appearance of exaggeration or posturing. Remember Shakespeare's advice to his players and rely on economy and simplicity to suggest the honesty and truthfulness of your character portraits. Of course, it will be important to read verse well and give a sense of "fine speaking" to the beauty and rhythm of Shakespeare's verse. Line interpretations should be precise, and have a clarity that captures the poetic grandeur of the blank verse familiar to the historical period.

Look closely at poetic images in the dialogue for textual clues that may help define your characters. These internal clues are the *score* that will help you orchestrate a flesh-and-blood portrait in audition. Pay particular attention to vocal sound, stress, or repetition motifs and remember that a majority of Shakespeare's scripts are written in *un-rhyming* verse that is punctuated with end rhyme or more formal couplets.

Blank Verse

The blank verse style of writing dialogue is a defining characteristic of the Elizabethan period, and requires agility and precision in voicing its rhythmical pattern. The pattern consists of five *unstressed* short sounds juxtaposed by five *stressed,* or long, sounds. This alternating series of short and long sounds is equivalent to ten *beats*. The stress in emphasis is always placed on the *second* sound (/), and each line ending concludes in a *strong* stress regardless of punctuation. The unstressed (X) sounds then serve as *counterpoint* to the long sounds. For example, if you were to chart the role of blank verse in the opening lines of Hamlet's familiar soliloquy, the following vocal blueprint might emerge.

```
To    be   or  not   to   be:  that  is   the  question:
X    /    X   /     X   /         /   X   X        /

Whether 'tis nobler in the  mind  to  suffer
    X     X    /    X   X    /    X    /

The  slings and  arrows of  outrageous fortune
X     /    X    /     X       /          /

Or   to take arms against a  sea  of  troubles,
 /   X   X   /    /       X  /    X       /

And  by  opposing end  them?
X    X     /      /    X
```

By charting individual lines of dialogue and identifying punctuation mark clues, your understanding of blank verse should allow you to make more informed choices on which words to stress, and which words or phrases to emphasize for vocal color. You may also discover a useful rehearsal technique for memorizing Shakespeare's long set speeches or soliloquies by remembering repetitious rhythms as they appear in a character's dialogue.

ADDITIONAL DIMENSIONS

In playing Shakespeare, strike a happy medium between Elizabethan practices and contemporary audition expectations. Frame a lively interpretation of the monologue character that avoids cliché or trite approaches to voice blank verse as if it were a poetry recitation. The character portrait should also not be delivered with stilted gestures, stiff-legged movement, or exaggerated poses to punctuate the character's action described in the dialogue. This is also sound advice for playing the period monologues that are included in Chapter Five.

It is especially important in playing Shakespeare for gestures and movement to appear fluid and spontaneous. The role of movement to suggest the heroic nature of the characters requires a relaxed body that moves with measured grace and style. In order to explore the role that gestures and movement play in Shakespeare, please review the Poetry-in-Motion exercise that follows. Your goal in the exercise is to *silently* voice the following passage from *Macbeth* Act I, Scene v using only subtle gestures and movements.

> Your face, my thane, is as a book where
> men
> May read strange matters. To beguile
> the time,
> Look like the time; bear welcome in
> your eye,
> Your hand, your tongue; look like the
> innocent flower,
> But be the serpent under 't.

Begin the exercise with a brief review of the passage to determine an appropriate age for the character, location for the setting, and mood being described. Perform the passage *silently* in a small, open space using only subtle gestures and movement to convey character age, location, and mood. Gestures and movements should be fluid but executed with vigor.

Now repeat the silent performance three times. With each repetition, eliminate gestures or movements that are not absolutely necessary to convey your interpretation of the passage. When all gestures and movements are refined to *suit the action to the word,* turn your attention to vocal elements that might enhance an interpretation of the passage. Please review the discussion of pitch, rate, and volume discussed earlier in the chapter before adding vocal elements to your interpretation.

Begin the second part of the exercise by identifying key words or phrases to vocally emphasize in your interpretation. When you have determined the role that pitch, rate, and volume will play in the character portrait, repeat the passage aloud three times in a conversational tone. Finally, incorporate refined gestures and movements developed earlier in the exercise and perform the passage three more times — vocally *and* physically — in a larger, open space. Review the Vocal Fine Tuning exercise in Chapter Two that describes the vocal qualities needed to voice the rhythm of poetic verse.

Now, are your gestures and movements clearly defined, natural, and relaxed? Is your voice conversational? Are your gestures and movements subtle enough to complement a conversational tone of voice? Does your performance build to a noticeable climax? Do you have meaningful variety in pitch, rate, and volume? When confident that voice and body are working *together,* repeat the passage a final time on videotape as an example of the fluid movement and conversational tone needed in playing Shakespeare.

AUDITION MONOLOGUES

The Shakespeare rehearsal period needs to focus on character interpretation and voicing subtle nuances of character meaning. Reading the complete script and defining a character's specific intention or motivation will give your audition an additional element of believability. Identify *active verbs* to immediately propel you into the action and given circumstances of the monologue, and you will capture the most significant moments in the life of the character being portrayed. Please review the discussion of active verbs in Chapter One for additional audition hints.

It is also crucial in the rehearsal period to explore a measure of risk-taking to discover imaginative stage business. Performance choices made in rehearsal should highlight both the *inner and outer* emotions or thoughts of the character, and reveal your own sensitivity to the action described in the monologue. Don't forget to set aside regular rehearsal time for warm-ups to voice Shakespeare's blank verse with a confident and crisp tone.

As You Like It (1599)
Act II, Scene vii

Jaques (Ja'kis), a sour and coldly cynical lord attending a banished Duke, arrives at court from an afternoon walk and spins a bizarre tale about meeting a "fool" in the forest. Although the embittered and resentful lord endures ridicule and humiliation from the Duke and his men, Jaques' blithe exterior and seemingly childish prattle adds an additional layer of wicked parody to the comic tale.

JAQUES: A fool, a fool! I met a fool i' the forest
A motley fool! — a miserable world! —
As I do live by food, I met a fool,
Who laid him down and bask'd him in the sun,
And rail'd on Lady Fortune in good terms,
In good set terms, and yet a motley fool.
'Good morrow, fool,' quoth I. 'No, sir,' quoth
he,
'Call me not fool till heaven hath sent me
fortune.'
And then he drew a dial from his poke,
And, looking on it with lack-lustre eye,
Says very wisely, 'It is ten o'clock:
Thus we may see,' quoth he, 'how the world wags:
'T is but an hour ago since it was nine,
And after one hour more 't will be eleven;
And so, from hour to hour, we ripe and ripe,
And then, from hour to hour, we rot and rot;
And thereby hangs a tale.' When I did hear
The motley fool thus moral on the time,
My lungs began to crow like chanticleer,
That fools should be so deep-contemplative,
And I did laugh sans intermission
An hour by his dial. — O noble fool!
A worthy fool! Motley's the only wear.

Note: Motley, a cloth garment composed of many patches of mixed color, was the traditional dress of a clown, fool, or jester in the historical period.

Later in the scene, the world-weary and melancholy Jaques laments the bitter and cynical view of a world in which human vanity corrupts and destroys. In one of Shakespeare's most quotable speeches, "The Seven Ages of Man," Jaques spins a sardonic vision of the inevitable fate that awaits mankind.

JAQUES: All the world's a stage,
And all the men and women merely players.
They have their exits and their entrances,
And one man in his time plays many parts,
His acts being seven ages. At first the infant,
Mewling and puking in the nurse's arms.
Then the whining schoolboy with his satchel
And shining morning face, creeping like snail
Unwillingly to school. And then the lover,
Sighing like furnance, with a woeful ballad,
Made to his mistress' eyebrow. Then, a soldier,
Jealous in honor, sudden, and quick in quarrel,
Seeking the bubble reputation
Even in the canon's mouth. And then the justice,
In fair round belly with good capon lined,
With eyes severe and beard of formal cut,
Full of wise saws and modern instances;
And so he plays his part. The sixth age shifts
Into the lean and slippered pantaloon,
With spectacles on nose and pouch on side,
His youthful hose, well saved, a world too wide
For his shrunk shank, and his big, manly voice,
Turning again toward childish treble, pipes
And whistles in his sound. Last scene of all,
That ends this strange, eventful history,
Is second childishness and mere oblivion,
Sans teeth, sans eyes, sans taste, sans everything.

Richard III (1592-1593)
Act I, Scene iv

To achieve his Machiavellian rise to power and accession to the throne of England, Richard, Duke of Gloucester, plots to have his brother Clarence, who stands before him in the royal line of succession, imprisoned in the Tower of London. While locked in his prison cell, Richard dispatches two murderers to kill his brother. In this edited excerpt, an anguished Clarence relates a "dream" he has had to his jailer — a nightmarish excursion into a dark underworld of tormented ghosts and hellish afterlife that foreshadows his own impending death.

CLARENCE: O, I have pass'd a miserable night, so full of fearful dreams, of ugly sights, that, as I am a Christian faithful man, I would not spend another such a night though 'twere to buy a world of happy days — so full of dismal terror was the time. Methoughts I saw a thousand fearful wrecks; a thousand men that fishes gnaw'd upon; wedges of gold, great anchors, heaps of pearl, inestimable stones, unvalued jewels, all scatt'red in the bottom of the sea; some lay in dead men's skulls, and in the holes where eyes did once inhabit, there were crept (as 'twere in scorn of eyes) reflecting gems, that woo'd the slimy bottom of the deep, and mocked the dead bones that lay scatt'red by. O then began the tempest to my soul! I pass'd (methought) the melancholy flood, with that sour ferryman which poets write of, unto the kingdom of perpetual night.

The first that there did greet my stranger soul was my great father-in-law, renowned Warwick, who spake aloud, "What scourge for perjury can this dark monarchy afford false Clarence?" And so he vanish'd. Then came wand'ring by a shadow like an angel, with bright hair dabbled in blood, and he shriek'd out aloud, "Clarence is come — false, fleeting, perjur'd Clarence, that stabb'd me in the field by Tewksbury: Seize on him, Furies, take him unto torment!" With that, methoughts, a legion of foul fiends environ'd me, and howled in my ears such hideous cries that with the very noise I, trembling, wak'd, and for a season after could not believe but that I was in hell, such terrible impression made my dream. Keeper, I prithee sit by me a while. My soul is heavy, and I fain would sleep.

A Midsummer Night's Dream (1595-1596)
Act III, Scene ii

In this delightful romantic comedy the mischievous sprite Puck has confused the command of Oberon, king of the fairies, and accidentally spread an elixir of love potion in the eyes of two young suitors, Demetrius and Lysander. Both dashing gallants awake and fall instantly in love with a companion, Helena, who is both confused and frustrated by such belated attention directed toward her. Here, Helena lashes out at the suitors for their cruelty and deception.

HELENA: O spite! Oh Hell! I see you all are bent
To set against me for your merriment.
If you were civil and knew courtesy,
You would not do me thus much injury.
Can you not hate me, as I know you do,
But you must join in souls to mock me too?
If you were men, as men you are in show,
You would not use a gentle lady so;
To vow, and swear, and superpraise my parts,
When I am sure you hate me with your hearts.
You both are rivals, and love Hermia;
And now both rivals to mock Helena.
A trim exploit, a manly enterprise,
To conjure tears up in a poor maid's eyes
With your derision! None of noble sort
Would so offend a virgin and extort
A poor soul's patience, all to make you sport.

Macbeth (1606)
Act II, Scene iii

The sun is just about to rise on the Macbeth household after a night of riotous feasting in honor of King Duncan, and someone is pounding at the front door. The Porter is drowsy and intoxicated as he shuffles forth to answer the call — unaware that at this very moment Macbeth has murdered King Duncan. The Porter, in a delirious haze, imagines he is the doorkeeper at the front gate of Hell, through which it was believed damned souls were first admitted, and the ensuing comic collision is a brief but howling romp across the stage.

PORTER: Here's a knocking indeed! If a man were porter of hell-gate, he should have old turning the key. *(Knocking within.)* Knock, knock, knock! Who's there, in the name of Beelzebub? Here's a farmer, that hanged himself on the expectation of plenty: come in time; have napkins now about you; here you'll sweat for't. *(Knocking within.)* Knock, knock! Who's there, in the other devil's name? Faith, here's an equivocator, that could swear in both the scales against either scale; who committed treason enough for God's sake, yet could not equivocate to heaven: O, come in, equivocator. *(Knocking within.)* Knock, knock, knock! Who's there? Faith, here's an English tailor come hither, for stealing out of a French hose: come in, tailor; here you may roast your goose. *(Knocking within.)* Knock, knock; never at quiet! What are you? But this place is too cold for hell. I'll devil-porter it no further: I had thought to have let in some of all professions that go the primrose way to the everlasting bonfire. *(Knocking within.)* Anon, anon! I pray you, remember the porter. *(Opens the gate.)*

Antony and Cleopatra (1606-1607)
Act V, Scene ii

With a theatrical flourish, the enchanting and exotic Cleopatra, Queen of Egypt, stages her own lavish death scene. Robed in cloak and crown by her trusted servants, Cleopatra prepares to commit suicide and join Marc Antony, her dead lover, in Cyndus where they first met and fell in love. As the fatal moment approaches, she tenderly caresses a basket of figs in which a poisonous asp is hidden and bows for a final curtain call like a finely chiseled statue of the love goddess she is.

CLEOPATRA: Give me my robe. Put on my crown. I have
Immortal longings in me. Now no more
The juice of Egypt's grape shall moist this lip.
(Charmian and Iras help her to dress.)
Yare, yare, good Iras, quick — methinks I hear
Antony call: I see him rouse himself
To praise my noble act. I hear him mock
The luck of Caesar, which the gods give men
To excuse their after wrath. Husband, I come.
Now to that name my courage prove my title
I am fire and air; my other elements
I give to baser life. So, have you done?
Come, then, and take the last warmth of my lips.
(She kisses them.)
Farewell, kind Charmian. Iras, long farewell.
(Iras falls and dies.)
Have I the aspic in my lips? Dost fall?
If thou and nature can so gently part,
The stroke of death is as a lover's pinch,
Which hurts and is desired. Dost thou lie still?
If thus thou vanishest, thou tell'st the world
It is not worth leave-taking.

Henry IV, Part 2 (1598)
Act II, Scene i

Mistress Quickly, the unflappable owner of the Boar's Head Tavern, has been taken advantage of, again, by the boisterous braggart Sir John Falstaff. He has trifled with her affection, neglected to pay his long overdue tavern tab, and fabricated fanciful tales to secure loans from the gullible Mistress Quickly when he was short of cash. She is now indignant and has enlisted the Lord Chief Justice and his officers to arrest Falstaff, demanding restitution for all he owes her.

MISTRESS QUICKLY: Good my lord, be good to me. I beseech you, stand to me. An't please your grace, I am a poor widow of Eastcheap, and he is arrested at my suit. He hath eaten me out of house and home; he hath pit all my substance into that fat belly of his: but I will have some of it out again, or I will ride thee o'nights like the mare. Marry, if thou wert an honest man, thyself and the money too. Thou didst swear to me upon a parcel-gilt goblet, sitting in my Dolphin-chamber, at the round table, by a sea-coal fire, upon Wednesday in Wheeson week, when the Prince broke thy head for liking his father to a singing-man of Windsor, thou didst swear to me then, as I was washing thy wound, to marry me and make me my lady thy wife.

Canst thou deny it? Did not goodwife Keech, the butcher's wife, come in then and call me "gossip Quickly?" Coming in to borrow a mess of vinegar, telling us she had a good dish of prawns, whereby thou didst desire to eat some, whereby I told thee they were ill for a green wound? And didst thou not, when she was gone downstairs, desire me to be no more so familiar with such poor people, saying that ere long they should call me "madam"? And didst thou not kiss me and bid me fetch thirty shillings? I put thee now to thy Book-oath: Deny it, if thou canst.

Timon of Athens (1607-1608)
Act IV, Scene i

Surrounded by fair-weather flatterers, Timon of Athens is a wealthy nobleman known for his unbridled generosity and extravagance. One by one, however, his friends soon desert him and creditors send agents to collect outstanding loans. In despair and humiliation, Timon abandons society and exiles himself in an abandoned cave outside of Athens where, digging for roots to gnaw, he curses his fate and voices bitterness against mankind.

TIMON: *(Digs.)* Nature, being sick of man's unkindness, should yet be hungry! Common mother, thou whose womb unmeasurable and infinite breast teems and feeds all; those selfsame mettle whereof thy proud child, arrogant man, is puffed engenders the black toad and adder blue, the gilded newt and the eyeless venomed worm, with all th' abhorred births, below crisp heaven whereon Hyperion's quick'ning fire doth shine — yield him who all thy human sons doth hate, from forth thy plenteous bosom, one poor root! Ensear thy fertile and conceptious womb; let it no more bring out ingrateful man! Go great with tigers, wolves, and bears; teem with new monsters whom thy upward face hath to the marbled mansions all above never presented! O, a root! Dear thanks! Dry up thy marrows, vines, and plough-torn leas, whereof ingrateful man with liquorish drafts and morsels unctuous greases his pure mind, that from it all consideration slips. Plague! I am sick of this false world, and will love naught but even the mere necessities upon't. Then, Timon, presently prepare thy grave. Lie where the light foam of the sea may beat thy gravestone daily. Make thine epitaph, that death in me at others' lives may laugh!

Henry IV, Part 2 (1598)

Shakespeare' remarkable male characters invariably attract actors who wish to stake a personal claim on these heroic stage figures. The practice of breeches parts, *however, has recently encouraged a more gender-neutral approach to playing Shakespeare. Breeches roles feature female actors as youthful male romantic heroes, sprites, or comic stock characters. The following two monologues are appropriate breeches roles that invite an imaginative approach to character interpretation. It is important, however, to keep in mind that this is* not *male impersonation. The roles should be played with the same irrepressible sense of humor and bright glimpses of comic timing that any actor might exhibit in translating an indelible character portrait from the page to the stage.*

Induction

The script opens with an *induction,* or prelude, as Rumor, dressed in a grotesque robe decorated with tongues, enters to recount the previous action on Henry IV, Part 1 and to set the mood for Part 2. This is Rumor's only appearance in the play but expectations are to grab the audience's attention and lay bare all the speculations, conjectures, and suspicions that will be unmasked later in the action.

RUMOR: Open your ears; for which of you will stop
The vent of hearing when loud Rumor speaks?
I from the orient to the drooping west,
Making the wind my post-horse, still unfold
The acts commenced on this ball of earth.
Upon my tongues continual slanders ride,
The which in every language I pronounce,
Stuffing the ears of men with false reports.
I speak of peace, while covert enmity
Under the smile of safety wounds the world;
And who but Rumor, who but only I,
Make fearful musters and prepared defence
Whiles the big year, swoll'n with some other
grief's,

Is thought with child by the stern tyrant war,
And no such matter? Rumor is a pipe
Blown by surmises, Jealousy's conjectures,
And of so easy and so plain a stop
That the blunt monster with uncounted heads,
The still-discordant wav'ring multitude,
Can play upon it. But what need I thus
My well-known body to anatomize
Among my household? Why is Rumor here?
I run before King Harry's victory,
Who in a bloody field by Shrewsbury
Hath beaten down young Hotspur and his troops,
Quenching the flame of bold rebellion
Even with the rebels' blood. But what mean I
To speak so true at first? My office is
No noise abroad that Harry Monmouth fell
Under the wrath of noble Hotspur's sword,
And that the King before the Douglas' rage
Stooped his anointed head as low as death.
This have I rumored through the peasant towns
Between that royal field of Shrewsbury
And this worm-eaten hold of ragged stone,
here Hotspur's father, old Northumberland,
Lies craft-sick. The posts come tiring on,
And not a man of them brings other news
Than they have learnt of me. From Rumor's
tongues
They bring smooth comforts false, worse than true
wrongs.

Epilogue

In marked contrast to the play's prelude, the epilogue is spoken by a dancer and has a more festive tone. The language abounds in musical wit, nonsense repartee, and innocent jests that undercut the melancholy of Rumor's opening speech. There is a light-hearted cabaret atmosphere about the epilogue and the audience can now leave the theatre knowing the characters have learned from their past mistakes, and are stronger and wiser than when we first met them.

DANCER: First my fear, then my curtsy, last my speech. My fear is your displeasure; my curtsy, my duty; and my speech to beg your pardons. If you look for a good speech now, you undo me; for what I have to say is of mine own making, and what indeed I should say will, I doubt, prove mine own marriage. But to the purpose, and so to the venture. Be it known to you, as it is very well, I was lately here in the end of a displeasing play, to pray your patience for it, and to promise you a better. I did mean indeed to pay you with this; which, if like an ill venture it come unluckily home, I break, and you, my gentle creditors, lose. Here I promised you I would be, and here I commit my body to your mercies. Bate me some, and I will pay you some, and, as most debtors do, promise you infinitely.

If my tongue cannot entreat you to acquit me, will you command me to use my legs? And yet that were but light payment, to dance out of your debt. But a good conscience will make any possible satisfaction, and so would I. All the gentlewomen here have forgiven me; if the gentlemen will not, then the gentlemen do not agree with the gentlewomen, which was never seen before in such an assembly. One word more, I beseech you. If you be not too much cloyed with fat meat, our humble author will continue the story with Sir John in it, and make you merry with fair Katherine of France; where, for anything I know, Falstaff shall die of a sweat — unless already he be killed with your hard opinions. For Oldcastle died a martyr, and this is not the man. My tongue is weary; when my legs are too, I will bid you good night, and so kneel down before you — but, indeed, to pray for the Queen. *(Dances, then kneels for applause.)*

The Tempest (1611)
Act I, Scene ii

The magician Prospero, Duke of Milan, and his daughter, Miranda, have been stranded for twelve years on a magical island after Prospero's jealous brother, Antonio, deposed him with the help of King Ferdinand. When Prospero landed on the island he freed the imprisoned Ariel, an androgynous spirit that can assume male or female form at will, who is now his servant. Ariel has just returned from creating a swirling tempest to cause the ship Antonio is traveling on to run aground on this very island. Here, Ariel reports his success to Prospero with a swaggering, whirlwind recreation of the tempest.

ARIEL: All hail great master! Grave sir, hail! I come
To answer thy best pleasure; be't to fly,
To swim, to dive into the fire, to ride
On the curl'd clouds, to thy strong bidding task
Ariel and all his quality.
Perform'd to point the tempest thy bade me.
I boarded the kin's ship; now on the beak,
Now in the waist, the deck, in every cabin,
I flam'd amazement: sometime I'd divide,
And burn in many places; on the topmast,
The yards and boresprit, would I flame distinctly,
Then meet, and join. Jove's lightning's, the precursors
O' th' dreadful thunder-claps, more momentary
And sight-outrunning were not: the fire and cracks
Of sulphurous roaring the most mighty Neptune
Seem to besiege, and make his bold waves tremble,
Yea, his dead trident shake!
Not a soul but felt a fever of the mad, and play'd
Some tricks of desperation. All but mariners
Plung'd in the foaming brine, and quit the vessel,
Then all afire with me: the King's son, Ferdinand,
With hair — upstarting — then like reeds, not hair —
Was the first man that leap'd cried, "Hell is empty,
And all the devils are here!"

The Merry Wives of Windsor (1600-1601)
Act II, Scene i

Mistress Page, an eccentric but wealthy dowager, has just received a love letter from that boisterous braggart and rascal Falstaff, who hopes to seduce her and secure money to pay his mounting debts. Mistress Page is outraged at Falstaff's presumptuous attitude and wicked mischief. Mistress Page's anger increases as she plots her own revenge for Falstaff's outrageous lack of decorum.

MISTRESS PAGE: What have I 'scaped love letters in the holiday time of my beauty, and am I now a subject for them? Let me see. *(She reads.)* "Ask me no reason why I love you, for though Love use Reason for his precision, he admits him not for his counselor. You are not young; no more am I. Go to, then, there's sympathy. You are merry; so am I. Ha, ha, then, there's more sympathy. You love sack, and so do I. Would you desire better sympathy? Let it suffice thee, Mistress Page, at the least if the love of soldier can suffice, that I love thee. I will not say 'pity me' — tis not a soldier-like phrase — but I say 'love me' ...

> By me, thine own true knight
> By day or night
> Or any kind of light,
> With all his might
> For thee to fight,
> John Falstaff"

O, wicked, wicked world! One that is well-worn to pieces with age, to show himself a young gallant! What an unweighted behavior hath this Flemish drunkard picked, in the devil's name, out of my conversation, that he dares in this manner assay me? Why, he hath not been thrice in my company. What should I say to him? I was then frugal of my mirth, heaven forgive me. Why, I'll exhibit a bill in the Parliament for the putting down of men. O God, that I knew how to be revenged on him! For revenged I will be, as sure as his guts are made of pudding!

. . . .

Later in the scene, Mistress Page's husband, Master Page, learns of Falstaff's outrageous behavior in writing the same letter to both his wife and the wife of his friend, Master Ford. Although Master Page has confidence in his wife's virtue and is not threatened by Falstaff's overtures, Master Ford is in such a jealous rage that he schemes to assume the name of "Master Brook" and meet Falstaff at a local tavern, offering him money to "woo" Mistress Ford on his behalf to test her fidelity.

MASTER FORD: What Epicurean rascal is this! My heart is ready to crack with impatience. Who says this is improvident jealousy? My wife hath sent him; the hour is fixed; the match is made. Would any man have thought this? See the hell of having a false woman! My bed shall be abused, my coffers ransacked, my reputation gnawn at; and I shall not only receive this villanous wrong, but stand under the adoption of abominable terms, and by him that does me this wrong. Terms! Names! Amaimon sounds well; Lucifer, well; Barbason, well; yet they are devils' additions, the names of fiends; but Cuckold! Cuckold! The devil himself hath not such a name.

Page will trust his wife; he will not be jealous. I will rather trust a Fleming with my butter, Parson Hugh the Welshman with my cheese, an Irishman with my aqua-vitae bottle, or a thief to walk my ambling gelding, than my wife with herself: then she plots, then she ruminates, then she devises; and what they think in their hearts they may effect, they will break their hearts but they will effect. God be praised for my jealousy! Eleven o'clock the hour. I will prevent this, detect my, wife, be revenged on Falstaff, and laugh at Page. I will about it; better three hours too soon than a minute too late. Fie, fie, fie! Cuckold! Cuckold! Cuckold!

Henry VIII (1612-1613)
Act III, Scene ii

The arrogant and corrupt Cardinal Wolsey, who publicly opposed the marriage of King Henry VIII to Anne Boleyn, has been stripped of his authority after it is revealed that he secretly amassed a considerable personal fortune from political blackmail. Here, the Cardinal reluctantly bids farewell to his position and power in a speech that laments the sin of pride.

CARDINAL WOLSEY: So farewell — to the little good you bear me. Farewell, a long farewell, to all my greatness! This is the state of man. Today he puts me forth the tender leaves of hopes; tomorrow blossoms, and bears his blushing honors thick upon him; the third day comes a frost, a killing frost, and when he thinks, good easy man, full surely his greatness is a-ripening, nips his root, and then he falls, as I do. I have ventures, like little wanton boys that swim on bladders, this many summers in a sea of glory, but far beyond my depth; my high-blown pride at length broke under me, and now has left me weary, and old with service, to the mercy of a rude stream that must for ever hide me. Vain pomp and glory of this world, I hate ye! I feel my heart new opened. O, how wretched is that poor man that hangs on princes' favors! There is betwixt that smile we would aspire to, that sweet aspect of princes, and their ruin, more pangs and fears than wars or women have, and when he falls, he falls like Lucifer, never to hope again.

As You Like It (1599)
Act V, Scene i

Touchstone, one of Shakespeare's most notorious "fools," is a cynical jester in the corrupt court of Duke Frederick. He likes to bedazzle simple minds with his courtly wit and willful command of language. He is now part of a wandering band of exiled courtiers seeking solace in the forest of Arden, and has fallen in love with Audrey, a country girl. William, a love-sick country boy, is also in love with Audrey, and when he inadvertently meets Touchstone his romantic illusions are shattered.

TOUCHSTONE: It is meat and drink to me to see a clown. By my troth, we that have good wits have much to answer for; we shall be flouting; we cannot hold. Good ev'n, gentle friend. Cover thy head, cover thy head; nay, prithee be cover'd. How old are you, friend? [Five and twenty.] A ripe age. Is thy name William? A fair name. Wast born in the forest here? Art thou wise? I do now remember a saying, "The fool doth think he is wise, but the wise man knows himself to be a fool." The heathen philosopher, when he had a desire to eat a grape, would open his lips when he put it into his mouth, meaning thereby that grapes were made to eat and lips to open. You do love this maid? Give me your hand. Art thou learned?

Then learn this of me: to have, is to have. For it is a figure in rhetoric that drink, being pour'd out of a cup into a glass, by filling the one doth empty the other. For all your writers do consent that *ipse* is he now, you are not *ipse,* for I am he. He, sir, that must marry this woman. Therefore, you clown — abandon — which is in the vulgar leave — the society — which in the boorish is company — of this female — which in the common is woman; which altogether is, abandon the society of this female, or, clown, thou perishest; or to thy better understanding, diest; or (to wit) I kill thee, make thee away, translate thy life into death, thy liberty into bondage. I will deal in poison with thee, or in bastinado, or in steel; I will bandy with thee in faction; I will o'errun thee withy policy; I will kill thee a hundred and fifty ways: therefore tremble and depart.

All's Well That Ends Well (1602-1603)
Act I, Scene i

Helena, a virtuous and highly principled young woman, is concerned about what she perceives to be a lack of ethical and moral values in her social circle. She is particularly distressed to observe that chastity is no longer considered a virtue in polite society. She asks Parolles, a self-proclaimed womanizer, how virtuous women like her may guard themselves against vile assaults on their reputation. Parolles' blunt response is an unapologetic indictment of chastity.

PAROLLES: It is not politic in the commonwealth of nature to preserve virginity. Loss of virginity is rational increase, and there was never virgin got till virginity was first lost. That you were made of is mettle to make virgins. Virginity, by being once lost, may be ten times found; by being ever kept, it is ever lost. 'Tis too cold a companion; away with it! There's little can be said in't. 'Tis against the rule of nature. To speak on the part of virginity is to accuse your mothers, which is most infallible disobedience. He that hangs himself is a virgin: virginity murders itself, and should be buried in highways, out of all sanctified limit, as a desperate offendress against nature. Virginity breeds mites, much like cheese; consumes itself to the very paring, and so dies with feeding his own stomach.

Besides, virginity is peevish, proud, idle, made of self-love — which is the most inhibited sin in the canon. Keep it not, you cannot choose but lose by it. Out with't! Within one year it will make itself two, which is goodly increase; and the principal itself not much the worse. Away with it! 'Tis a commodity will lose the gloss with lying: the longer kept, the less worth. Off with't while 'tis vendible. Answer the time of request. Virginity, like an old courtier, wears her cap out of fashion, richly suited but unsuitable, just like the brooch and the toothpick, which wear not now. Your date is better in your pie and your porridge than in your cheek, and your virginity, your old virginity, is like one of our French withered pears: it looks ill, it eats drily, marry, 'tis a withered pear — it was formerly better, marry, yet 'tis a withered pear. Have nothing to do with it!

The Two Gentlemen of Verona (1593)
Act II, Scene iii

The two gentlemen of Verona are Valentine and Proteus, both of whom are dashing young gallants seeking more exciting life experiences. However, it is the comic subplot featuring Launce, the clownish servant to Proteus, that delighted Elizabethan audiences. Master to a poorly trained mutt named Crab, the sheepish Launce has unbridled devotion to his dog and family as he tearfully informs them he is accompanying Proteus to the Imperial court.

LAUNCE: Nay, 'twill be this hour ere I have done weeping; all the kind of the Launces have this very fault. I have received my proportion, like the prodigious son, and am going with Sir Proteus to the Imperial's court. I think Crab, my dog, be the sourest-natured dog that lives: my mother weeping, my father wailing, my sister crying, our maid howling, our cat wringing her hands, and all our house in a great perplexity, yet did not this cruel-hearted cur shed one tear: he is a stone, a very pebble stone, and has no more pity in him than a dog. Why, my grandma, having no eyes, look you, wept herself blind at my parting. Nay, I'll show you the manner of it.

This shoe is my father: no, this left shoe is my father: no, no, this left shoe is my mother: nay, that cannot be so neither: yes, it is so, it is so, it hath the worser sole. This shoe, with the hole in it, is my mother, and this my father; a vengeance on't! there 'tis: now, sit, this staff is my sister, for, look you, she is as white as a lily and as small as a wand: this hat is Nan, our maid: I am the dog: no, the dog is himself, and I am the dog — Oh! The dog is me, and I am myself; ay, so, so. Now come I to my father; Father, your blessing: now should not the shoe speak a word for weeping: now should I kiss my father; well, he weeps on. Now come I to my mother: O, that she could speak now like a wood woman! Well, I kiss her; why, there 'tis; here's my mother's breath up and down. Now come I to my sister; mark the moan she makes. Now the dog all this while sheds not a tear nor speaks a word; but see how I lay the dust with my tears.

As You Like It (1599)
Act III, Scene v

In the magical forest of Arden, Rosalind, an attractive young maiden wounded by the arrows of failed love, stumbles upon the saucy shepherdess Phebe and fellow shepherd Silvius. Now disguised as the dashing and handsome male Ganymede, Rosalind rebukes the amorous advances of the country bumpkin Phebe and lectures her on the true meaning of love. Phebe, in turn, is struck "love sick" for the suave and handsome stranger as romance swirls in the air!

PHEBE: Think not I love him, though I ask for him.
'Tis but a peevish boy. Yet he talks well.
But what care I for words? Yet words do well
When he that speaks them pleases those that hear.
It is a pretty youth — not very pretty —
But sure he's proud; and yet his pride becomes him.
He'll make a proper man. The best thing in him
Is his complexion; and faster than his tongue
Did make offence, his eye did heal it up.
He is not very tall; yet for his years he's tall.
His leg is but so-so; and yet 'tis well.
There was a pretty redness in his lip,
A little riper and more lusty-red
Than that mixed in his cheek. 'Twas just the difference
Betwixt the constant red and mingled damask.

There be some women, Silvius, had they marked him
In parcels as I did, would have gone near
To fall in love with him; but for my part,
I love him not, nor hate him not. And yet
Have I more cause to hate him than to love him
For what had he to do to chide at me?
He said mine eyes were black, and my hair black;
And now I am remembered, scorned at me.
I marvel why I answered not again.
But that's all one. Omittance is no quittance.
I'll write to him a very taunting letter,
And thou shalt beat it. Wilt thou, Silvius?

Much Ado About Nothing (1598-1599)
Act II, Scene ii

Set in romantic Messina on the idyllic island of Sicily, Don Pedro, an Italian prince, and his deputies have just returned from a successful battle and been invited by Leonato, the governor of Messina, to stay for a month of celebration. The main interest in the play, however, is the gender tug-of-war between Benedict and Beatrice. Benedict, Don Pedro's deputy, is an avowed bachelor who inflames Beatrice by voicing male anxieties about women who are deceitful and unfaithful. Beatrice, Leonato's niece, is a free-thinking young woman who enrages Benedict with her views on men who are egocentric and paranoid. Here, Benedict reveals his bleak views on love and marriage.

BENEDICT: I do much wonder that one man, seeing how much another man is a fool when he dedicates his behaviors to love, will, after he hath laugh'd at such shallow follies in others, become the argument of his own scorn by falling in love — and such a man is Claudio. I have known when there was no music with him but the drum and the fife, and now had he rather hear the tabor and the pipe; I have known when he would have walk'd ten mile afoot to see a good armor, and now will he lie ten nights awake carving the fashion of a new doublet; he was wont to speak plain and to the purpose (like an honest man and a soldier), and now he is turned orthography — his words are a very fantastical banquet, just so many strange dishes.

May I be so converted and see with these eyes? I cannot tell; I think not. I will not be sworn but love may transform me to an oyster, but I'll take my oath on it, till he have made an oyster of me, I shall never be made such a fool. One woman is fair, yet I am well; another is wise, yet I am well; another virtuous, yet I am well; but till all graces be in one woman, one woman shall not come in my grace. Rich she shall be, that's certain; wise, or I'll none; virtuous, or I'll never cheapen her; fair, or I'll never look on her; mild, or come not near me; noble, or not I for an angel; of good discourse, an excellent musician, and her hair shall be of what color it please God!

A Midsummer Night's Dream (1595-1596)
Act V, Scene i

Shakespeare's earliest comedy is also one of the most adventurous, introducing not only the supernatural world of sprites and spirits but also the colorful "rude mechanicals." This happy band of working-class laborers have arranged to perform a mercifully short classical scene from "Pyramus and Thisby" for the Duke of Athens' wedding. They are now in rehearsal learning their lines to play the roles with genuine insight and emotional honesty. What follows, of course, is a side-splitting parody of naïve and inexperienced performers in agonizing and artless distress.

Here are two "death duos" sure to leave you laughing out loud. In the first, the weaver Nick Bottom as Pyramus is to meet his true love Thisby at Ninny's tomb late at night. He discovers her stained mantle instead and, thinking she is dead, takes his own life in a raging fit of sorrow. In the second, enter Francis Flute the bellows-mender as Thisby, who was late for the rendezvous after being frightened away by a lion, played by Snug the joiner. Overcome with grief when spying "dead" Pyramus, Thisby wails and moans until it is her time to bid farewell, which she does by stabbing herself in the chest to end this farcical interlude. As Shakespeare indicated earlier in the play, "The course of true love never did run smooth!"

PYRAMUS: Sweet Moon, I thank thee for thy sunny beams;
I thank thee, Moon, for shining now so bright;
For, by thy gracious, golden, glittering gleams,
I trust to take of truest Thisby sight.
But stay, O spite!
But mark, poor knight.
What dreadful dole is here?
Eyes, do you see?
How can it be?
O dainty duck! O dear!
Thy mantle good,
What, stain'd with blood!
Approach, ye Furies fell!
O Fates, come, come,
Cut thread and thrum;
Quail, crush, conclude, and quell!
O wherefore, Nature, didst thou lions frame?
Since lion vile hath here deflow'r'd my dear,
Which is — no, no — which was the fairest dame
That liv'd, that lov'd, that lik'd, that look's with cheer.
Come, tears, confound,
Out, sword, and wound
The pap of Pyramus;
Ay, that left pap,
Where heart doth hop. *(Stabs himself.)*
Thus die I, thus, thus, thus.
Now am I dead,
Now am I fled;
My soul is in the sky.
Tongue, lose thy light;
Moon, take thy flight.
Now die, die, die, die, die. *(Pyramus dies.)*

. . . .

THISBY: This is old Ninny's tomb. Where is my love?
Asleep, my love?
What, dead my dove?
O Pyramus, arise!
Speak, speak. Quite dumb?
Dead, dead?
A tomb must cover thy sweet eyes.
These lily lips,
This cherry nose,
These yellow cowslip cheeks,
Are gone, are gone!
Lovers, make moan.
His eyes were green as leeks.
O Sisters Three,
Come, come to me.
With hands as pale as milk;
Lay them in gore,
Since you have shore
With shears his thread of silk.
Tongue, not a word.
Come, trusty sword,
Come, blade, my breast imbrue! *(Stabs herself.)*
And farewell, friends.
Thus Thisby ends.
Adieu, adieu, adieu. *(Thisby dies.)*

Henry V (1599)
Act III, Scene i

This history play, based on the life of King Henry V — the wild,
undisciplined "Prince Hal" depicted in Henry IV *— focuses on events*
immediately before and after the Battle of Agincourt (1415) as England
embarks on another failed conquest of France. There are a number of
familiar minor characters in Henry's army — Pistol, Nym, and
Bardolph from the Henry IV *plays — and the boisterous braggart,*
Falstaff, whose death is briefly detailed later in the play. In the

following monologue a young boy gives an unflattering account of the company of soldiers in Henry's army.

BOY: As young as I am, I have observed these three swashers. I am boy to all three; but all three, though they would serve me, could not be man to me; for indeed three such antics do not amount to a man. For Bardolph, he is white-livered and red-faced; by the means whereof 'a faces it out, but fights not. For Pistol, he hath a killing tongue and a quiet sword; by the means whereof 'a breaks word and keeps whole weapons. For Nym, he hath heard that men of few words are the best men, and therefore he scorns to say his prayers, lest 'a should be thought a coward; but his few bad words are matched with as few good deeds, for 'a never broke any man's head but his own, and that was against a post when he was drunk.

They will steal anything, and call it purchase. Bardolph stole a lute-case, bore it twelve leagues, and sold it for three halfpence. Nym and Bardolph are sworn brothers in filching, and in Calais they stole a fire-shovel. I knew by that piece of service the men would carry coals. They would have me as familiar with men's pockets as their gloves or handkerchiefs; which makes much against my manhood if I should take from another's pocket to put into mine; for it is plain pocketing up of wrongs. I must leave them and seek some better service. Their villainy goes against my weak stomach, and therefore I must cast it up.

Sonnets

Shakespeare's sonnets are also a potential source of audition material that call for a short reading of verse to demonstrate skill in interpretation and phrasing. The following sonnets are rich in performance hints, compact in thought, lend themselves to any age or type, and may be played by female or male actors. The sample sonnets should be voiced as a direct address to the audience.

Sonnet 27

Weary with toil, I haste me to my bed,
The dear repose for limbs with travel tired.
But then begins a journey in my head,
To work my mind, when body's work expired.
For then my thoughts, from far where I abide,
Intend a zealous pilgrimage to thee,
And keep my drooping eyelids open wide,
Looking on darkness which the blind do see.
Save that my soul's imaginary sight
Presents thy shadow to my sightless view,
Which, like a jewel hung in ghastly night,
Makes black night beauteous and her old face new.
Lo, thus by day my limbs, by night my mind,
For thee and for myself no quiet find.

Sonnet 71

No longer mourn for me when I am dead
Than you shall hear the surly sullen bell
Give warning to the world that I am fled
From this vile world with vilest worms to dwell;
Nay, if you read this line, remember not
The hand that writ it, for I love you so,
That I in your sweet thoughts would be forgot,
If thinking on me then should make you woe.
O, if (I say) you look upon this verse,
When I (perhaps) compounded am with clay,
Do not so much as my poor name rehearse,
But let your love even with my life decay;
Lest the wise world should look into your moan,
And mock you with me after I am gone.

Sonnet 94

They that have pow'r to hurt and will do none,
That do not do the thing they most do show,
Who, moving others, are themselves as stone,
Unmoved, cold, and to temptation slow —
They rightly do inherit heaven's graces,
And husband Nature's riches from expense;
They are the lords and owners of their faces,
Others but stewards of their excellence.
The summer's flow'r is to the summer sweet,
Though to itself it only live and die;
But if that flow'r with base infection meet,
The basest weed outbraves his dignity:
For sweetest things turn sourest by their deeds;
Lilies that fester smell far worse than weeds.

CHAPTER FIVE
PLAYING THE PERIOD

"Theatre, like the fresco, is art fitted to its time and place ...
Therefore, it is above all else the human art, the living art."

— *Theatre of the People,* Romain Rolland

John Dryden, seventeenth century poet and playwright, defined the spirit of playing the period with his candid observation that societal attitudes, lifestyles, and manners are the substance and form of the historical times as they are portrayed in drama and literature. Dryden's point is that drama and literature mirror and then reflect the attitudes of the period in which they are written, and is the most accurate recorded history of the life and times of the people who are chronicled in those times.

The monologues included in this chapter – late seventeenth to nineteenth centuries and modern – represent a number of historical periods and feature prominent social, political, or moral themes of the period. In some instances authors lampoon or ridicule the pompous customs or conventions of their day. In other instances authors hold the mirror up to life to call attention to significant issues of the period. The historical periods here are, for the most part, outside the time frame of the monologues included in individual chapter headings of the book.

The immediate appeal of period scripts is that they provide alternative choices for those occasional requests to include a non-classical or non-modern monologue in an audition. Period scripts are also a refreshing departure from standard classical or Shakespeare monologues and have the added ingredients of biting social satire, intriguing storylines, peculiar mannerisms, and romantic misadventures. It should not surprise you that most of the period scripts are comic, or that each author's slings and arrows are aimed at the pretentious manners and social values of their respective periods.

The hallowed traditions of period society and its leading thinkers are comic targets as well. There is a familiar theme in period monologues: expose the silly, posturing antics of those who appear to take themselves and their own opinions much too seriously. Society's exaggerated sense of proper decorum and undue restraint leads period characters to rebellious and reckless acts of defiance as they flaunt their "bad" conduct and "unpolished" manners.

THE TIMES

There is a range of period drama and non-dramatic literature to choose from in this chapter. Comedies of manner, for example, depict aristocratic society of the seventeenth and eighteenth centuries engaged in witty exchanges of dialogue while displaying elegant social graces and sophisticated behavior. More complex social topics with universal themes — personal values, human dignity, social responsibility — surface in the march toward realism in the mid-nineteenth century and the modern era that follows in the early twentieth century.

Major movements in theatre history are included as well and feature representative excerpts from naturalism — a nineteenth century French version of realism that emphasized a more sordid view of life — and some early seeds of absurdism, a twentieth century movement made popular by existential authors who depicted human life devoid of meaning and at the cruel mercy of a mysterious fate.

Although there is an uneven degree of buffoonery, slapstick, and witty repartee in period scripts, each one has a familiar ring of satire. Laughter, of course, is the primary concern of most period authors but there is also a serious intent to make the audience *think* while they also enjoy a hearty laugh. Beneath the convenient masks they wear, each monologue character delights in pointing out flaws they happen to observe in others, and even the slightest social mishap is treated with reckless scorn.

Period characters endure scathing ridicule for their social indiscretions, but at the end of the play all is well that ends well — and the characters are restored to a healthy balance of humility in a predictable "happy ending." It is only foolish or silly characters that refuse to reject hypocrisy who suffer and are rudely cast out of society. Period scripts, then, expose the audience to the shallowness and superficiality of fictitious stage characters. It is only after the curtain has fallen that the audience realizes they may, in fact, have been laughing at themselves as well.

Typical playhouses had pit, box, and gallery stages that framed a forestage placed in front of a carved proscenium arch. There was a large main stage for the playing space, orchestra pit, decorated house curtain, and candles placed in elaborate chandeliers or, later, oil lamps to serve as footlights. *Both* the actors and the audience were illuminated. The Restoration Theatres (1660-1685) introduced four spaced pairs of wing flats, or shutters, placed in grooves on the stage floor that could be pushed together to form intricate indoor or outdoor backgrounds. Scenery was generally placed upstage and scenic practices included colorful wings, drops, borders, and shutters. The average seating capacity of a typical playhouse was 1200.

Acting took place on the apron in front of the proscenium arch. Actors and actresses — *yes,* women now appear on the stage! — dressed in fashionable clothes of the period and might pose on gilded chairs or recline on sumptuous beds. A number of actors "owned" the roles they played, and authors began to write scripts tailored to the vocal or physical talents of star performers. Surrounding all this glitter was an arsenal of stage machinery and special effects so heroic characters could be seen descending to earth on cloud machines or crossing raging rivers in a boat.

PERIOD STYLE

A review of the letters, diaries, and playbills of the period suggest there was little illusion of reality at work in the acting style. Actors were frequently seen in profile speaking directly to the audience in presentational postures, and no effort was made to disguise storylines that were trivial rather than heroic. Characters were either unduly good or unjustly evil, and wayward characters repented their sins — usually in the last act — and pledged to embrace morality as the newfound guiding principle of their lives.

Some authors tried to arouse the audience's pity or sympathy, but then arbitrarily invoked *poetic justice* to punish the bad and reward the good. Other authors sacrificed dramatic license in their use of *sentiments,* or moral proverbs, to depict virtue's triumph over vice. Unlike Shakespeare, period authors rarely permitted their characters to hold the mirror of nature up to themselves, or to seriously reflect on their own shallowness.

Sentiments expressed by reformed characters provided invaluable moral lessons to the audience, and offered public testimony that their sins had been washed away. Sentiments were more frequently directed at pretentious *fops* who sparkled in the current male fashion of the day and perfumed themselves with orange water at night. The nastiest barbs, however, were directed at foreigners and country bumpkins from the provinces. Typical period sentiments might include Richard Brinsley Sheridan's pronouncements in *The Rivals* that "a circulating library in a town is as an evergreen tree of diabolical knowledge" or "'tis safest in matrimony to begin with a little aversion."

Sophisticated comedies of the period relied heavily on stock characters to mirror societal attitudes, lifestyles, and manners. Authors were barely able to appease the audience's insatiable appetite for such stock characters as the forlorn poet, stylish rake, dowdy spinster, double-dealer, Herculean hero, coy mistress, and profligate son. Witches and comic old women, however, continued to be played by men until the end of the seventeenth century.

Period audiences also reflected the historical times. Theatre patrons chatted incessantly and at times strolled around the playhouse during a production to greet friends. To some patrons, the theatre was where one went to see *and* to be seen. Other patrons viewed the theatre as a social occasion to meet associates, gossip, or make rude comments aloud. For a few patrons, attending the theatre was an excuse to sport the latest fashion, conduct some secretive business, or pursue a fleeting rendezvous with the leading actress.

HISTORICAL VIEWS

In spite of nineteenth century critic Michel St. Denis' remark that there is *no* difference in the performance approach to period or contemporary scripts — "it's only that they do not take place on the same level" — period actors were frankly non-realistic and their character portraits would appear stiff and unnatural in comparison to modern acting techniques. The size and shape of the period playhouse itself may have encouraged a more formal and stylized approach to period acting and emphasized the vocal and physical attributes of performers.

For example, male actors were asked to portray exotic heroes dressed in periwigs and waistcoats, while female heroines were clothed in fashionable dresses layered with multiple petticoats. Actors appear to have intoned the poetic passages of lyrical period tragedies in the same manner that classical actors are thought to have chanted choral odes. There are also historical chronicles that describe popular actors who often paused abruptly *during* a speech or scene to encourage audience applause.

Actors performing verse scripts, usually written in rhymed couplets, modeled their role-playing on the social behavior of the times as well, exhibiting an exquisite degree of elegance and grace in movement. A period actor's facial expression appears to have been the most useful tool to define character attitude or mood — when not competing, of course, with a decorative costume that mirrored the current fashion.

Audience expectations for entertainment and frivolity were extremely high. The most accurate appraisal is that of Thomas Davies, an eighteenth century pamphleteer, who wrote that period audiences " … look upon the theatre as a place of amusement; they do not expect to be alarmed with fear and terror, or wrought upon by scenes of commiseration; but are surprised into the feeling of those passions, and shed tears because it cannot be avoided. The theatre is a place of instruction only by *chance*."

MODERN APPROACHES

Unlike the approaches to playing classical Greek or Shakespeare monologues discussed in Chapter Three and Chapter Four, period monologues do not easily lend themselves to complex character portraits. That is why it is crucial in playing the period to focus on vocal delivery, particularly the nuance of *word play* that may help to define a character's intention or motivation. Remember that in period monologues what is said is not nearly as important as *how* it is said.

At first, you may feel awkward or self-conscious focusing exclusively on word play to define a period character's attitude or mood in a monologue. But keep in mind that period scripts require significant vocal variety to capture the speaking rhythm of a character's dialogue. Vocal sounds will need to be placed "forward" in the mouth to achieve good enunciation, and an expressive range of pitch, rate, and volume are essential to achieve a more comfortable speaking style. Any neglect of vocal variety or crisp, articulate speech will only lead to an unpolished period audition.

Playing the period requires careful attention and focus on stage presence and a relaxed, yet alert, posture with head held high and arms resting comfortably at your side. Period portraits in comedy of manners monologues in particular will need to exhibit elegance and sophistication. Rehearsal time is an excellent opportunity to pursue period dance or music to enhance graceful gestures and stylish movement. Rehearsal time should also be set aside to explore the role that period fans, walking sticks, snuff-boxes, spectacles, or handkerchiefs might play in an audition.

Your first role in playing the period should be *actor as detective*. Begin by collecting information related to the historical times of each monologue. Review manners, mores, and social customs as part of your role-playing preparation. Historical sources that might add an ingredient of authenticity to an audition include memoirs and illustrated books on period fashion or theatre design sketches of period costumes. You may also need to consider museum visits, recordings, film documentaries, music recitals, lectures, and portrait studies to capture a glimpse of the historical times depicted in the monologues of your choice. Take advantage of any opportunity to review historical artifacts that may have imaginative clues for period character interpretation or performance.

AUDITION MONOLOGUES

The following monologues should provide a challenging opportunity for you to blend period styles and contemporary acting techniques into a memorable audition. Be very selective in the use of period styles, and do not attempt to duplicate every element learned from your detective work. Careful monologue selection, discriminating performance choices, and attention to detail are the primary ingredients needed to provide a glimpse of the historical times suggested in a period character portrait.

Playing period characters in an honest and realistic manner — without artifice or cliché — is the audition goal. Identify character actions or thoughts suggested in the monologues and express each simply and directly. Read the complete script and arm yourself with a strong sense of character intention and motivation. Although you will become more aware of different period acting styles through detective work, your own style of acting should give only a hint of the historical period. Remember that a successful period audition features a *here-and-now* believable character, not a *there-and-then* period reenactment.

The Happy Prince (1888)
by Oscar Wilde

This whimsical fairy tale pays tribute to endearing romance and eternal purity. In the city square of a small idyllic town stands the statue of a handsome prince that is much admired, especially by young lovers. One day a sad swallow happens to fly into town looking for his feathered friends to console him after a doomed romance. Exhausted from his journey, the swallow falls asleep at the feet of the Happy Prince. Awakened when drops of water begin to fall on his wings, the sparrow is amazed to discover that it is the statue, now very much alive, crying tears of sorrow.

HAPPY PRINCE: I am the Happy Prince. When I was alive and had a human heart, I did not know what tears were, for I lived in the Palace of Sans-Souci, where sorrow is not allowed to enter. Round the garden ran a very lofty wall, but I never cared to ask what lay beyond it, everything about me was so beautiful. So I lived, and so I died. And now that I am dead they have set me up here so high that I can see all the ugliness and the misery of my city, and even though my heart is made of lead yet I cannot choose but weep.

Far away in a little street there is a poor house. One of the windows is open, and through it I can see a woman seated at a table. Her face is thin and worn. She has coarse, red hands, all pricked by the needle, for she is a seamstress. She is embroidering passion-flowers on a satin gown for the loveliest of the Queen's maids-of-honour to wear at the next Court-ball. In a bed in the corner of the room her little boy is lying ill. He has a fever, and is asking for oranges. His mother has nothing to

135

give him but river water, so he is crying. Little swallow, will you not bring her the ruby out of my sword-hilt? My feet are fastened to this pedestal and I cannot move.

Don Juan (1665)
by Moliére

The legend of the handsome Don Juan, who appreciates feminine beauty wherever and whenever he sees it, is based on his insatiable quest to frolic in the passion that women inspire in him. This immortal rake is very light on his feet, constantly being chased by those he has wronged in the past — or by their angry fathers, brothers, uncles, cousins, and even priests! In a frank conversation with Sganarelle, his man-servant, Don Juan scoffs at the ludicrous notion that a man can love only one woman at a time and offers his own recipe on the subject.

DON JUAN: Would you have a man bind himself to the first girl he falls in love with, to give up the world for her, and to have eyes for no one but her? A fine thing to be sure, to pride yourself on some false honor of fidelity, to lose yourself in one passion forever, and to be blinded from your youth to all other beautiful women! No: constancy is only for fools.

Every beautiful woman has the right to charm us, and the woman who has the advantage of being the first one we meet should not deprive other women of their just claims over our hearts. It doesn't matter if I'm already engaged; the love I have toward one so fair does not bind me to do injustice to all the others; my eyes still see the merit in them all, and I pay the homage and tribute that Nature demands on us. I cannot refuse my love to any beautiful woman I behold.

Besides, the first stirrings of love have an indescribable charm, and the true pleasure of love consists in its variety. It's a delightful adventure to overcome the heart of a young beauty; to see day and day the progress you make; to shrink with sweet words, tears, and sighs the innocent modesty of a heart which is unwilling to yield; and to combat, inch by inch, all the little obstacles she places in the path of our passions; to overcome the scruples in which she places so much honor; and to lead her, step by step, to where we always intended to lead her.

In short, there is no pleasure more wonderful than triumphing over the resistance of a beautiful woman. In this matter, I have the ambitions of a conqueror, who flies from victory to victory, and who cannot bring himself to put limits on his hunger. There is nothing that can control my impetuous desires. I have a heart big enough for me to love the whole world, and, like Alexander, I could wish for other worlds to conquer as well.

A Matter of Husbands (1923)
by Ferenc Molnar

In this sophisticated kiss-and-don't-tell confession, Sara, a famous period actress cloaked in tart one-liners offers her considerable expertise to all young ingénues who may find themselves falsely accused of playing the role of the "other woman." With the flair of a femme savant, she points to the inevitable signposts that cleverly mask a fanciful, though fabricated, love affair with an actress. It is, after all, just a matter of husbands.

SARA: It happens to every actress who is moderately pretty and successful. It's one of the oldest expedients in the world, and we actresses are such conspicuous targets for it! There is scarcely a man connected with the theatre who doesn't make use of us in that way some time or another — authors, composers, scene designers, lawyers, orchestra leaders, even the managers themselves. To regain a wife or sweetheart's affections all they need to do is invent a love affair with one of us. Usually we don't know a thing about it. But even when it is brought to our notice we don't mind so much. At least we have the consolation of knowing that we are the means of making many a marriage happy which might otherwise have ended in the divorce court.

(With a gracious little laugh) It seems plausible. You fancy your husband in an atmosphere of perpetual temptation, in a backstage world full of beautiful sirens without scruples or morals. One actress, you suppose, is more dangerous than a hundred ordinary women. You hate us and fear us. None understands that better than your husband. And so he plays on your fear and jealousy to regain the love you deny

him. He writes a letter and leaves it behind him on the desk. He orders flowers for me by telephone in the morning and probably cancels the order the moment he reaches his office.

By the way, hasn't he a lock of my hair? They bribe my hairdresser to steal from me. It's a wonder I have any hair left at all. And hasn't he left any of my love letters lying around? Don't be alarmed. I haven't written him any. I might have if he had come to me frankly and said: "I say, Sara, will you do something for me? My wife and I aren't getting on so well. Would you write me a passionate love letter that I can leave lying around at home where she may find it?" I should certainly have done it for him. I'd have written a letter that would have made you weep into your pillow for a fortnight. I wrote ten like that for a very eminent playwright once. But he had no luck with them. His wife was such a proper person she returned them all to him unread.

The Drummer (1705)
by Joseph Addison

Lady Truman, recently widowed after a happy marriage, suddenly finds herself pursued by a host of ardent suitors. While they may be serious, Lady Truman simply dismisses them as a worthless tribe of faddish fellows who delight most in their own pretentious manners. Mr. Tinsel's romantic fortunes, however, may hold some merit as Lady Truman slyly admits in her undeniably generous and praiseworthy confession.

LADY TRUMAN: Women who have been happy in a first marriage, are the most apt to venture upon a second. But, for my part, I had a husband so every way suited to my inclinations that I must entirely forget him before I can like another man. I have now been a widow but fourteen months, and have had twice as many lovers, all of them professed admirers of my person, but passionately in love with my jointure. I think it is a revenge I owe my sex, to make an example of this worthless tribe of fellows, who grow impudent, dress themselves fine, and fancy we are obliged to provide for them.

But of all my captives, Mr. Tinsel is the most extraordinary in his kind. I hope the diversion I give myself with him is unblameable. I'm sure 'tis necessary to turn my thoughts off from the memory of that dear man, who has been the greatest happiness and affliction of my life. My heart would be a prey to melancholy, if he did not find these innocent methods of relieving it. Now, Mr. Tinsel, there's a wild fellow. 'Tis a thousand pities he should be lost; I shall be mighty glad to reform him.

The Swan Song (1888)
by Anton Chekhov

In this bittersweet farce — Chekhov's first play based on his short story of the same title — an aging alcoholic comedian, Vasili Svietovidoff, travels the hinterlands performing melodramatic skits that delight the local rustics. Small, cramped makeshift theatres are his venue, and he stumbles on stage each night with no thoughts of eventual retirement. In this monologue Vasili shares his first memory of love with one of the stagehands.

VASILI SVIETOVIDOFF: When I first went on the stage, in the first glow of passionate youth, I remember a woman loved me for my acting. She was beautiful, graceful as a poplar, young, innocent, pure, and radiant as a summer dawn. Her smile could charm away the darkest night. I remember, I stood before her once, as I am now standing before you. She had never seemed so lovely to me as she did then, and she spoke to me so with her eyes — such a look! I shall never forget it, no, not even in the grave; so tender, so soft, so deep, so bright and young! Enraptured, intoxicated, I fell on my knees before her, I begged for my happiness, and she said, "Give up the stage!"

Give up the stage! Do you understand? She could love an actor, but marry him — never! I was acting that day, I remember — I had a foolish, clown's part, and as I acted, I felt my eyes being opened; I saw that the worship of the art I had held so sacred was a delusion and an empty dream; that I was a slave, a fool, the plaything of the idleness of strangers. I understood my audience at last, and since that day I have not believed in their applause, or in their wreathes, or in their enthusiasm. Yes, Nikitushka! The people applaud me, they buy my photograph, but I am a stranger to them. They don't know me. I am as the dirt beneath their feet. They are willing enough to meet me ... but allow a daughter or a sister to marry me, an outcast, never! I have no faith in them.

The Bachelor's Soliloquy (1897)
by Phineas Garrett

This playful parody of Hamlet's classic soliloquy "To be or not to be" offers a juicy recipe of sarcasm and irony, with frothy undertones of sugar-coated truth, to all confirmed bachelors who fear they may succumb to an indecent proposal of marriage. In an unabashed paean to the single life, the Bachelor's adamant refusal to surrender to the ceaseless bombardment of marital bliss gets funnier as it goes along, and is lethal in its coldly savage assault.

BACHELOR: To wed, or not to wed — that is the question: Whether 'tis nobler in a man to suffer the slings and sorrows of that blind young archer; or fly to arms against a host of troubles, and at the altar end them. To woo — to wed — no more; and by this step to say we end the heartache, and the thousand hopes and fears the single suffer — 'tis a consummation devoutly to be wished. To woo — to wed — to wed — perchance repent! — ay, there's the rub; for in that wedded state, what woes may come when we have launched upon that untried sea must give us pause.

There's the respect that makes *celibacy* of so *long* life; for who would bear the quips and jeers of friends, the husband's pity, and the coquette's scorn, the vacant hearth, the solitary cell, the unshared sorrow, and the void within, when he himself might his redemption gain with a fair damsel. Who would beauty shun to toil and plod over a barren heath; but that the dread of something yet beyond — the yet undiscovered country, from whose bourne no bachelor returns — puzzles the will and makes us rather bear those ills we have than fly to others that we know not of! Thus forethought does make cowards of us all, and thus the native hue of resolution is sickled o'er with the pale cast of thought, and numberless flirtations, long pursued, with this regard, their currents turn awry and lose the name of marriage.

The Second Mrs. Tanqueray (1893)
by Arthur Wing Pinero

Paula, an artful trickster who married widower Aubrey Tanqueray to advance her place in society, is the notorious "woman with a past." The second Mrs. Tanqueray, however, is ill-equipped to deal with the tedium of country life, rejection by her husband's daughter from a first marriage, and the misery of a mismatched marriage. Paula's anxiety finally causes her marriage to fail and she begins a slow, torturous descent into madness. She rejects Aubrey's offer of a trip abroad as a way to escape past events, and darkly alludes to her own plan to reconcile a sordid past … suicide.

PAULA: I believe the future is only the past again, entered through another gate. You must see now that, do what we will, go where we will, you'll be continually reminded of — what I was. I see it … Of course I'm pretty now — and a woman, whatever else she may be, is always — well, endurable. But even now I notice that the lines of my face are getting deeper, so are the hollows about my eyes. I hate paint and dye and those messes, but, by-and-by, I shall drift the way of the others; I sha'n't be able to help myself.

And then, some day — perhaps very suddenly, under a strange, fantastic light at night or in the glare of the morning — that horrid, irresistible truth that physical repulsion forces on men and women will come to you, and you'll sicken of me. You'll see then, at last, with other people's eyes, you'll see me just as your daughter does now, as all wholesome folks see women like me. And I shall have no weapon to fight with — not one serviceable little bit of prettiness left me to defend myself with! A worn-out creature — broken up, very likely, some time before I ought to be — my hair bright, my eyes dull, my body too thin or too stout, my cheeks raddled and ruddled — a ghost, a wreck, a caricature, a candle that gutters, call such an end what you like!

Frankenstein (1833)
by Mary Shelley

Frankenstein, the novel, has little to do with the horrific images of blood and guts that have been popularized in film. Mary Shelley's historical novel depicts the eerie Creature with compassion and sympathy. It was only a consequence of the continual rejection and irritability he suffered while his creator failed to respond to his very human *desires that the Creature gradually grew into a malignant beast. Here is a haunting portrayal of the Creature's vulnerability when, in the novel, he tenderly requests a female companion.*

CREATURE: I expected this reception. All men hate the wretched. How, then, must I be hated, who am miserable beyond all living things! Yet you, my creator, detest and spurn me, thy creature, to whom thou art bound by ties only dissoluble by the annihilation of one of us. How dare you sport thus with life? Do your duty toward me, and I will do mine toward you and the rest of mankind. If you will comply with my conditions, I will leave them and you at peace. Have I not suffered enough that you seek to increase my misery? Life, although it may be an accumulation of anguish, is dear to me, and I will defend it.

Remember, thou hast made me more powerful than thyself. But I will not be tempted to set myself in opposition to thee. I am thy creature and I will be even mild and docile to my natural lord and king, if thou wilt also perform thy part, the which thou owest me. I am the fallen angel whom thou drivest from joy for no misdeed. Everywhere I see bliss from which I alone am irrevocably excluded. If the multitude of mankind knew of my existence, they would do as you do and arm themselves for my destruction. Yet it is in your power to recompense me.

Let your compassion be moved and do not disdain me. I was benevolent and good. Misery made me a fiend. Make me happy and I shall again be virtuous. We may not part until you have promised to comply with my request. I am alone and miserable. Man will not associate with me, but one as deformed and horrible as myself would not deny herself to me. My companion must be of the same species and have the same defects. A female. This being you must create.

The Wonder:
A Woman Keeps a Secret (1714)
by Susanna Centlivre

This domestic comedy is unique not only for its unconventional views on a woman's right to choose her husband, but also for the simple fact that its author is one of the few known female playwrights in the period. The storyline is typical of domestic comedies: a headstrong father figure stands in the way of his daughter's marital bliss. Isabella's scheming father, Don Lopez, arranges a marriage between his daughter and Don Guzan, a decrepit and deluded — but wealthy — old man. Isabella, a bold and headstrong young lady would rather become a nun to avoid this inescapable disaster.

ISABELLA: The thought of a husband is as terrible to me as the sight of a hobgoblin. To be forced into the arms of an idiot, a "sneaking, sniveling, driveling, avaricious fool" who has neither person to please the eye, sense to charm the ear, nor generosity to supply those defects. Ah, what pleasant lives women lead in England, where duty wears not fetter but inclination! The custom of our country enslaves us from our very cradles, first to our parents, next to our husbands, and when Heaven is so kind to rid us of both these, our brothers still usurp authority, and expect a blind obedience from us; so that maids, wives, or widows, we are little better than slaves to the tyrant man. Therefore, to avoid their power, I resolve to cast myself into a monastery. There will be no man to plague me!

A Woman of No Importance (1893)
by Oscar Wilde

In this dark comedy Mrs. Allonby, a flirtatious woman with a reputation for impolite indiscretion, sketches a satiric portrait of the "ideal man" a married woman should take for a lover. She has abundant wit to match her juicy tidbits of gossip, much to the delight of an adoring fan club. Here, Mrs. Allonby's verbal onslaught covers everything from how a man should treat a married woman to how to extol a woman's virtues to greatest advantage. She is charming but alarming as she reveals the secrets every woman of no importance already knows.

MRS. ALLONBY: The Ideal Man! Oh, the Ideal Man should talk to us as if we were goddesses, and treat us as if we were children. He should refuse all our serious requests, and gratify every one of our whims. He should encourage us to have caprices, and forbid us to have missions. He should always say much more than he means, and always mean much more than he says. He should never run down other pretty women. That would show he had no taste, or make one suspect that he had too much. If we ask him a question about anything, he should give us an answer all about ourselves. He should invariably praise us for whatever qualities he knows we haven't got. But he should be pitiless, quite pitiless, in reproaching us for the virtues that we have never dreamed of possessing.

And yet he should be always ready to have a perfectly terrible scene, whenever we want one, and to become miserable, absolutely miserable, at a moment's notice, and to overwhelm us with just reproaches in less than twenty minutes, and to be positively violent at the end of half an hour, and to leave us for ever at a quarter of eight, when we have to go and dress for dinner. And when one has seen him for really the last time, and he has refused to take back the little things he has given one, and promised never to communicate with one again, or to write one any foolish letters, he should be perfectly broken-hearted, and telegraph to one all day long, and send one little notes every half-hour by a private hansom, and dine quite alone at the club, so that everyone should know how unhappy he was.

After a whole dreadful week, during which one has gone about everywhere with one's husband, just to show how absolutely lonely one was, he may be given a third last parting, in the evening, and then, if his conduct has been quite irreproachable, and one has behaved really badly to him, he should be allowed to admit that he has been entirely in the wrong, and when he has admitted that, it becomes a woman's duty to forgive him, and one can do it all over again from the beginning, with variations.

Cyrano de Bergerac (1897)
by Edmond Rostand

Cyrano de Bergerac, a proud and patriotic nobleman serving as a soldier in the French Army, is also a brash and bombastic man with an extremely large nose. Although he is an expert duelist, gifted poet, and versatile musician, Cyrano is plagued by ridicule and scorn because of his prominent proboscis. Having fallen in love with the beautiful Roxanne, a distant cousin, Cyrano's insecurity and self-doubt forbids him to dream of ever finding true love.

CYRANO: My old friend — look at me.
And tell me how much hope remains for me
With this protuberance! Oh, I have no more
Illusions! Now and then — bah! I may grow
Tender, walking alone in the blue cool
Of evening, through some garden fresh with flowers
After the benediction of the rain;
My poor big devil of a nose inhales
April … and so I follow with my eyes
Where some boy, with a girl upon his arm,
Passes a patch of silver … and I feel
Somehow, I wish I had a woman too,
Walking with little steps under the moon,
And holding my arm so, and smiling. Then
I dream — and I forget …
And then I see
The shadow of my profile on the wall!

The Beaux' Strategem (1707)

by George Farquhar

Kate Sullen was married off at a tender young age by her parents to Squire Sullen, a bumbling blockhead, and was forced to abandon fashionable London to live with him and Lady Bountiful, who spends her time conjuring up herbal medicines, at their dreary country estate in the rural town of Lichfield. Trapped in a loveless marriage to a man she despises, Kate shares the misery of marital bliss in a pungent description of her husband's bedtime manner.

KATE SULLEN: O sister, sister! If you ever marry, beware of a sullen, silent sot, one that's always musing but never thinks. There's some diversion in a talking blockhead; and since a woman must wear chains, I would have the pleasure of hearing 'em rattle a little. Now you shall see, but take this by the way. He came home this morning at his usual hour of four, wakened me out of a sweet dream of something else, by tumbling over the tea-table, which he broke all to pieces; after this man and he had rolled about the room, like sick passengers in a storm, he comes flounce into bed, dead as a salmon into a fishmonger's basket; his feet as cold as ice, his breath hot as a furnace, and his hands and his face as greasy as his flannel night-cap. O matrimony! He tosses up the clothes with a barbarous swing over his shoulders, disorders the whole economy of my bed, leaves me half naked and my whole night's comfort is the tuneable serenade of that wakeful nightingale, his nose! Oh, the pleasure of counting the melancholy clock by a snoring husband!

The Man Who Married a Dumb Wife (1915)

by Anatole France

Leonard, a local municipal court barrister, finds himself in dire straits: the bloom is gone from the rose of his marriage, and he has been left with a dumb wife! It appears his wife, Catherine, is not able to attract the bribes and gifts other judges are receiving because their wives are more clever and cunning in their solicitation schemes. The

*time has come, obviously, to bring down the curtain on this marriage
and Leonard states his bill of particulars for our amusement.*

LEONARD: My wife is dumb. Quite dumb. I admit, I noticed it
before we were married. I couldn't help noticing it, of course, but it
didn't seem to make so much difference to me then as it does now. I
considered her beauty, and her property, and thought of nothing but the
advantages of the match and the happiness I should have with her. But
now these matters seem less important, and I do wish she could talk;
that would be a real intellectual pleasure for me and, what's more, a
practical advantage for the household.

What does a judge need most in his house? Why, a good-looking
wife, to receive the suitors pleasantly and, by subtle suggestions, gently
bring them to the point of making proper presents so that their cases
may receive — more careful attention. People need to be encouraged
to make proper presents. A woman, by clever speech and prudent
action, can get a good ham from one, and a roll of cloth from another;
and make still another give poultry or wine. But this poor dumb thing
Catherine gets nothing at all. While my fellow judges have their
kitchens and cellars and stables and store-rooms running over with
good things, all thanks to their wives, I hardly get wherewithal to keep
the pot boiling.

You see what I lose by having a dumb wife. I'm not worth half as
much ... And the worst of it is, I'm losing my spirits, and almost my
wits, with it all. When I hold my wife in my arms — a woman as
beautiful as the finest carved statue, at least so I think — and quite
silent, that I'm sure of — it makes me feel odd and uncanny. I even ask
myself if I'm holding a graven image or a mechanical toy, or a magic
doll made by a sorcerer, not a real human child of our Father in Heaven.
Sometimes, in the morning, I am tempted to jump out of bed to escape
from bewitchment. Worse yet! What with having a dumb wife, I'm
going dumb myself. Sometimes I catch myself using signs, as she does.
The other day, on the Bench, I even pronounced judgment in
pantomime, and condemned a man to the galleys, just by dumb show
and gesticulation!

The Old Bachelor (1693)

by William Congreve

In this comedy of manners by William Congreve we see the blossoming talent of a young author whose brittle wit and pungent social commentary are already ripe with satire on the social times in which he lives. The Prologue, spoken in the original script by a female, unveils the self-portrait of an author who is charming and genuine, but somewhat still in awe of his fledgling career.

PROLOGUE (FEMALE):

How this vile world is chang'd! In former days,
Prologues, were serious speeches, before plays;
Grave solemn things, as graces are to feasts;
Where, poets beg'd a blessing, from their guests.
But now, no more like suppliants, we come;
A play makes war, and prologue is the drum:
Arm'd with keen satyr, and with pointed wit,
We threaten you who do for judges sit,
To save our plays, or else we'll damn your pit.
But for your comfort, it falls out to day,
We've a young author and his first born play;
So, standing only on his good behaviour,
He's very civil, and entreats your favour.
Not but the man has malice. Would he show it,
But on my conscience he's a bashful poet;
You think that strange — no matter, he'll out grow it.
Well, I'm his advocate — by me he prays you,
(I don't know whether I shall speak to please you)
He prays — O bless me! What shall I do now!
Hang me if I know what he prays, or how!
And 'twas the prettiest prologue, as he wrote it!
Well, the deuce take me, if I han't forgot it.
O Lord, for Heavens sake excuse the play,
Because, you know, if it be damn'd to day,
I shall be hang'd for wanting what to say,
For my sake then — but I'm in such confusion,
I cannot stay to hear your resolution.

The Phantom of the Opera (1911)
by Gaston Leroux

*The novel, allegedly based on a true story, combines all the gothic
ingredients of horror, mystery, romance, and murder in late nineteenth
century Paris at the Opera Garnier — and is, of course, the text source
of Andrew Lloyd Webber's longest-running Broadway musical of the
same title. The Opera Garnier is haunted by a "ghost," actually a
horribly deformed musical genius named Erik, who has taken on a
young singer, Christine Daae, as a protégé. Erik, the "Angel of Music,"
tutors Christine through the wall of her remote dressing room and she
then mysteriously achieves stardom when she replaces the lead singer
who unexpectedly falls ill during a rehearsal for* Faust. *Here, Christine
describes her fateful encounter with the phantom of the opera to Raoul,
her true love.*

CHRISTINE: I had heard him for three months without seeing
him. The first time I heard it I thought it was as the voice of an angel.
I had never got the Angel of Music whom my poor father had promised
to send me as soon as he was dead. I thought that it had finally come,
and from that time onward, the voice and I became great friends. It
asked leave to give me lessons every day. The voice seemed to
understand mine exactly, to know precisely where my father had left
off teaching me. It was a curious thing, but, outside the dressing-room,
I sang with my ordinary, every-day voice and nobody noticed anything.

I did all that the voice asked. It said, "Wait and see; we shall
astonish Paris!" It was then that I saw you for the first time one evening
in the house. I was so glad that I never thought of trying to conceal my
delight when I reached my dressing-room. Unfortunately, the voice was
there before me and soon noticed, by my air, that something had
happened. I saw no reason for keeping our story secret or concealing
the place which you filled in my heart. Then the voice was silent. I
called to it, but it did not reply. The next day, I went back to my
dressing-room and the voice was there. It spoke to me with great
sadness and told me plainly that, if I must bestow my heart on earth,
there was nothing for the voice to do but go back to Heaven. I feared
nothing so much as that I might never hear it again. I swore to the voice

that you were no more than a brother to me nor would be, and that my heart was incapable of earthly love.

At last, the voice said to me, "You can now, Christine Daae, give to men a little of the music of Heaven," I don't know how it was that Carlotta did not come to the theatre that night nor why I was called upon to sing in her stead; but I sang with a rapture I had never known before, and I felt for a moment as if my soul were leaving my body! Suddenly I heard a long, beautiful wail which I knew well. It is the plaint of Lazarus when, at the sound of the Redeemer's voice, he begins to open his eyes and see the light of day. And then the voice began to sing the leading phrase, "Come! And believe in me! Whoso believes in me shall live! Walk! Whoso hath believed in me shall never die!" I cannot tell you the effect which that music had upon me. It seemed to command me to come to it.

Then, I was outside my dressing-room without knowing how! I was in a dark passage and was frightened. It was quite dark, but for a faint red glimmer at a distant corner of the wall. I cried out. My voice was the only sound, for the singing and the violin had stopped. And, suddenly, a hand was laid on mine ... or rather a stone-cold, bony thing that seized my wrist and did not let go. I cried out again. An arm took me round the waist and dragged me toward the little red light, and then I saw that I was in the hands of a man wrapped in a large cloak and wearing a mask that hid his whole face. I made one last effort; my limbs stiffened, my mouth opened to scream, but a hand closed it, a hand which I felt on my lips, on my skin ... a hand that smelt of death. Then I fainted away.

The Beggar's Opera (1728)
by John Gay

This ballad opera popularized London low-life in the eighteenth century and set the stage for later musicals that glamorized the lives of wayward criminals and seedy vagabonds of the night. Macheath and his ruthless gang of cutthroats create an underworld of love, lust, and violence that is seductive in its risqué charm. Here, the brash Macheath greets his "street ladies" and then improvises an inspired and joyful dance in a swirl of music.

MACHEATH: I must have women! There is nothing unbends the mind like them! Dear Mrs. Coaxer. You look charmingly today. I hope you don't want the repairs of quality, and lay on paint. Dolly Trull! Kiss me, hussy! Are you as amorous as ever? You are always so taken up with stealing hearts, that you don't allow yourself time to steal anything else. Mrs. Vixen, I'm yours! I always loved a woman of wit and spirit. They make charming mistresses, but plaguey wives. Oh, Betty Doxy! Come hither, turtledove. Do you drink as hard as ever? You had better stick to good wholesome beer; for in troth, Betty, strong waters will in time ruin your constitution. You should leave those to your betters. What! And my pretty Jenny Diver too! As prim and demure as ever! There is not any prude, though ever so high bred, hath a more sanctified look; but with a more mischievous heart! Ah! Thou art a dear artful hypocrite, Mrs. Slammekin! As careless and genteel as ever! All you fine ladies, you know your own beauty. But see, here's Suky Tawdry come to contradict what I was saying. Everything she gets one way, she lays out and then back. Why, Suky, you must keep at least a dozen tallymen. Thou hast a most agreeable assurance, girls; and art as willing as a turtle. But hark! I hear music. The harper is at the door. "If music be the food of love, play on!" Ere you seat yourselves, ladies, what think you of a dance?

Adam and Eve's Diaries (1906)
by Mark Twain

These "Two by Twain" sketches feature excerpts from the author's separately published diaries of Adam and Eve, juxtaposed here to reveal comic impressions the characters have in meeting each other for the first time in the Garden of Eden. There is enough biting wit and daring insolence here to suggest that Adam and Eve may soon come to discover that they were made for each other.

ADAM: The new creature with the long hair is a good deal in the way. It is always hanging around and following me about. I wish it would stay with the other animals. Cloudy today; think we shall have rain … *We?* Where did I get that word? I remember now — the new creature uses it. This morning found the new creature trying to clod apples out of that forbidden tree. I wish it would not talk; it is always talking right at my shoulder, right at my ear, and I am used only to sounds that are more or less distant from me. The new creature also names everything that comes along, before I can get in a protest. And always the same pretext is offered — it *looks* like the thing.

There is the dodo, for instance. Says the moment one looks at it one sees at a glance that it "looks like a Dodo." It will have to keep that name, no doubt. Dodo! It looks no more like a dodo than I do! I built me a shelter against the rain, but could not have it to myself in peace. The new creature intruded. When I tried to put it out it shed water out of the holes it looks with, and wiped it away with the back of its paws, and made a noise such as some of the other animals make when they are in distress. I escaped last Tuesday night, and traveled two days, and built me another shelter in a secluded place, and obliterated my tracks as well as I could, but she hunted me out by means of a beast which she has tamed and calls a wolf, and came making that pitiful noise again, and shedding that water out of the places she looks with. I was obliged to return with her, but will presently emigrate again when the occasion offers.

.   .   .   .

EVE: I am almost a day older now. It must be so, for if there was a day-before-yesterday, I was not there when it happened; or I should remember it. It could be, of course, that it did happen and I was not noticing it. It will be best to start right now, and not let the record get confused. Some instinct tells me that these details are going to be important to the historian some day. We are getting along very well now, Adam and I, and getting better and better acquainted. He does not try to avoid me any more, which is a good sign, and shows that he likes to have me with him. He is up in the tree again. Resting, apparently. When I found that I could talk I felt a new interest in it, for I love to talk, all day, and in my sleep, too. I tag around after him and have to do all the talking, because he's shy, but I don't mind.

I tried to get him some of those apples, but I cannot learn to throw straight. During the last day or two I have taken all the work of naming things off his hands, and this has been a great relief to him, for he has no gift in that line, and he is evidently very grateful. Whenever a new creature comes along I name it before he has time to expose himself by an awkward silence. In this way I have saved him many embarrassments. Now I purposefully keep away from him in the hope that he will get lonely, but he has not. I shall talk with the snake. He is very kindly disposed ...

Money (1840)
by Edward Bulwer-Lytton

Graves, a crunchy curmudgeon of a man, has a cynical view of recent tabloid tales of deceit and deception that have made their way into — of all sacred places — the daily newspapers! His sensibilities are inflamed and outraged at the disparaging advertisements and editorials that are being published. Graves' dissection of news reporting is a passionate critique that treads a fine line between a scathing letter to the editor and a paid political advertisement. Hold the presses! This is an informative and trendy theatrical page-turner.

GRAVES: Ay — read the newspapers! — They'll tell you what this world is made of. Daily calendars of roguery and woe! Here, advertisements from quacks, money-lenders, cheap warehouses, and spotted boys with two heads! So much for dupes and imposters! Turn to the other column — police reports, bankruptcies, swindling, forgery, and a biographical sketch of the snub-nosed man who murdered his own three little children at Pentonville. Do you fancy these but exceptions to the *general* virtue and health of the nation? — Turn to the leading article! And your hair will stand on end at the horrible wickedness or melancholy idiotism of that half of the population who think differently from yourself. In my day I have seen already eighteen crises, six annihilations of agriculture and commerce, four overthrows of the Church, and three last, final, awful, and irremediable destructions of the entire Constitution! And that's a newspaper — a newspaper — a newspaper!

Epicoene, or The Silent Woman (1609)
by Ben Jonson

Morose, a cantankerous old miser with an obsessive hatred of noise, has plans to disinherit his profligate nephew Dauphine by marrying Epicoene, an apparently sweet and innocent young lady who is exceptionally quiet and reserved. He, of course, is unaware that Dauphine has secretly plotted this mismatch for his own mercenary gain. True Wit, a confidante and well-meaning friend, offers Morose a shrewd accounting of the disadvantages of marriage at his age, regardless of the virtues of the young lady involved. After adding up the assets and subtracting the deficits, the final balance sheet suggests this is a marriage already on the rocks.

TRUE WIT: Alas, sir, I am but a messenger: I but tell you what you must hear. It seems your friends are careful after your soul's health, sir, and would have you know the danger (but you may do your pleasure, for all them, I persuade not, sir). If, after you are married, your wife do run away with a vaulter, or the Frenchman that walks upon ropes, or him that dances the jig, or a fencer for his skill at his weapon, why it is not their fault; they have discharged their consciences: when you know what may happen. Nay, suffer valiantly, sir, for I must tell you all the perils that you are obnoxious to.

If she be fair, young, and vegetous, no sweetmeats ever drew more flies; all the yellow doublets and great roses in the town will be there. If foul and crooked, she'll be with them, and buy those doublets and roses, sir. If rich, and that you marry her dowry, not her, she'll reign in your house, as imperious as a widow. If noble, all her kindred will be your tyrants. If fruitful, as proud as May, and humorous as April; she must have her doctors, her midwives, her nurses, her longings every hour; though it be for the dearest morsel of man.

If learned, there was never such a parrot; all your patrimony will be too little for the guests that must be invited to hear her speak Latin and Greek: and you must lie with her in those languages too, if you will please her. If precise, you must feast all the silenced brethren, once in three days; salute the sisters, entertain the whole family, or wood of 'em; and hear long-winded exercises, singings, and catechizings, which you are not given to, and yet must give for: to please the zealous matron your wife, who, for the holy cause, will cozen you, over and above. You begin to sweat, sir? But this is not half, in faith: you may do your pleasure notwithstanding, as I said before, I come not to persuade you.

The Relapse (1696)
by John VanBrugh

In its turbulent stage history, this Restoration comedy of manners gem has been frequently attacked for its unveiled messages in defense of women's rights in marriage and jarred conservative opinions on the subject well into the eighteenth century. The enduring humor of the script is the pretentious fool Lord Foppington, laughable for his gross period affectation but mean-spirited enough to make even his own generation wince. Here, Lord Foppington discourses ad nauseam on his daily routine and extols the conversation with himself to a bored and weary party of guests.

LORD FOPPINGTON: To my mind the inside of a book, is to entertain one's self with the forced product of another man's brain. Now, I think, a man of quality and breeding, may be much diverted with the natural sprouts of his own. Once he comes to know this town, he finds so many better ways of passing away the four and twenty hours, that 'twere ten thousand pities he should consume his time in reading. For example, Madam, my life; my life, Madam, is a perpetual stream of pleasure, that glides through with such a variety of entertainments, I believe the wisest of our ancestors never had the least conception; not that I pretend to be a beau; but a man must endeavour to look wholesome, lest he makes so nauseous a figure in the side-box, the ladies should be compelled to turn their eyes upon the play.

So at ten o'clock, I say, I rise. Now, if I find it a good day, I resolve to take a turn in the park, and see the fine women; so huddle on my clothes, and get dressed by one. If it be nasty weather, I take a turn in the chocolate house; where, as you walk, Madam, you have the prettiest prospect in the world: you have looking glasses all around you — But

I'm afraid I tire the company. Not at all? Why then, ladies, from thence I go to dinner at Lacket's, and there you are so nicely and delicately served, that, stop my vitals, they can compose you a dish, no bigger than a saucer, shall come to fifty shillings; between eating my dinner, and washing my mouth, ladies, I spend my time, till I go to the play; where till nine o'clock, I entertain myself with looking upon the company; and usually dispose of one hour more in leading them out.

There's twelve of the four and twenty pretty well over. The other twelve, Madam, are disposed of in two articles: in the first four I toast myself drunk, and in t'other eight I sleep myself sober again. Thus, ladies, you see my life is an eternal round O of delights.

The Rivals (1775)
by Richard Brinsley Sheridan

Mrs. Malaprop, an opinionated dowager and guardian to Lydia Languish — a wealthy teenage heiress — isn't pleased to learn that her niece refuses to marry the socially prominent son of Sir Anthony Adverse. Sir Anthony is persuaded that Lydia's home schooling has seduced her, and restates his universal opinion that no young lady in polite society should become educated. Mrs. Malaprop vigorously defends her decision to educate Lydia in a comic tirade of twisted words and broken thoughts that have since been termed malaprop-isms, *words that* sound *like the word intended, but* mean *something entirely different and provoke unintentional misunderstanding and merriment.*

MRS. MALAPROP: Fie, fie, Sir Anthony, you surely speak laconically! Observe me, Sir Anthony. I would by no means wish a daughter of mine to be a progeny of learning; I don't think so much learning becomes a young woman; for instance — I would never let her meddle with Greek, or Hebrew, or Algebra, or Simony, or Fluxions, or Paradoxes, or such inflammatory branches of learning — neither would it be necessary for her to handle any of your mathematical, astronomical, diabolical instruments.

But, Sir Anthony, I would send her, at nine years old, to a boarding-school, in order to learn a little ingenuity and artifice. Then, Sir, she

should have a supercilious knowledge in accounts — and as she grew
up, I would have her instructed in geometry, that she might know
something of the contagious countries — but above all, Sir Anthony,
she should be mistress of orthodoxy, that she might not misspell, and
mispronounce words so shamefully as girls usually do; and likewise
that she might reprehend the true meaning of what she is saying. This,
Sir Anthony, is what I would have a woman know — and I don't think
there is a superstitious article in it.

The Way of the World (1700)
by William Congreve

*Often regarded as a social satire on greed and lust, this comedy of
manners play could just as easily be seen as a period soap opera,
perhaps titled "As the World of the Idle Rich Turns." Mirabell, a
handsome man of impeccable taste, desires to marry Millamant, an
equally attractive woman with a rather considerable family inheritance
to her credit. In this "pre-nuptial" speech, Mirabell states his
conditions for marrying Millamant in a written contract focused more
on grandiose notions of proper behavior than on true love.*

MIRABELL: I covenant that your acquaintance be general; that
you admit no sworn confidant, or intimate of your own sex; no she-
friend to screen her affairs under your countenance, and tempt you to
make trial of a mutual secrecy. No decoy-duck to wheedle you a fop-
scrambling to the play in a mask — then bring you home in a pretended
fright, when you think you shall be found out — and rail at me for
missing the play, and disappointing the frolic which you had to pick me
up, and prove my constancy.

Item, that you continue to like your own face, as long as I shall; and
while it passes current with me, that you endeavor not to new-coin it.
To which end, together with all vizards for the day, I prohibit all masks
for the night, made of oil-skins, and I know not what — hogs' bones,
hares' gall, pig-water, and the marrow of a roasted cat. In short, I forbid
all commerce with the gentlewoman in what d'ye call it court. Item, I
shut my doors against all bawds with baskets, and pennyworths of

muslin, china, fans, atlases, etc. Item, when you shall be breeding — which may be presumed with a blessing on our endeavors — Item, I denounce against all strait lacing, squeezing for a shape, till you mould my boy's head like a sugar-loaf, and instead of a man-child, make me father to a crooked billet.

Lastly, to the dominion of the tea-table I submit — but with proviso, that you exceed not in your province; but restrain yourself to native and simple tea-table drinks, as tea, chocolate, and coffee: as likewise to genuine and authorized tea-table talk — such as mending of fashions, spoiling reputations, railing at absent friends, and so forth — but that on no account you encroach upon the men's prerogative, and presume to drink healths, or toast fellows; for prevention of which I banish all foreign forces, all auxiliaries to the tea-table, as orange-brandy. All aniseed, cinnamon, citron, and Barbadoes waters, together with ratafia, and the most noble spirit of clary — but for cowslip wine, poppy water, and all dormitives, those I allow. These provisos admitted, in other things I may prove a tractable and complying husband.

The War of the Worlds (1898)
by H. G. Wells

H. G. Wells' frightening futuristic novel of an impending martian invasion offers a dark and desolate image of war and the impending doom of mankind. There is no stirring call to all of good conscience and good will to reawaken their sense of individual or collective responsibility in the time of crisis — just a disturbing view of impending annihilation. Here, a soldier rallies his comrades to prepare for final judgment day in the face of the alien attack.

SOLDIER: This isn't a war. It never was a war, any more than there's war between man and ants ... That's what we are now — just ants. Here's intelligent things, and it seems they want us for food. First, they'll smash us up — ships, machines, guns, cities, all the order and organization. All that will go. At present we're caught as we're wanted. A Martian has only to go a few miles to get a crowd on the run. And I saw one, one day, out by Wandsworth, picking houses to pieces and routing among the wreckage. But they won't keep on doing that. So soon as they've settled all our guns and ships, and smashed our railways, and done all the things they are doing over there, they will begin catching us systematic, picking the best and storing us in cages and things ... Lord! They haven't begun on us yet. Don't you see that? Cities, nations, civilizations, progress — that's all over. That game's up. We're beat ... Those who mean to escape their catching must get ready. I'm getting ready.

The Easiest Way (1909)
by Eugene Walker

Elfie, an attractive chorus girl with limited talent, took "the easiest way" out years ago and allowed herself to become a kept woman by several men. When she learns that Laura, a young actress friend in the same business, has lost her heart to a handsome newspaper man who knows nothing of her past life, Elfie delivers a sober sermon about the strong bonds of sisterhood that exist between women like them ... and the lives they lead.

ELFIE: Was it my fault that time made me older and I took on a lot of flesh? Was it my fault that the work and the life took out the color, and left the makeup? Was it my fault that other pretty young girls came along, just as I'd come, and were chased after, just as I was? Was it my fault the cabs weren't waiting any more and people didn't talk about how pretty I was? And was it my fault when he finally had me alone, and just because no one else wanted me, he got tired and threw me out flat — cold flat? It almost broke my heart. Then I made up my mind to get even and get all I could out of the game.

The thing to do is to lie to all men — they all lie to you. Protect yourself. You seem to think that your happiness depends on this. Now do it. Listen. Don't you realize that you and me, and all the girls that are shoved into this life, are practically the common prey of any man who happens to come along? Don't you know that they've got about as much consideration for us as they have for any pet animal around the house, and the only way that we've got it on the animals is that we've got brains. This is a game, Laura, not a sentiment. Do you suppose this Madison — now don't get sore — hasn't turned these tricks himself before he met you, and I'll gamble he's done it since. A man's natural trade is a heartbreaking business. Don't tell me about women breaking men's hearts. The only thing they can ever break is their bankroll.

The Historical Register (1736)
by Henry Fielding

The biting parody of this non-dramatic narrative lies in its almost contemporary suggestion that, perhaps, once sacred virtues like modesty, patriotism, and honesty are now simply commodities regularly for sale to the highest bidder on both the public and private auction block. Soliciting a fair price on treasured virtues is, of course, a job for an experienced Auctioneer, who must maintain a sense of urgency in spite of the author's satirical point of view.

AUCTIONEER: I dare swear, gentlemen and ladies, this auction will give general satisfaction. It is the first of its kind which I have had the honor to exhibit, and I believe I may even challenge the world to produce some of the curiosities which this choice cabinet contains. Gentlemen and ladies, this is Lot 1: a most curious remnant of political honesty. Who puts it up gentlemen? It will make you a very good cloak. You see it's both sides alike, so you may turn it as often as you will. Come — five pounds for this curious remnant. I assure you, several great men have made their birthday suits out of the same piece. It will wear forever and never be the worse for wearing. Five pounds is bid. Nobody more than five pounds for this curious piece of political honesty? Five pounds. No more? *(Knocks.)* Sold to Lord Both Sides. Lot 2: A most delicate piece of patriotism, gentlemen. Who bids? Ten pounds for this piece of patriotism? Sir, I assure you several gentlemen at court have worn the same. 'Tis a quite different thing within to what it is without. You take it for the old patriotism, whereas it is indeed like that in nothing but the cut; but, alas, sir, there is a great difference in the stuff. But, sir, I don't propose this for a town suit. This is only proper for the country. Consider, gentlemen, what a figure this will make at an election. Come — five pounds? One guinea? *(Silence)* Put patriotism aside. Lot 3: Three grains of modesty. Come, ladies, consider how scarce this valuable commodity is. Half a crown for all this modesty? Is there not one lady in the room who wants any modesty? It serves mighty well to blush behind a fan with, or to wear under a lady's mask at a masquerade. *(Silence)* What? Nobody bid? Well, lay modesty aside.

The Negotiations of Medieval Marriage
by Tom Smith

Set in a creepy castle, this contemporary parody of period lords and ladies is ruthless in its comic spin on the manners of medieval courtship, and skewers historical views of marriage. Sir Gallenfield, a dashing young gallant with striking good looks that would have dazzled King Arthur's court, has come to negotiate his terms of marriage with the fair maiden Lady Fenecia before their nuptials. Lady Fenecia, — no damsel in distress! — is a lusty and forthright young woman determined to plot her own course for the marriage that lies ahead. In the medieval madness that follows, Sir Gallenfield and Lady Fenecia relentlessly deluge each other with delightfully infuriating and obstinate insults — so much so that any lingering illusions of a happy-ever-after-ending are doomed to comic failure!

(Lady Fenecia is pacing nervously. Sir Gallenfield enters.)

SIR GALLENFIELD: Lady Fenecia, I presume? *(Bowing)* I am Sir Gallenfield.

LADY FENECIA: *(Curtsies.)* Charmed.

SIR GALLENFIELD: I'm glad you're not too thin. The plague has completely turned me off skinny wenches. *(She glares at him.)* Excuse me: "ladies."

LADY FENECIA: Your teeth are the perfect shade of yellow. I feel our parents made a good match.

SIR GALLENFIELD: There are some things I feel I must tell you before our nuptials. First, I eat meat. Vegetarianism is for cows. Secondly, I require my suit and chainmail be polished at least once a week, preferably on Sundays. Finally, let's not pretend I will be faithful to you alone. I will be with you only when I'm in the township, but anytime I travel outside our kingdom, I am free to see whomever I please. You, however, are required to stay chaste at all times to everyone save me. I trust that's acceptable?

LADY FENECIA: Perfectly. *(Beat.)* However, I too have certain items that need to be discussed. First, once a week, usually Fridays after my chores, I go out with the other maidens for some grog at the local inn. I will continue to do so, even after our nuptials. Secondly, if you are coming home late from a day on the battlefield, you must send me a note via carrier pigeon to tell me so. If you do not, and you come home with the smell of brew on your breath, you will not be welcomed in our bedchamber. Finally, you must put the chamber pot under the bed every time you use it. You may not leave it out for me to step in or trip over. Agreed?

SIR GALLENFIELD: What if I send the pigeon and he gets lost? Or he cannot find you because you are out with your maidens? You can't possibly expect me to —

LADY FENECIA: In such a case, you are to arrive home as soon as possible, completely sober, with roses in hand.

SIR GALLENFIELD: *(Reluctantly)* Agreed. *(Pulls out a contract, which she pushes away.)*

LADY FENECIA: I'm not yet through. Now, about your mother ...

SIR GALLENFIELD: What about her?

LADY FENECIA: I don't want her checking in on us every minute. Tell her she may visit our dwelling twice a year: once in the spring, and once around the holy days. Under no circumstances is she to call upon us uninvited.

SIR GALLENFIELD: I will agree to that if you agree that no matter how heinously I behave, you are never to compare me to your last lord. Most especially in the ways of love. You will not speak of how much taller, fitter or more stately he was, nor are you ever to refer to our relationship as "the next best thing," "better than dying alone," "slightly less atrocious than a dragon's breath," or "somewhat between being scalded alive in the world's largest vat of candle wax and being forced to roll around in stinging nettles then leaping into highly salted sea water."

LADY FENECIA: Agreed.

SIR GALLENFIELD: Here is the contract. Sign there. *(Points.)* And there. Initial this. And once more. I look forward to a long and happy life together as — *(Writing on the contract)* Sir and Lady Gallenfield.

LADY FENECIA: Gallenfield? But I am going to keep my maiden name. We will be — *(Crossing out the names and rewriting.)* Sir Gallenfield and Lady Fenecia.

SIR GALLENFIELD: Nonsense! You must take my name as your own. All the other knights will laugh at me!

LADY FENECIA: I don't want to change all my monogrammed handkerchiefs just because of some medieval tradition.

SIR GALLENFIELD: You must! I demand it!

LADY FENECIA: Whoa! Who are you to demand anything? You're fortunate I even agreed to this marriage. If my father hadn't —

SIR GALLENFIELD: Who are you to talk? Look at you. My swayback horse has more attractive curves.

LADY FENECIA: That does it! *(Tears up the contract.)* Find some other "wench" to polish your suit. Or maybe you can marry your horse, since he's the only creature on this earth foolish enough to put up with you! *(Storms out.)*

SIR GALLENFIELD: Wenches!

CHAPTER SIX
PLAYING THE CONTEMPORARY

"Contemporary drama is all about life ...
with just the dull bits cut out."

— Alfred Hitchcock, *Musings*

Period satirist Oscar Wilde (1856-1900) wrote in his *Confessions* that while he enjoyed writing plays, he really looked forward to " ... acting in [his] own plays for the simple pleasure that they are so much more real than my *life*." Contemporary authors, however, appear to be less self-centered and more reclusive in such public displays. They are also more introspective and unassuming in depicting stage figures that speak directly to our capacity to understand life as it is lived day-to-day.

Contemporary scripts are particularly challenging for actors that want to add a fresh flavor and firm texture of directness and simplicity to their audition. Authors writing in the contemporary period — familiar as well as unfamiliar — challenge today's actors when they depict authentic characters and present an unbiased look at the world that surrounds us. Contemporary authors also take a more candid, almost photographic, approach to writing scripts that offer intimate character snapshots that include the beautiful as well as the ugly, and the physical as well as the spiritual.

THE TIMES

Today's scripts owe much of their contemporary impetus to Henrik Ibsen (1828-1906), known to all as the Father of Modern Drama, and Emile Zola (1840-1902), known to most as the Father of Naturalism. Each of these playwrights in his time wrote scripts with ordinary characters, simple facts, and non-heroic actions. Although they addressed relevant social issues with merciless clarity, there was none of the artifice or oratory that had defined previous periods of theatre. The immediate result of this "modern" approach to theatre was the emergence of scripts that no longer depicted what had been imagined or wished but, rather, what is and what is *not* true-to-life.

164

Ibsen's familiar scripts were accurate depictions of the nineteenth century world in which he lived. He identified universal themes like the struggle for personal dignity, conflict between man and society, and the need to adopt a new morality that would not inhibit or restrict individual freedom of expression. Ibsen also discarded a number of literary practices that had been part of the theatrical landscape since the classical period. Poetic verse, tragic hero, soliloquy, aside, chorus, and direct address to the audience were abandoned in favor of non-heroic characters, plain language, and familiar, everyday actions depicted in realistic settings that revealed life as it is *lived* on a daily basis.

Ibsen's bold vision in promoting an activist theatre enabled him to call attention to social forces that appeared to unduly influence character behavior, especially ethical or moral strictures. These restraints, he believed, prevented those of little stature from achieving their rightful evolutionary place in the universe or determining their own fate. Ibsen's influence on contemporary theatre is his ability to capture vivid images of authentic people who are heroic only in their basic goodness and honesty, while still remaining oppressed by forces outside themselves.

PERIOD INFLUENCES

Although Zola's thoughts on naturalism are not as original as Ibsen's views on realism, he also remains a dominant force in contemporary theatre. Influenced by the historian Hippolyte Taine (1828-1893) and philosopher Auguste Comte (1828-1893) — both of whom explored the inherent relationship of heredity and environment — Zola was interested in the role that theatre might play as a pseudo-scientific study of the human condition. He argued that the only way to understand a stage figure's *action* (motivation) or *thought* (intention) was to study the social forces at work in the character's life.

Zola's experimental approach to naturalism as a dramatic technique is best expressed in the following excerpt from his book, *The Experimental Novel:*

> I am waiting for them [the realists] to rid us of fictitious characters, which possess no value as human data. I am waiting for the surroundings to help determine the characters, and for the characters to act according to the logic of the facts. I am waiting for the painting of life in an exact reproduction to take place on the stage.

To lead the way, Zola adapted his popular novel *Therese Raquin* (1873) for the stage to dramatize the tragic story of a frustrated wife, Therese, and her lover, Laurent, whose illicit love for each other eventually drives them to drown Therese's invalid husband.

The naturalistic elements of the script focused on the increasing anxiety, fear, and guilt the lovers experience as they live under the accusing eyes of the dead husband's paralyzed mother. The predictable ending of the script is a calculated slow, agonizing mental and emotional deterioration of the lovers that reaches a climax with their eventual suicide. Although Zola's rebellion against period dramas of the early nineteenth century was a literary one, the basic ingredients of naturalism he encouraged, in both acting and staging, have become a fellow traveling companion to realism in contemporary theatre.

PERIOD STYLE

Subtle influences of Ibsen and Zola can easily be measured in this chapter of monologues. There are some that model Ibsen's "problem play" and deal with a specific ethical, moral, or social issue. There are some that mirror Zola's "raw slice of life" dramas and depict the squalid side of life. There are also a number of reflected elements of both Ibsen and Zola to depict average, everyday characters speaking directly and sincerely about the *truth* of their lives without any false façade of pretense or self-loathing.

In stark contrast to previous theatre periods, contemporary scripts appear to make a more conscious attempt to define character action, attitude, or mood in common vernacular. For example, the language of some characters is so often punctuated with colloquialisms, slang, or profanity that it is sometimes difficult to catch a glimpse of their self-worth. The repetitive use of broken phrases, incomplete thoughts, or even extended moments of silence to suggest familiar conversation styles may also make it difficult to clearly define a character's intention or motivation.

Today's authors are so firmly rooted in the now that the graphic experiences they describe are immediate and have the additional benefit of being rooted in the present tense. In addition, they appear to be more aware of lessons learned from personal life experiences and are more sensitive in accurately translating those lessons into multi-dimensional stage figures. The results are well defined character portraits with distinctive behaviors, colorful dialogue, and persuasive voices that are as believable as any of those found in the natural world.

Although contemporary authors still work within the dramatic framework of their own unique writing style, they are also modern *image-makers* who transform the familiar into the theatrical. Image-makers take basic truths recognized by all and translate them into word pictures or visual symbols that capture a true sense of life as they know it and live it every day. They are much more interested in small, even insignificant souls than the cosmic mysteries of human destiny or comic social foibles pursued so relentlessly by authors in earlier periods of theatre.

HISTORICAL VIEWS

Playing the role in contemporary period offers an almost risk-free approach to an audition. There is, of course, a marked degree of *method madness* in today's theatre as actors mix-and-match acting techniques to meet the demands of both the director and the script. Indeed, "A rose is a rose is a rose" the poet Gertrude Stein might say of today's acting styles. Some actors continue to define their role-playing in theories of beats, objective memory, or personal association to give character portraits more expressive and thoughtful distinction. Other actors prefer to focus on the basic performance principles of improvisation or theatre games to give an imaginative flair or inventive subtext to their stage figures.

Regardless of the acting technique you choose to define contemporary characters, these words of caution by the distinguished stage and film actor Raymond Massey may prove useful: "Good actors, like good plays, are made of flesh and blood, not just bundles of tricks." Remember that one of the primary goals of the modern actor is to be honest and truthful in an audition, so avoid "bundles of tricks" and insatiable urges to call attention to oneself, either through conceit for lack of script analysis or cliché for lack of rehearsal. Do not confuse a caricature with a character. When you are able to approach a contemporary audition from this perspective, your monologue characters will have a spark of intuition and intensity that is life-like and memorable.

MODERN APPROACHES

Eliminate all extraneous details and focus on a single performance goal to create an illusion of reality that what is seen or heard is familiar and spontaneous. Exhibit a resonant tone of delivery and relaxed sense of movement that suggests a sense of purpose and active character engagement. Place emphasis on an intimate acting style and minimize stage business and movement. Engage in real-life observations to model character portraits. Sharpen interpretation skills by identifying authentic character actions based on everyday events and incidents. Avoid playing stereotypes that lack dimension and diversity.

Today's audition challenge is to act instinctively and to make daring choices that build moment-to-moment anticipation. Explore the *interior monologue* of the character to better understand the intention or motivation of each action and reaction in the monologue. Shape character portraits by your own lived experiences. Pursue an emphatic identification and response to the character's words, phrases, and thoughts for the most meaningful expression of honesty and truthfulness. Finally, promote the look and feel of the character as a *self-portrait* at an audition.

AUDITION MONOLOGUES

The monologues in this chapter represent a broad sampling of scripts that address familiar issues like petty deceptions, turbulent relationships, and the inevitable search for meaning and purpose in life. Minimum narrative defines the characters, so be very selective in performance choices, and explore a more subtle acting style, with emphasis upon subtext, than you may have used in performing monologues in the previous chapters. Remember to avoid overly precise use of the voice, refrain from highly theatrical movement, and eliminate all extraneous details that are not an integral part of the character portrait or that may become a potential source of distraction in an audition.

Spell #7 from Three Pieces
by Ntozake Shange

This is one of a series of gut-wrenching vignettes, set in a seedy bar in St. Louis, featuring African-American artists and musicians unburdening their souls in a series of poignant soliloquies. Maxine, a mature woman of extraordinary spirit, struggles to conceal her despair and emotional numbness as she paints a haunting and stark portrait of what it really means to live in Black America.

MAXINE: the pain I succumbed to each time a colored person did something that I believed only white people did waz staggering. My entire life seems to be worthless/ if my own folks aren't better than white folks/then surely the sagas of slavery & the jim crow hadn't convinced anyone that we were better than them. I commenced to buying pieces of gold/14 carat/24 carat/18 carat gold/every time some black person did something that waz beneath him as a black person & more like a white person. I bought gold cuz it came from the earth/& more than likely it came from south africa/where the black people are humiliated & oppressed like in slavery. I wear all these things at once/to remind the black people that it cost a lot for us to be here/our value/can be known instinctively/but since so many black people are having a hard time not being like white folks/I wear these gold pieces to protest their ignorance/their disconnect from history. I buy gold with a vengeance/each time someone appropriates my space or my time without permission/each time someone is discourteous or actually cruel to me/if my mind is not respected/my body toyed with/I buy gold & weep. I weep as I fix the chains round my neck/my wrists/my ankles. I weep cuz all my childhood ceremonies for the ghost-slaves have been in vain. Colored people can get polio & mental illness. slavery is not unfamiliar to me. no one on this planet knows/what I know abt gold/abt anything hard to get & beautiful/anything lasting/wrought from pain. No one understands that surviving the impossible is sposed to accentuate the positive aspects of a people.

Reckless
by Craig Lucas

Set in a cold, sterile consulting office, this "birth therapy" session probes a young doctor's struggle to get her anguished patient to experience again *the trauma of being born. The unnamed doctor explores a series of clinical techniques to discover the place where the patient's pain began. The session grows increasingly more aggressive as the doctor tries to unlock suppressed dreams — and delusions — so her patient can finally release tormented memories of the past.*

FOURTH DOCTOR: This is very important, Cheryl. We've talked about the birth scream. It is a terrible shock to be torn away in a shower of blood with your mother screaming and your home torn open and the strange doctor with his rubber hands slapping you with all his might and the cold light piercing the dark, the warm beautiful wet dark, the silent murmuring safe dark of Mummy everywhere and Daddy, everything is one and everything is sex and we are all together for eternity and we are happy and nothing ever passes through your mind but good thoughts until suddenly this squeezing is going on around you and everyone is pushing and pulling and cold steel tongs pinch your skin and pull you by the top of your head and you don't want to go, no, you don't want to leave your home where you're always floating in and your mother's heart is always beating for something unknown and cruel where people are cold and you're stinging now, everything is breaking, it makes you want to scream, Cheryl, makes you want to scream the scream of all ages, scream of the greatest tragedy of all time and your mummy is screaming and your daddy is screaming and now all the doctors are screaming and everything's blinding you as you're torn away and they're hitting you and they throw you up in the air and you open your eyes and your mother is covered in blood and you scream, Cheryl, scream, scream, scream, Cheryl, SCREAM, SCREAM!!! *(Pause.)*

All right, we'll try it again.

Napalm the Magnificent:
Dancing with the Dark
by David S. Craig

Lurking in the shadowy corners of every theatre is the gaunt figure of a tortured genius whose fiery outbursts and feigned indignations elicit groans of disbelief and repulsion from actors and directors alike: the theatre critic. Hiding behind a makeshift shield of anonymity, the critic inflicts verbal wounds that can only be healed by the sword that inflicted them.

CRITIC: Well you see ... *(Puffs.)* I'm a theatre critic. I've seen a thousand plays in the past three years and I've only liked the first act of one. It was a production of *The Tempest*. Prospero made his entrance crawling out of the mud. English director. God they know Shakespeare ... sometimes. The thing is, I don't know why I keep going. Obviously, I don't enjoy it. I much prefer going to movies. A good movie is great, a bad movie is funny. A good play is rare, a bad play leaves me depressed for weeks. I just can't keep opening myself up like that and still be critical. That's why I developed a system. First, I always read the press release and make up my mind before I go. That way I have an opinion in case I arrive late, or leave early or just drift off in the middle, which, let's face it, happens. Then, I always dismiss the content. If the issue is evident, I say the playwright has gone too far. If it isn't, I say the playwright hasn't gone far enough. It saves me grappling with issues I don't understand. After all, I can only write from experience and my experience is seeing six to eight plays a week. What do I like? [...] Deciding what's good and bad. Being the public judge of the cultural agenda. Sleeping in every morning, I don't know. What'd I'd really like to do is write a cheap sex thriller and use a pseudonym. But who has the time to do what they really want. Naturally, in my frame of mind, being critical is a lot easier than being positive. In fact, when I see people at the theatre enjoying themselves I just assume they're friends of the actors, or from out of town. And then a bad review usually gets a better headline, which means a better place in the entertainment section, but I'm not influenced by those considerations. I just don't really like theatre anymore. In fact, I can't remember why I ever did.

You Could Die Laughing
by Billy St. John

Lucinda Tate, an over the hill stand-up comedienne, has been invited by the reclusive television producer Jacque St. Yves to his isolated lodge off the coast of Canada along with ten other has-been comics to audition for a role in his new situation comedy series. Lucinda's audition pushes antic humor to its limits as her daffy one-liners snap, crackle, and pop.

LUCINDA: You want to know about me? Sure, I'll tell you. Lucinda Tate's the name. My life is an open book. It's titled: "In the Garden of Love, I Keep Picking the Stinkweeds." I've had every kind of spouse: the louse, the grouse, the souse, and the mouse. The louse was my first husband, Irving. We had the ideal marriage — for about ten minutes. I should have realized something was wrong when he and my maid of honor both disappeared from the reception for over an hour, but I was young and naïve. It was two years before I came to realize that Irving was chasing anything in a skirt ... and I had a closet full of slacks. I showed Irving the door; my mistake was letting husband number two, George, come through it — George, the grouse. He groused about everything — my cleaning, my washing, my ironing, my cooking ... my cooking ... my cooking ... Hey, I never claimed to be Betty Crocker. Heck, I can't even keep up with Mrs. Paul. Eventually, I gave George some coupons for fast-food restaurants and sent him on his way.

That brings us to husband number three, Benny the souse. Benny had a drinking problem. I don't joke about Benny because that kind of problem is no laughing matter. I just mention him to keep the record straight. I'm happy to say he later got help and is doing well. My fourth and latest husband Willard was a mouse. As in timid. How timid was he, you ask ... Willard was so shy he blushed at the sight of a plucked chicken ... so shy that at parties he'd stand very still in a corner and hope people would mistake him for a statue ... so shy that he kept his socks on when he trimmed his toenails. As you can tell, I'm an out-there kind'a gal, so Willard and I were not what you'd call compatible. I was fire, he was ice, and whenever I got near him, he started to puddle.

When he eventually asked me for a divorce, I had to agree it was a good idea. Actually, he didn't "ask" me, he left a note in my shoe. We untied the knot and went our separate ways. So, Stanley, if you still want a date, look me up when we get back to the states. I'm in the Yellow Pages under "Desperate."

Thank You for Flushing My Head in the Toilet
And Other Rarely Used Expressions
by Jonathan Dorf

This is a complex psychological story of a young, apparently harmless, student who stumbles upon an injured bird lying near the birdbath in his backyard. The first impression of this poignant picture is heartbreaking as the student gently lifts the fallen comrade and appears poised to play Dr. Doolittle making a house call. Without warning, however, the episode takes a disturbing turn and erupts in sudden rage and fury that snaps the bonds of common humanity.

BLUEBIRD STUDENT: There's a birdbath in my yard. In the back. We get robins, sparrows, pigeons. A lot of pigeons. Sometimes there's a cardinal. And squirrels. Yes, I know they're not birds, but maybe the squirrels think they are. I mean there's flying squirrels — right? I've never seen one, but flying squirrels exist. Right?
(Beat.)
I like watching the birds. The real birds. The way they all kinda twitch their heads forward.
(Demonstrates a pecking motion.)
It's like they're talking to each other. Saying how's your day and how's the weather and would you like worms with that order? Sometimes when I'm bored, I make up what they'd say. Like this one pigeon, he's complaining about his taxes to a sparrow, and the sparrow's like, "dude, maybe if you spent more time working and less time looking for handouts in the park …"
(Beat.)

I'm supposed to put water in the birdbath once a week. Today's my day. And the birds are there talking about the weather and their kids and there's a duck talking about how his cousin bought the farm and got served up in orange sauce last week. And the other birds are saying how sad that is and how sorry they are, only this one bird's not talking. He's not even in the bath. He's wet, like he was there, but he's not in there. He's on the ground under the bath, and he's trying to hop up, only he can't. There's something wrong with his left wing. He can't flap it like the right one. And he's spinning around in a circle, like he's break dancing — only he's not.

(Beat. Achilles enters silently and watches.)

I go over to the bath, and they all scatter when I get close. Except for the break dancing bird. It's a bluebird — I don't remember when I've ever seen a bluebird in our backyard, and now there's one spinning like a merry-go-round under the birdbath. He's beautiful. He's flapping his right wing like crazy, but the poor little guy can't go anywhere. And he's going nuts when I pick him up in my hands. I hold him real tight so he won't scratch me, and I've got my thumb and finger around his neck to keep him from biting. "Don't worry, little bird. I've got you." And I hold him.

(Beat.)

The phone rings in the house. I'm the only one home, but I don't move. I've got this beautiful, living thing in my hands, and that's more important than —

(Beat.)

The longer I hold him, the less he fights. He knows he's safe. I'm like the Dr. Doolittle of my backyard.

(Beat.)

And then I start to squeeze my finger and thumbs together. Around his neck. Around its neck. Tighter and tighter. The bluebird starts going crazy. I know it can't breathe, and I don't stop. I keep going — because I can. I keep going until it's — It feels good. It feels good, because for once in my life, I'm not the bird.

Sorrows and Rejoicings
by Athol Fugard

Two women meet in a remote rural village in the desert region of southern Africa after the funeral of David, an exiled, leukemia-stricken, radical white poet who has returned to his homeland to die. One woman, Allison, is white and the other woman, Marta, is black, and the mother of David's adult daughter Rebecca. The two women appear to have only one thing in common: their devotion and love for the same man. During a hot and humid afternoon of reconciling secrets of the past and renewing family ties, Marta and Rebecca finally come to terms with the painful reality that if the world around you is to change, you must change yourself first.

REBECCA: What's the matter with you, Mommy! Don't you understand anything? You taught me never to say that word! Have you forgotten? No "father," no "daddy," no "pa" … "because we must protect him Rebecca." Have you forgotten the little girl who came crying to you because the other children had been teasing her again?
"Who is your daddy, Rebecca?"
"Where is your daddy, Rebecca?"
Have you forgotten wiping away her tears — and yours! — and telling her the big secret about who she was which was no secret at all because everybody knew? Have you forgotten making her promise that when he came back one day she would pretend she didn't know who he was?
Well, I kept my promise, Mommy. But it wasn't easy, because if you really want to know something, when I stood there in front of him I wanted to say it. Yes, I wanted to say "Father" more than I've wanted to say anything in my whole life. But I didn't! Because you had taught me I mustn't. *(Pause.)*
You've been so blind and selfish. All you've ever thought about was your own precious love. You've sacrificed your life for it and you would do that to mine as well if I let you. No, Mommy, I am not going to. I am going to live my own life the way I want to. *(Pause. Her anger is spent. She approaches her mother hesitantly in a timid attempt at reconciliation.)*

You're right, Mommy, he's dead and buried. So why don't you now try to live your own life, as well. Stop dreaming in here. Say good-bye to this house and its ghosts. There's nothing left for you in here. Lock up like you say, give her your big bunch of keys and come back to the location with me. There's a real life waiting for you there, with real people, our people.

Relative Strangers
by Sheri Wilner

Marie Barrett is a disillusioned and troubled young woman in a state of perpetual trauma. Her limited sensibilities have been numbed by the grinding insecurity of not knowing the significance of her own life. Marie is one of the world's "lost souls," desperately trying to reconcile her troubled present and her emotionally deprived childhood. Her failure to find happiness has left her hopelessly lonely and estranged from society.

MARIE: I know you must think I'm a weirdo, but I'm not. I don't have a mother, you see. It's something I'm aware of every second of the day. Like if I didn't have any arms or legs ... or skin. She died during childbirth. They say as soon as I emerged — as soon as I took my first breath, she took her last. She really was only a vessel for me if you think about it — just like this place. She received me, took me to a destination and then I emerged, disembarked and she was gone. Lame metaphor, I know, but the mind — my mind — needs ways to understand, to make sense. I'm always feeling so ... lost — like everyone in the world has a map that I don't have. Sometimes, I find I just don't know how to get around. Like there's vital information I don't have access to. Letters missing from my alphabet, you know? But now, all of a sudden ... here you are. I know this is lousy timing given your situation, but there's too much I need to know.

The Profession
by Walter Wykes

Eugene, an enigmatic young man of mystery with a devilishly mesmerizing gaze, has recently escaped from a secret, diabolical guild known only as "The Profession," whose malevolent "handbook" threatened to assert its insidious control over every aspect of his well-ordered life. Eugene takes refuge in a public park where he carefully guards his only clue to the meaning of existence from a mute, strangely familiar and possibly deranged, vagrant. In the idleness and inanity that follows, what distinguishes fantasy from reality has yet to be determined.

EUGENE: Hey! Don't touch that! That's my orange! MINE!!! *(Eugene wrenches his orange from the VAGRANT.)* Sorry. I'm sorry. I … I don't mean to be stingy. I'm sure you're very hungry, but I can't allow you to eat this orange. It's just that … well, it's … it's the key to everything! I know that doesn't seem to make much sense. I don't understand it quite yet myself. But one has to have faith, you know, that … well, that everything will come clear in the end. *(Pause.)*

It … it must be nice to be a halfwit. A vagrant, I mean. A wanderer. You don't have to contemplate. If you're hungry, you eat. Everything's basic. Primitive. Nothing to confuse the issue. No one to push you around … tell you what to do. Maybe … maybe I should join you! *(Eugene chuckles. No response from the VAGRANT.)* Hey … maybe … maybe I should! They'd never find me then! And if they did … well, they wouldn't recognize me! I'll bet people don't even give you a second look, do they? They probably cross the street when they see you coming! That's it! That's the answer! I'll be an outcast! What do you think? *(The VAGRANT snorts.)*

What's so funny? I could be an outcast! I … I admit I don't have much experience, but I've always thought of myself as living on the fringes, you know. I'm an outlaw at heart! Once, when I was five or six … don't tell anyone, but … I once stole a whole handful of comic books from a retarded boy that lived down the street! Lifted them right under his nose! *(A beat.)* All right. I … I took them back the next day, but it's the thought that counts! *(A beat.)* You're not impressed. *(A beat.)* I guess maybe a … a true outcast only takes what he needs to survive. Is that it? You probably have your own code of conduct. Like the samurai. But I … I could learn! You could teach me! *(The VAGRANT snorts.)* I think I'd make a respectable outcast! *(Pause.)*

All right, what's … what's wrong with me? Is it the shoes? You're right — shoes might draw attention! Shoes are much too mainstream for me anyway! I've never really liked them! They chafe your feet! Give you blisters! *(Eugene removes his shoes.)* There! *(The VAGRANT stares at Eugene's feet.)* I … I suppose I should get rid of the socks too? *(He does.)* There! You see — I'm willing to make sacrifices. I don't ask for special treatment. I just want to be a regular outcast like everyone else. *(The VAGRANT stares hard at Eugene.)* What? *(Eugene begins to fidget.)* What is it? The pants? Just tell me what to do. I'm willing to do whatever it takes. Only I … I don't have anything else to wear. This is all I've got. I admit, it's a bit dressy for your average outcast, but … I … I could dirty it up a bit. A few properly placed smudges, a rip here and there, and you won't recognize it! *(Eugene attempts to rip his coat.)*

This … ahh … this is … good … good fabric. Maybe if I try the seams. *(He tries the seams … no luck.)* Oh! Wait! I've got it! We could trade! You want to trade? You know, they say well dressed panhandlers are much more successful! People are more likely to give you a few dollars if you're wearing a coat and tie because they know you must really be in a bind! I … I know it doesn't make much sense, but it's a proven fact! *(Eugene begins to take off his clothes.)* Just … just take off your clothes. I'll even throw in the shoes. And the socks, if you'd like. They're a little smelly, but … *(The VAGRANT takes Eugene's shoes. Sniffs them.)* Believe me, you won't be sorry. Those are very expensive shoes! Some kind of fancy leather. My … my wife, Ibid, bought them for me … *(Eugene pauses.)* Ibid … *(He stares at the pants in his hands for a long moment.)* She … she has very good taste in … in clothes. *(Silence. Overcome with sadness, Eugene sits on the bench. Finally, after a long moment, he offers the VAGRANT his pants.)*

Here. Take them. *(He does.)* You want the coat too? Take it! And the tie! Take it all! I don't need it anymore! There! I feel much better now! Free! So this is what it's like to be an outcast! *(The VAGRANT snorts.)* What? I … I still don't qualify? But I've met all the requirements. I mean, I'm sure there are some spiritual aspects that I'll … I'll have to grow into … certainly. I mean, I'm sure there are several levels of vagrancy and … and I can't expect to attain the highest levels right away. These things take time. I'm sure you've been at it for years, and you want to protect your status by making newcomers serve a … a sort of apprenticeship so to speak. And I'm willing to do that! I'm committed for the long term! But surely I qualify as at least a Level One outcast! I mean, one has to have some kind of assurance that one is moving in the right direction! After all, I've given up everything! I've sworn off all material possessions! *(The VAGRANT stares at Eugene's orange.)*

What? *(Eugene clutches the orange tightly.)* You don't mean this? It's not for material reasons that I'm attached to it! It's what the orange represents! Why can't I be an outcast with an orange? Where is it written that an outcast can't own a little piece of fruit? *(The VAGRANT holds up his hand — points to it.)* What? *(The VAGRANT points to his hand.)* Your hand. *(The VAGRANT nods — pantomimes opening a book.)* Reading. Hand — reading? Braille? Blind? *(The VAGRANT shakes his head no.)* Book. *(The VAGRANT nods.)* Hand. Book. *(A beat. Horrified.)* The handbook? *(The VAGRANT nods emphatically.)* No! Oh, no! *(The VAGRANT does a mad dance, clapping wildly.)* You're lying! There is no handbook! I refuse to believe it! It's a lie! A fabrication! You just want me to feel I've been left in the dark! Well, I … I won't have it! Do you hear? I won't have it! I refuse to cooperate! How do you like that?

Lillian
by David Cale

The stage is bare except for a stool, microphone, and small wooden table with a vase of yellow chrysanthemums and a glass of water as Lillian slowly enters, holding a single bloom and moves center stage to the microphone. She is a sophisticated Englishwoman who appears oddly out of place. Lillian clings to her private secrets as she weaves memory, sadness, and testimony into an intricate tapestry of darkness and light that reveals the lyrical grace of a woman full of quiet strength and gentle virtue.

LILLIAN: Chrysanthemums are considered to be late bloomers. Originating in China, they date back as far as five hundred years B.C. The wild native version of the species has now almost disappeared. Having been completely overshadowed by its more colorful domesticated relative. For optimum results, chrysanthemums require a clay soil, a sunny yet cool location, ideally facing south, and loam. They are what's known as short-day plants, meaning they are light sensitive and produce buds only as the days become shorter and the nights grow longer. To improve the quality of the flowers the first bud that appears should be pinched, that's according to most chrysanthemum experts, in whose ranks I now number myself, thereby increasing the radiance of the subsequent flowers. *(She places the bloom on the stool.)*

The other day I overheard a landscape gardener talking to a woman I know who designs plaster gnomes to put on your front lawn: a garden ornament whose appeal has frankly always eluded me. Anyway the landscape gardener says, "I realized recently that I have been mildly depressed for the last fifteen years." The gnome lady asked, "How come you only realize that now?" He answered, "Because I don't feel that way anymore." It's funny what you just happen to overhear.

I wonder if it's true that all the secrets of our lives are whispered into our ears at birth. That the secrets then attach themselves to our unconscious. As years pass occasionally a secret will break free, and make its way up into our daily thoughts. They are then referred to as premonitions. I think we know everything that's going to happen to us. People come into your life for a reason. There are no accidents. There's nothing haphazard about it. Or coincidental. What may seem random at the time, I think in the end has a kind of correctness. *(She picks up the flower.)*

I mean, in retrospect, when you look back on your life, if you're able to be honest with yourself, I think you come to realize, it could not have happened any other way.

(Lights fade. She places the single bloom in the vase.)

Carol Mulroney

by Stephen Belber

Ken, a mature African-American man in a continual search for love, hides behind a compulsive and controlling façade to conceal his genuine warmth and humanity. He is a romantic at heart, but firmly grounded in the harsh reality of failed merry-go-round relationships that end in rejection. In this direct address to the audience, Ken talks about his friend Carol, who recently died, and we see a humble man whose charity and goodness has never been truly appreciated or understood.

KEN: I've always been a huge admirer of sadness; of sad people, of people who don't understand something very … vital. *(Beat.)* We live in a world where sadness is devalued, where sad people are considered … incompetent. And maybe we are, for there are many ways to be happy and you'd think that we would just embrace one, but … *(Beat.)* Carol had sadness running through her veins like bad blood. Consequently, I was drawn to her immediately. I dunno. I just wanna love them; the sad people like Carol. I just want to love. Because that's what I'm good at — maybe the only thing I have, this skill of love — this will *to* love. I love to love. I do. I love it. *(Pause.)* The problem is that the world tends not to love me back. Which makes me very sad. *(Pause.)* And it's a great disappointment because it *should*; the world, or certain people in it, they should love me back. And I get so mad at them when they don't. Because I know I know how to solve them, to help *solve* their sadness. But it's like at some point they just stop listening; like they get too close to the edge … and they lose their ability to focus. *(Almost whispering)* And I get so angry … that this beautiful, sad person standing in front of me can't see how much potential happiness I'm offering them. *(Pause.)* It's like … "Why can't you just be […] happy?" *(Pause.)* When of course I already know the answer. Which is that sometimes you just miss the train.

Belle

by Florence Gibson

Set in the Reconstruction Era of 1865, this searing saga traces the flight of two freed slaves, wife Belle and husband Bowlyn, from rural Georgia to New York in search of a prosperous life. Instead of finding acceptance and opportunity in their new lives, however, Belle and Bowlyn must once again confront the haunting specters of their past: prejudice, poverty, and racism. Here, Bowlyn stands on a street corner in shantytown and rages against the unexpected turn of events as he struggles to salvage his self-identity and dignity in a cruel world where he is defined by an inescapable destiny that has misshaped him.

BOWLYN:
I will provide for you.
Because I am MAN.
It were my *dream* to have a horse and buggy.
(Beginning to speak to the passersby.)
I had a horse. And that horse was mine. But it was taken from me.
Now I ain't used to speechifyin' my life, but my life is just that: mine.
A life like any other, and so to be honoured. And for that I am tellin' it.
I work always, to raise my family. This is to be the truth of my life —
To provide for my family. Because I am a man.
And because I am a man, I know no man should lead the life I led ... back
Before freedom ... my daddy they'd hired out — *they'd* get paid for his field
Work on another farm — *his* work.
But me.
Never could hire me out.
Shut my face like a box lid, white boss screamin', and I would not. Would.
Not. *(Pause.)*

So the bit was placed in my mouth, and the lash put to my back,
    and I was
Forced to plough the furrow true as a beast — and yet I was a
    man! (Pause.)
Because I am a man, I have the right to provide for my family,
    to see my
Children fed, my home safe and myself free to serve the country
    in which
I live. And I tell you, these are the things that I will do — because
    I am a man.

Miss Witherspoon
by Christopher Durang

Miss Witherspoon, a mature woman who finds the world too terrifying, recently committed suicide. She now finds herself in an Eastern afterlife with an Indian guide named Maryamma … and refuses a next reincarnation back to earth. Her monologue is a chilling testament for the present — and perhaps future — but is chock-full of karma and life lessons for all who claim to be alarmed about the future of the planet.

VERONICA: Well, I'm dead. I committed suicide in the 1990s because of Skylab. Well, not entirely, but that's as sensible an explanation as anything.

Most of you don't remember what Skylab was … I seem to have had a disproportionate reaction to it, most people seemed to have sluffed it off.

Skylab was this American space station, it was thousands of tons of heavy metal, and it got put into orbit over the earth sometime in the seventies.

Eventually the people on board abandoned it, and it was just floating up there; and you'd think the people who put it up there would have had a plan for how to get it back to earth again, but they didn't. Or the plan failed, or something; and in 1979 they announced that Skylab would eventually be falling from the sky in a little bit — this massive thing the size of a city block might come crashing down on your head as you stood in line at Bloomingdale's or sat by your suburban pool, or as you were crossing the George Washington Bridge, etc., etc.

And the experts didn't think it through, I guess. Sure, let's put massive tonnage up in the sky, I'm sure it won't fall down. Sure, let's build nuclear power plants, I'm sure we'll figure out what to do with radioactive waste eventually.

Well, you can start to see I have the kind of personality that might kill myself.

I mean throw in unhappy relationships and a kind of dark, depressive tinge to my psychology, and something like Skylab just sends me over the edge.

"I CAN'T LIVE IN A WORLD WHERE THERE IS SKYLAB!" — I sort of screamed this out in the airport as I was in some endless line waiting to go away to somewhere or other.

So I died sometime in the nineties. Obviously it was a delayed reaction to Skylab.

So I killed myself. Anger turned inward they say. But at least I got to miss 9/11.

If I couldn't stand Skylab, I definitely couldn't stand the sight of people jumping out of windows. And then letters with anthrax postmarked from Trenton. And in some quarters people danced in the streets in celebration. "Oh lots of people killed, yippee, yippee, yippee." God, I hate human beings. I'm glad I killed myself.

You know, in the afterlife I'm considered to have a bad attitude.

Dirty Story
by John Patrick Shanley

Pulitzer Prize playwright John Patrick Shanley offers a bold satire with a deeper level of political subtext. Brutus, an arrogant but successful writer, has befriended aspiring writer, Wanda, whose talent he describes as "wretched." Their uncommon relationship deteriorates when Wanda surprisingly moves in with Brutus and begins to refer to herself as "Israel." As territorial wars escalate, Brutus resembles a certain character in the Middle East now wearing an Arab headdress as he records a "Good-bye Video."

BRUTUS: Take number seventeen: "The Good-bye Video." *(He gets into character.)* How long can a man live off good memories? How long before he needs something new? The time is now. I want to say ... to my father ... when you see this, I am already dead. You never appreciated my scholarship. I know that. You called me a girl for reading books. Well, I'm not reading books anymore. I am a man of fiction now. Perhaps you will raise your opinion of me. To my mother: You are no doubt shedding fat tears of sorrow and regret and counting the insurance money you've collected. For the many times you did not love me, for valuing my death more than my life, I want to say to you: I am in Paradise. I am surrounded by virgins and candy and raisins and God is here with me and He doesn't like you very much. But I am not angry anymore. I speak to you from a place beyond anger. I am free. To my wider family, I want to say look at me, how terrific it is to be me, and why don't you all just hope to be as brave and good as I am. And good-bye. And cut. *(Drops character.)*

The Play About the Baby
by Edward Albee

This absurdist comedy revolves merrily around a young couple who have just had a baby, and the strange turn of events when they are visited by a mysterious older man and woman. The Woman, crotchety and outrageously theatrical, sparkles with farcical extravagance, but also has jarring outbursts of dark but good-natured emotional terrorism. Here, the Woman introduces herself to the audience, but has little to say as her words shoot off like fireworks.

WOMAN: Well. I ... uh ... well, I suppose you'd like to know who I am, or why I'm here.

I'm not an actress; I want you to know that right off, although why you'd think I *was,* I mean automatically think I *was,* I don't know, though I *am* a trifle ... theatrical, I suppose, and no apologies *there.* I *was* Prince Charming in our all-girl production of *Snow White,* and while the bug may have bitten, it never took.

(Chuckles.)

Nor — and forgive the seeming discontinuity here — nor am I from the press. That's the first thing I want you to know — well, the second, actually, the first being … having been …

(Trails off; starts again.)

Oh, I am a very good cook, among other things. I became that to please my husband, my *then* husband, who was in the habit of eating out, by which he meant … alone … without *me.* It occurred to *me* that if I … well, it was no good: Alone, to him, meant *specifically* not with *me,* though with others, with lots of others. And the great feasts I'd prepare … would be for *me.* Alone. I became quite heavy, which I no longer am, and unmarried, which I am to this day. I trust he is still eating alone … all by himself … facing a wall.

(Pause.)

No matter. Really: From the very first week, come dinnertime, he would put the paper under his arm, say "Bye, bye," or whatever, and … no matter. I *have* had journalistic dreams, though I am not a journalist — dreams of *being* a journalist, that is, and quite awake; not asleep. I went so far one time as to take a course; and my assignment was to interview a *writer,* to try to comprehend the "creative mind" as they call it.

(Firm gesture)

Don't try! Don't even give it a thought! There seems to be some sort of cabal going on the part of these so-called creative people to keep the process a secret — a deep dark secret — from the rest of the world. What's the matter with these people? Do they think we're trying to steal their tricks? ... would even *want* to!? And all I wanted to do was … understand! And, let me tell you!, getting through to them — the creative types? — isn't easy. I mean even getting at them. I wrote politely to seven or eight of them, two poets, one biographer, a couple of short story writers, one female creator of "theatre pieces," etcetera, and not one of them answered. Silence; too busy "creating," I guess.

Eleanor
by Sean David Bennett

Eleanor Roosevelt, the reigning grande dame of period politics and immovable force in the social justice movement of the 1940s, sits comfortably in an overstuffed armchair facing the audience. A news reporter has commented to the First Lady that her wartime trip to visit injured and wounded servicemen in the Pacific showed great courage in the face of the burgeoning conflict unleashed on civilization. Eleanor's response is heartfelt in a manner full of emotional resonance that probes deeply into the question of who she really is inside, as opposed to the image she presents to the outside world.

ELEANOR: Courageous? Where on earth did you get the idea that I was courageous? I thought you — of all people — could see beyond a headline. "First Lady Visits Coal Miners," "First Lady Defies Daughters of the American Revolution." Wonderful headlines, I'll admit — and, of course — Franklin found them useful. But that's all they were. Headlines. Nothing more. Life, as you know, is a bit more complicated. I simply tried to be of use to my husband. He did what he had to do in order to remain in office, and I did what I could to make that office live up to its responsibilities.

There were times, of course, when we did not always see eye to eye. The Civil Rights Movement, for instance. Franklin knew how fast he could move, but I was always there, the thorn in his side, the pea under the pillow, making sure — however slowly — he kept going in the direction we needed to go. But, it wasn't courage that moved me to act, or some sense of responsibility blown all out of proportion. It was simply the right thing to do.

The incident you mention — the time in 1944 when I flew out to the Pacific to visit our troops — I felt it was my duty. The men were all too badly wounded to be flown home, and with my own boys serving, I felt that, by going, I represented all their mothers. I don't recall the question of courage entering into it. I was too busy with all the preparations to think about it. Franklin was more concerned for my safety than I was.

187

I can recall that trip as if it had taken place yesterday. I remember there was a hospital on Guam, for instance, where I was escorted through the wards by the tallest, most handsome officer I have ever laid eyes upon. At the end of the tour, I began to feel a little weak, and tired from all the traveling. All I could think of was getting back to the base and soaking my feet. As we walked down the corridor, there were some wounded men who had been segregated from the larger units. The Colonel who was escorting me said, "There's no need to go into any of these rooms, Mrs. Roosevelt. These men aren't expected to make it through."

But as we walked toward the front door, a man called out my name. "Mrs. Roosevelt, Mrs. Roosevelt — please." In the room to the right of me was a man so horribly disfigured that I could only stand where I was and not look at him. The top of his head had been blown away, and blood was oozing through the bandages. "Please … " He kept saying it and I kept standing there — my heart, my mind, were rigid with horror.

I did not want to go to him. Then, as if under their own power, I felt my legs begin to move — and, before I knew it, I was standing alongside his bed. He reached his arm out to me, and I felt my arm reach for his — as if it had been willed to do so by a power greater than myself. When I could finally bring myself to look into his eyes, I saw my own son's eyes — and I knew why I had made the trip. "Please, Mrs. Roosevelt — tell me that I don't have to die in this room — not with all the cockroaches, and the rats. Please tell me I won't have to die here."

But, of course, I couldn't do that — I could only stand there and hold his hand. We were both crying. In the silence, I could almost hear the tears as they ran down my face. I couldn't bring myself to tell him the lie he wanted to hear. We were, after all, in the real world — both of us knew that. To be in that room together — just the two of us — and to be able to see beyond the bandages, the broken body — was impossible.

That's when I recalled a passage from the Bible. I couldn't tell you if it was Luke or John, or what. I'm not all that well versed in the Bible. It was about the crucifixion. What must it have been like for Mary — to stand at the foot of the cross and watch the life go out of her child? Would she have lied to him, or would she have remained silent until, at last, he said the words, "It is done." That was all my mind could understand at that moment. When I looked at the boy again, he was dead.

Courage: Can you call it courage when you know the truth and fail to speak?

Tightrope Time: Ain't Nuthin' More Than Some Itty Bitty Madness Between Twilight & Dawn
by Walter Borden

This complex and compelling symbolic drama, subtitled "Git it out of your system," evokes universal sensibilities of race and recrimination in the 1980s. The Minister of Defense, emissary from an unknown realm, spews radical activism to alleviate the black man's burden. Although the Minister is a baffling enigma, his defiant attitude and rousing call for resistance is passionate and persuasive.

MINISTER OF DEFENSE: I recall how just the other day this white man had the nerve to say to me: sir, he says, life is a banquet; enjoy yourself. Well, I looks this fool right into his eye and I says: sir, how many times have we been led to the banquet table only to be told we could get our victuals in the kitchen? How many times have we watched you wrap your lips around the giblets of sweet contentment while we have been asked to gnaw upon the drumstick of despair? How many times, I said, are we forced to accept the chocolate and not the mousse? Well, that same idiot looked at me with this Simple Simon grin across his face and said: My goodness, sir, I could be wrong, but you seem somewhat perplexed. What possibly could be the matter?

[...] We will no longer be deceived. It is the eleventh hour — and the heat is on! We are ready to do whatever is necessary to redeem our right to sit down at the banquet of life with the rest of the human family. We are prepared to fight, and fight we will!

We will fight you on the street corners,
And in the pool halls.
We will fight you on the dance floors,
And at the back of the bus.

Bobrauschenbergamerica
by Charles L. Mee

Bob, an emotionally distraught and unpredictable loner who committed a triple murder — stabbing his sister, her husband, and their small son in a horrific and mercilessly brutal spree of manic-depression — is now working for a pizza delivery service. We meet him here for the first time when he is asked if he thinks that dark "episode" will ever become part of his past. Bob's cryptic response is a selfish and insensitive denial that is mesmerizing.

BOB, THE PIZZA BOY: In the first three or four years there was a couple of nights where I would stay up thinking about how I did it, you know. And what they said ... they told me later there were something like thirty stab wounds in my sister, but uh, I remember distinctly I just cut her throat once. That was all, you know, and I don't know where the thirty stab wounds came from. So that might have been some kind of blackout thing. You know, I was trying to re-re-re-uh, re-uh, uh, resurrect the uh, the crime — my initial steps, etcetera. You know, and uh, and uh, I took, as a matter of fact, it came right out of the, I was starting the New Testament at the time, matter of fact I'm about the only person you'll ever meet that went to, to do a triple murder with a Bible in his, in his pocket, and, and, listening to a radio. I had delusions of grandeur with the radio. Uh, I had a red shirt on that was symbolic of, of some lines in Revelations in the, in the New Testament. Uh, I had a red motor ... as a matter of fact, I think it was chapter six something, verses three, four or five, or something where, uh, it was a man, it was a man. On a red horse. And, and, a man on a red horse came out, and uh, and uh, uh, and he was given a knife, and unto him was given the power to kill and destroy. And I actually thought I was this person. And I thought that my red horse was this red Harley Davidson I had. And I wore ... it was just, you know, it was kind of a symbolic type of thing. And, and, and uh, you know, uh, after the murders I thought the nephew was, was the, was a new devil or something, you know. This, this is pretty bizarre now that I think back on it. I thought he was a new devil and uh, uh. I mean basically I love my sister, there's no question about that. But at times my sister hadn't come through, uh, for me. You know and I was in another one of these manic attacks. And uh, and uh, uh, uh, you know, uh, I was just you know, I mean I was fed up with all this, you know, one day they treat me good and then they tell all these other people that I was a maniac and watch out for me and etcetera and like that. And uh, uh, so I went to them that night to tell them I was all in trouble again, you know, and could they put me up for the night, you know, and they told me to take a hike and uh, so, uh, believing that I had the power to kill, uh, you know, that was that for them. You know. I mean when family turns you out, that's a real blow. You know. But uh, back to the original subject of forgiveness. If I forgive myself, I'm forgiven. You know that's essentially the answer. I'm the captain of my own ship. I run my own ship. Nobody can crawl in my ship unless they get permission. I just *(He nods)* "over there." You know. "I'm forgiven." You know. *(Laughs.)* It's as simple as that. You know. You're your own priest, you're your own leader, you're your own captain. You know. You run your own show, a lot of people know that.

A Delicate Balance
by Edward Albee

This Pulitzer Prize script has a simple, but melodramatic, storyline: a husband, Tobias, and wife, Agnes, whose marriage has become a reckless misadventure, and Agnes' alcoholic sister, Claire, who lives with them, receive a surprise visit from their daughter, who is now recovering from a fourth failed marriage, and their odd couple best friends, who storm in and lock the door! There is poison in every decanter as the characters toast self-loathing, loss of innocence, and their own demons before finally discovering a simple truth: life's "delicate balance" is a blurred line between sanity and madness. In one of the few sane moments, Claire shares a recent incident to call attention to the severity of her own problems.

CLAIRE: Well, I had an adventure today. Went into town, thought I'd shake 'em up a little, so I tried to find me a topless bathing suit. Yes, I did. I went into what's-their-names', and I went straight up to the swim-wear, as they call it, department and I got me an eighteen-nineties schoolteacher type, who wondered what she could do for me. And I felt like telling her, "Not much, sweetheart" ... But I said, "Hello, there, I'm in the market for a topless swimsuit." "A what, Miss?" she said, which I didn't know whether to take as a compliment or not. "A topless swimsuit," I said. "I don't know what you mean," she said after a beat. "Oh, certainly you do," I said, "no top, stops at the waist, latest thing, lots of freedom." "Oh, yes," she said, looking at me like she was seeing the local madam for the first time, "those." Then a real sniff. "I'm afraid we don't carry ... those." "Well, in that case," I told her, "do you have any separates?" "Those we carry," she said, "those we do." And she started going under the counter, and I said, "I'll just buy the bottom of one of those." She came up from under the counter, adjusted her spectacles and said, "What did you say?" I said, "I'll buy the bottom of one of those." She thought for a moment, and then she said, with ice in her voice, "And what will we do with the tops?" "Well," I said, " Why don't you save 'em? Maybe bottomless swimsuits 'll be in next year." Then the poor sweet thing gave me a look I couldn't tell was either a D-minus, or she was going to send me home with a letter to my mother, and she said, sort of far away, "I think you need the manager." And off she walked.

Fences
by August Wilson

Rose, a strong-willed African-American woman whose emotional life has become as barren as an untilled garden, is married to Troy Maxson, a former star in the Negro Baseball League. Troy is now working as a garbage man, and remains bitter that he was unfairly excluded from the major leagues during his prime. He sees the world — and Rose — as "fences" which confine him. Rose, in a blistering but heartbreaking outburst, strains herself to persuade Troy to take a hard look at their eighteen year marriage that has survived against incredible odds in spite of his unhappy experiences in life.

ROSE: I been standing with you! I been right here with you, Troy. I got a life, too. I gave eighteen years of my life to stand in the same spot with you. Don't you think I ever wanted other things? Don't you think I had dreams and hopes? What about my life? What about me? Don't you think it ever crossed my mind to want to know other men? That I wanted to lay up somewhere and forget about my responsibilities? That I wanted someone to make me laugh so I could feel good? You not the only one who's got wants and needs. But I held onto you, Troy. I took all my feelings, my wants and needs, my dreams … and I buried them inside you. I planted a seed and watched and prayed over it. I planted myself inside you, and waited to bloom. And it didn't take me no eighteen years to find out the soil was hard and rocky and it wasn't never gonna bloom.

But I held onto you, Troy. I held you tighter. You was my husband. I owed you everything I had. Every part of me I could find to give you. And upstairs in that room ... with the darkness falling in on me … I gave everything I had to try and erase the doubt that you wasn't the finest man in the world. And wherever you was going … I wanted to be there with you. 'Cause you was my husband. 'Cause that's the only way I was gonna survive as your wife. You always talking about what you give … and what you don't have to give. But you take, too. You take … and don't even know nobody's giving!

My Children! My Africa!
by Athol Fugard

Athol Fugard occupies a unique position in South African drama: he is a white playwright who captures the agony of racial conflict and biting injustice of native black South Africans. This monologue explores the tragic consequences of the friendship and personal attraction between Isabel Dyson, a white high school student, and Thami Mbikwana, her African classmate, as they confront each other over a recent attack in which Mr. M., an unarmed, defenseless man, was killed.

THAMI: *(Abandoning all attempts at patience. He speaks with the full authority of the anger inside him.)* Stop it, Isabel! You just keep quiet now and listen to me. You're always saying you want to understand us and what it means to be black … well if you do, listen to me carefully now. I don't call it murder, and I don't call the people who did it a mob and yes, I do expect you to see it as an act of self-defense … listen to me! ... blind and stupid but still self-defense.

He betrayed us and our fight for freedom. Five men are in detention because of Mr. M's visit to the police station. There have been other arrests and there will be more. Why do you think I'm running away?

How were those people to know he wasn't a paid informer who had been doing it for a long time and would do it again? They were defending themselves against what they thought was a terrible danger to themselves. What Anela Myalatya did to them and their cause is what your laws define as treason when it is done to you and threatens the safety and security of your comfortable white world. Anybody accused of it is put on trial in your courts and if found guilty they get hanged. Many of my people have been found guilty and have been hanged. Those hangings we call murder!

Try to understand, Isabel. Try to imagine what it is like to be a black person, choking inside with rage and frustration, bitterness, and then to discover that one of your own kind is a traitor, has betrayed you to those responsible for the suffering and misery of your family, or your people. What would you do? Remember there is no magistrate or court you can drag him to and demand that he be tried for that crime. There is no justice for black people in this country other than what we make for ourselves. When you judge us for what happened in front of the school four days ago just remember that you carry a share of the responsibility for it. It is your laws that have made a simple decent black people so desperate that they turn into "mad mobs."

The Lucky Spot
by Beth Henley

Set in the sleepy backwoods town of Pigeon, Louisiana, during the depths of the Great Depression in 1934, this offbeat story features headstrong Sue Jack. She is a volatile woman with a vicious temper who has been in jail three years for pushing a woman over the balcony to her death for "messing with her husband," Hooker. Home on Christmas parole, Sue Jack unexpectedly drops in at the ramshackle "Lucky Spot" dance hall that Hooker recently won in a card game, and hopes to rekindle the flames of their smoldering relationship.

SUE JACK: I'm not the same as I was. Go on and look at me. You see, I'm not the same. I'm not the same one who kept on hurting you by drinking, and brawling and gambling it all away. And I'm not the young, laughing girl you married with the rosy cheeks and pretty hands. I guess I'm not sure who I am. And, I tell you, it's been making me feel so strange. When I was in prison, the only belonging I had was this old photograph of myself that was taken just before I ran off from home. In it I'm wearing this straw hat decorated with violets and my hair's swept back in a braid and my eyes, they're just ... shining ... I used to take out that picture and look at it. I kept on pondering over it. I swear it confused me so much, wondering where she was — that girl in the picture. I could not imagine where she'd departed to — so unknowingly, so unexpectedly. *(A pause.)* Look, I won't drink or yell or fight or shoot pool or bet the roosters or — . Please, I don't wanna lose any more. I'm through throwing everything away with both fists.

Dedication; or, The Stuff of Dreams
by Terrence McNally

Lou, a pompous patron of the arts, runs a struggling children's theatre company in an old run-down ex-vaudeville hall. Although he has come to the end of the road in his career, Lou still has spirited memories of his colorful life in the topsy-turvy world of theatre. He also has a playwright for whom he has a lingering and rather obsessive dislike — William Shakespeare.

195

LOU: I hate Shakespeare. I don't know anyone who's honest who doesn't. In the first place, there's too many words. He said so himself: "Words, words, words." And what are they talking about? "Speak English," I want to yell at the actors. No, instead you get yada yada yada yada in iambic pentameter for six and a half hours. And the plots! People getting murdered because they lost a handkerchief. Women playing men and no one notices. "What's with the high voice, buddy? And what are those, pray tell, oh shepherd youth? Look like hooters to me." The plays are so confusing people don't even know what period to set them in. The Scottish Play on the North Pole in 3005 — I'm sorry, I'm very confused. I don't deny Shakespeare wrote a lot of great lines. "To be or not to be," "Et tu, Brute?" "Let's kill all the lawyers." It's just the […] plays you have to sit through to get to them! King Lear or Dumbo, there's no contest.

The Mineola Twins
by Paula Vogel

Myrna and Myra are identical twin sisters, but polar opposites in their views on a wide range of controversial issues. The schism between them is treated as an allegory representing the political and social views of the left and right in the United States. In this dark metaphor Myrna, the good twin, invokes the biblical story of the "Prodigal Son" to describe her estranged sister, Myra.

MYRNA: You know the story of the Prodigal Son? This man had two sons, right, and one worked hard in the fields from dawn to dusk. He never gave his parents cause to worry. […] The Prodigal Son got into trouble with the law. He had to hide in this foreign land far across the borders, and a price was on his head. And he thought — wait a minute, I'll bet I can get Mom sorry for me, and she'll dip into the old man's pockets when he's asleep. And so he came dragging home in clothes that hadn't been washed in weeks. And his aged parents bailed him out. They drew his bath water. They washed his clothes. And they barbecued up filet mignon. And do you know what the Good Son felt, when he came home from the fields and saw his evil brother getting the ticker-tape parade? *What am I, ground chuck?* [...] The Good Brother bided his time, and then went to the cops in the other country and turned his sorry brother in. Took the reward, and invested it. And then, he got control of his father's business. He sent his parents to a nice, clean nursing home where they had arts therapy. And when the Prodigal Son was finally released from the hoosegow, he had to beg in the marketplace, until the Prodigal Son finally died. And the Good Son danced and danced. Happy Ending!

Employees Must Wash Hands ...
Before Murder
by Don Zolidis

Torok, an under-the-counter manager of a low-end, no frills food restaurant, is a callous and unfeeling supervisor who indulges all his own excesses at the expense of those he supervises. Here, the weasel gives a rare glimpse of corporate management style as he conducts an orientation session to introduce a new employee to the Burgatorium way of doing business.

TOROK: Good. Now, in the Burgatorium team, we like to do things a certain way. Before you do something, ask yourself this question: Will someone sue me? If the answer to that question is no, then you go ahead and do it. If the answer to that question is yes, do it very quietly. And then sign your name to it. And then sign this form releasing the store of any responsibility. *(He produces a form. TOROK guides the new employee over to the counter area.)*

You got your counters here, this is where we talk to the customers, and then the customers eat their stuff over there and then run to the restrooms, which are located on either side of us — Behind the counter is the kitchen area, which is where the magic happens. You are gonna start out in the kitchen, and if you can handle it, you just might move up to the counter. The counter, though, requires a whole different skill set. Like pressing buttons. And talking. But most important: listening. Because if you look at the customers, they just might tell you what they want. And then you have to press buttons. And talk some more. It's complicated.

A lot of people go to school a long time to learn these skills. *(He stares at her.)* Perhaps this short instructional video will help you understand the history of Burgatorium. I'm going to go play solitaire on my computer to pass the time and deaden my soul.

Decisions, Decisions
by Ken Friedman

This comic duologue offers an intimate glimpse at a young actor's debut role in a New York theatre production after three years of cattle calls. Bert, a waif-like adolescent type, is enjoying his budding career success as he shares the unexpected good news with Karen, his free-spirited friend. Karen insists that Bert perform his lines for her, and Bert reluctantly agrees — and so begins this comedy of errors that captures the theatrical spirit of what "now let's make believe" is all about.

KAREN: It's a great opportunity; grab it.

BERT: But, Karen, I don't know if it's the right one.

KAREN: Bert, for God's sakes, your first role in New York after three years. Grab it and make it work.

BERT: Right. You're right. Thank you.

KAREN: I mean, are you nude? Do you eat body parts? What?

BERT: Well, first of all, it's a play about the Korean war.

KAREN: The what war?

BERT: Korean.

KAREN: Drama or comedy?

BERT: Drama.

KAREN: The Korean War? Is it fictional?

BERT: No, there actually was one.

KAREN: Really? I never heard of it.

BERT: See?

KAREN: That doesn't mean anything. It could be one of those quiet wars with a large cult following. Who was in it?

BERT: Us and Korea. China and maybe Ireland. I couldn't tell.

KAREN: Okay. Reputable countries. So, what is your problem?

BERT: Well, who's going to come and see it?

KAREN: No one. It's a showcase. Have you read the script?

BERT: Twice.

KAREN: Good?

BERT: I have no idea. I asked the director what it meant.

KAREN: Before you read it, or after you read it?

BERT: Before. I didn't want to read it and still not know.

KAREN: Smart. Very professional. And he said?

BERT: He's not quite sure, but he thinks it's a metaphor.

KAREN: I like that. I respect any director that can turn what he doesn't understand into a metaphor. I think a heartfelt vagueness is essential to the success of any play. Are you a soldier?

BERT: Yes. I open the show.

KAREN: Fantastic.

BERT: With three lines.

KAREN: To open the show? Good. Very good.

BERT: No, I have three lines for the entire show. The curtain rises. I'm in a foxhole. I stand and shout: "Look! An eagle! A free bird in flight. How I envy your proud plumage!" That's it.

KAREN: That's a very nice speech.

BERT: And BANG! I get it. A sniper. Off-stage. And after that I lie there. Dead. That's it. I'm dead.

KAREN: For how long do you lie there or is it lay?

BERT: Either way, two hours. No intermission. Two hours of my back to the audience. The director doesn't want them to see my face, because my nose could twitch. So I ask, Karen ... do you think that this is the New York debut that will advance my career?

KAREN: Bert, are you crazy? A lot of actors would kill for that role. Do the lines. I want to hear. Do them. Do them. Please. *(He reveals a huge script.)*

BERT: Performance level? From beginning to end?

KAREN: Yes. Let's find out what they mean.

BERT: *(He prepares.)* Okay ... I'm not really sure, yet. But, here goes ... *(He lies down, gets up.)* Wait! Help me. Be the eagle. Fly. Fly like an eagle.

KAREN: Good idea. Focus on me. I'm on my perch. Here I go! I'm flying. Do eagles make sounds?

BERT: If they want to, sure.

KAREN: *(She flies around.)* Cooo … Cooo. Watch the birdie.

BERT: No, no. You're flying like a parakeet. Be grand. Big wings. Swoop. Soar. Better. Much better. Yes!

KAREN: Ready? Here I come. The form, the face of a hunter. *(She is flying. He jumps to his feet.)*

BERT: Look! An eagle! A free bird in flight. How I envy your proud plumage!

KAREN: Gunshot!

BERT: Bang. Aggghhh … aghhhhhh … *(He twists as he is falling.)*

KAREN: Ohhhhh. *(She too is falling.)*

BERT: MA! I'M DYING! I love you … Maaa. Ohhhhh. *(He hits the floor, she lands on top of him. They get up.)* Well?

KAREN: Wow! You must do the part! You were so real.

BERT: Thank you. Did you like the ad-lib? About my mother? I had to do it. But, what were you doing? It was my scene and you landed on me.

KAREN: He shot me, too. I couldn't help it. I was so into it. But, you were communicating so much of … you know, death, pain, grief. All that stuff.

BERT: I feel it. I wasn't sure, but now I know. I'm an actor. And I must act!

KAREN: No question about it. You can do this. It may be three lines, but on your resume, it'll look like a lead.

BERT: Thank you, Karen. I needed to hear that. Now, this brings me to my next question.

KAREN: What? What else is there?

BERT: Should I invite agents?

KAREN: Absolutely. They leave at intermission anyway. Bert, you haven't mentioned my eagle.

BERT: Very good. Very helpful. You had a real sense of bird.

KAREN: Thank you. And call your parents and let them know.

BERT: I'll have to write. They just got an unlisted number. Then it's settled. I'm going to do it. My first play in New York. It may not be much, but after my lines, I'll get plenty of much needed rest. I just hope I don't fall asleep.

KAREN: And, you don't know. In this business, you never know.

BERT: It could lead to something. Come on, let's get out of here and go rent a movie. Look, look an eagle in flight. I'll take the script. I may want to make some changes. *(They exit.)*

CHAPTER SEVEN
PLAYING THE MUSICAL AND THE MEDIUM

*"Music expresses that which cannot be said,
and on which it is impossible to be silent."*

— Victor Hugo

Part One:
PLAYING THE MUSICAL

Musical theatre has been one of the most popular forms of live entertainment for the past sixty years. Between riveting songs and lively dance numbers, musicals are shaped by elaborate production elements from beginning to end. A supporting chorus of singers in bright costumes, a troupe of agile dancers in intricate formations, colorful lighting, revolving stage, characters suspended in flight, and spectacular scenic effects in the blink of an eye continue to captivate audiences. Until recently, however, serious theatre critics tended to dismiss musicals as simply, "sound and fury, signifying nothing."

Some continue to refer to this art form as "musical comedy," but modern musicals contain such an intense depth of emotion and thought that we may now need to think of them as something much more than a script or book set to music. Even previous critics have begun to recognize the artistic achievement that is possible when story *(Phantom of the Opera)*, characters *(Rent)*, music *(Dream Girls)*, dance *(A Chorus Line)*, and spectacle *(Beauty and the Beast)* are integrated in a sparkling way that is full of dash and energy, but also proves to be thought provoking.

HISTORICAL VIEWS

Although the earliest roots of musical theatre are found in eighteenth century comic operettas and later vaudeville revues, American musical theatre evolved more slowly. Since the first "true American musical," *The Black Crook* (1866), dance has been as important as music to interpret the storyline of a script or book. For a long time, however, musical "dance" consisted of well-drilled lines of scantily-clad chorus girls stepping, kicking, and whirling as they paraded in front of the audience.

The first significant appearance of dance that helped an audience interpret a storyline in musical theatre was the stirring "dream ballet" choreographed by Agnes de Mille in the 1943 production of *Oklahoma!* With the recent emergence of contemporary choreographers trained in ballet, jazz, tap, and modern techniques, today's musical theatre dance is used frequently to define character emotions and thoughts. Expectations for musical theatre have changed little from the early 1940s and as a result the artistic and commercial success of a new musical may well depend on its ability to strike a familiar chord of audience appeal based on the following criteria.

Character

Musicals rely on popular stereotypes that are easily recognized by an audience. The most common are the betrayed woman (Luisa in *Rent*), star-crossed lovers (Tony and Maria in *West Side Story*), romantic hero (Sky Masterson in *Guys and Dolls*), fun trickster (Nathan Detroit in *Guys and Dolls*), idealistic dreamer (Don Quixote in *Man of La Mancha*), chronic cynic (Frederick in *A Little Night Music*), innocent heroine (Christine in *Phantom of the Opera*), comic old man (Major General in *The Pirates of Penzance*), comic con artist (Bloody Mary in *South Pacific*), staunch nonconformist (Tevye in *Fiddler on the Roof*), wise confidante and side-kick (Col. Pickering in *My Fair Lady*), happy schemer (Max Bialystock in *The Producers*), domineering mother (Rose in *Gypsy*), heroic rebel (Jean Valjean in *Les Miserables*), and arch-villain (Jud in *Oklahoma!*).

Language

Musical characters speak prose in short and simple sentences that quickly move the storyline to the next song or musical number. Short exchanges of dialogue are then interspersed with recitative and lyrical song, either solo or ensemble. An interesting perspective of recent musicals has been the focus on social change, human values, and new interpretations of traditional religious, political, or moral issues — *Sweeney Todd, The Color Purple, Wicked, Monty Python's Spamalot*. Characters in musicals usually find themselves in unfortunate, yet comic, situations — failed love affair, family feud, dead end job, or shattered dream — but resolve their problems through ingenuity and a little good luck. Songs, of course, are voiced in complicated rhymes and intricate rhythms to indicate characters that triumph over their plight and achieve a measure of personal dignity as a result of the struggle.

Movement

Movement is agile in non-singing scenes and establishes relationships. In non-speaking scenes, movement is choreographed with complex dance combinations that include tap, jazz, modern, and ballet to give the storyline tempo and express character attitude or mood. The role of movement in musicals frequently depends on the choreographer's design for the production and the actor's ability to discover character intention or motivation in dialogue during non-singing and non-dancing scenes.

Spectacle

Spectacle is the ultimate theatrical tool for a musical! It spotlights the characters, swiftly changes the scene, utilizes awe-inspiring stage machinery, and propels the storyline to its climactic finale. Scenery that flies, glides, turns, or disappears is essential for musical transformations from one locale to another. The elaborate use of turntables, slides, projections, and film sequences add an additional flavor to the musical production. Costume changes are also frequent, and the emphasis is on bright hues and glittering fabric.

Time

The passage of musical time elapses quickly *between* scenes and acts. Unlike the chronological time structure in most theatre scripts, musicals compress time and action to heighten suspense and build momentum. Suspending time allows a musical to condense a series of unrelated incidents or events into one scene, or to highlight a number of individual events simultaneously. For example, several months need to elapse between Act I and Act II of *My Fair Lady* to allow Eliza Doolittle time to learn proper diction; and more than ten years elapse in *Jesus Christ Superstar* to account for historical events depicted in the *Old Testament*.

Versatility

Audience expectations that actors exhibit versatility and vitality in their role-playing have not changed over the years. Long-running productions — *Cats, Les Miserables, A Chorus Line, The Lion King, Miss Saigon* — feature roles that require a strong singing voice, extensive dance training, especially jazz, modern, and tap, and gymnastic ability for tumbling, falling, and stage combat. Actors also need the ability to read complex music scores and display vocal variety in speaking roles. There is even a need for today's musical actors to acquire skills in circus techniques, improvisation, magic tricks, and pantomime as part of a competitive audition.

AUDITION OVERTURE

An interesting analogy might be drawn between the structure of a musical and the architectural design of a modern building. Both the musical author and the architect begin their initial design plans with a solid foundation capable of supporting the emerging structure. Both calculate dimensions, size, and scope that will give the musical or the building its inner strength and outer beauty. In initial planning stages, both author and architect allow ample time for revision or redesign of the project. The foundation of a musical production is plot, which includes exposition, complication, and resolution.

Exposition, background information needed to understand character actions and relationships, occurs briefly in the first scene of a musical and serves as an introduction to the storyline. For example, in

The King and I we learn early in Act I that the arrogant King of Siam has sent for a Welsh schoolmistress, Anna, to educate his numerous children and wives. This introductory exposition propels the storyline through a number of songs, scenes, and acts to its happy ending: Anna dutifully instructs the children and wives, but also teaches the King an invaluable lesson in how to show gratitude and humility.

Complication, real or imagined obstacles that create conflict or inhibit a character from achieving desired goals and objectives, occurs toward the middle of a musical. It is complication that provides the impetus for characters to take action, which is then resolved at some later time in the last half of the musical. In *West Side Story,* Tony and Maria fall instantly and hopelessly in love, but the complication of their affair is a violent street gang confrontation that quickly accelerates the musical's irreconcilable ending.

Resolution, knitting together previous character actions, situations, and relationships to conclude the storyline, occurs toward the end of the musical. The final resolution dissolves any conflict developed in the complication and reconciles the characters. In *Gypsy,* for example, an ambitious and aggressive mother, Rose, reluctantly realizes in the resolution that her daughters need freedom to make their own decisions and vows to cease interfering in their lives.

As you become more familiar with the structure of musicals, it should not surprise you that there is a solid foundation built on the seamless and sequential arrangement of dialogue and song. Each scene and act also evolves from what has preceded it, and character attitudes or moods follow a similar pattern. Like the stage actor, the musical actor begins a study of the script or book by asking *who, what, when, where,* and *why* of characters to discover their intention, motivation, and point of view in the storyline.

PRE-AUDITION PREPARATION

The focus of this chapter is on musical etiquette and the preparation skills an actor needs to be successful in an audition. Rather than an introduction to singing techniques or voice training, this chapter is an exploration of musical theatre audition expectations. Preparing for a musical theatre audition is very similar to the analysis, character building, and rehearsal approaches used at traditional theatre auditions.

There are, however, a number of differences you will need to anticipate. The musical storyline presents an abbreviated version of character description and detail. There are also fewer plot complications or reversals that help to clarify a character's intention or motivation. For example, a traditional musical format may include the following brief outline.

- The opening scene introduces the principal character(s) and reveals a conflict that must be resolved as the plot unfolds.
- The plot is simple and features a number of individual or ensemble songs rather than dialogue to advance the storyline.
- The storyline is embellished with ensemble or solo dances, reprises, and elaborate technical displays that frame character intention or motivation.
- Character development focuses on emotional content rather than intellectual or psychological points of view.
- With few exceptions, there is a predictable "happy ending" or at least a reconciliation of apparent conflict.

Although musical storylines may appear slick and superficial at times, there is still an opportunity for actors to present an incisive and vivid character portrait that mirrors reality. Musicals featuring characters that perform mock-heroic deeds (*The Man of La Mancha*), succeed against all odds (*Jersey Boys*), commit silly blunders (*You're A Good Man, Charlie Brown*), exhibit courage (*Shrek*) or cowardice (*Avenue Q*), rush to judgment (*Hairspray*), or simply display basic human emotions (*Mamma Mia!*) are all ripe vehicles for a three-dimensional audition.

Before proceeding to the discussion of an audition blueprint, it is important to point out some of the basics to anticipate as you begin your preparation. First, you should have an understanding of musical theatre practices, terms, and techniques. That means being familiar with musical theatre styles of performance as well. Second, you should be disciplined in your preparation and rehearsal. That means being able to exhibit efficiency in acting and singing to suggest a competent and well-trained performer. Third, you should be fresh and original in your character interpretation. That means giving your audition an added dimension of vitality and an indescribable "life spirit" that radiates self-confidence.

Character Building

Character building begins by paying careful attention to dialogue and song. You may find it helpful to make a performance chart of potential mannerisms or traits revealed in individual speeches or songs to flesh-out individual character portraits. Here are some of the questions you need to answer in character building: What stage business does the character frequently repeat? Where does the character appear to place priorities? What is the character's emotional and mental state of mind? What do the song lyrics suggest about a character's attitude or mood? Which of the character's primary objectives appear in each scene or song? What other characters appear to influence your character the most or least? What three adjectives define the character's point of view?

Role-Playing

Your own personality should be the initial source to mold and give life to a musical character. Explore your personality to discover role-playing techniques that encourage use of *both* the voice and body as expressive instruments to help define distinctive character portraits. Cultivate an inventory of sensory and emotional responses that might be appropriate for audition songs. Remember that role-playing begins with a detailed study of the character in the *complete* script or book of the musical.

MUSICAL AUDITION BLUEPRINT

Musical theatre is a heightened form of theatre, one in which characters reach such a high pitch of emotion that the only form of expression available is a song or a dance. To provide an overview of a typical musical theatre audition and introduce a common vocabulary for the discussion that follows, here is a list of key topics you will need to review for an audition. Understanding the basic ingredients of a *libretto* — words or text of spoken dialogue and lyrics of the songs — styles of performance, and rigorous audition demands will prepare you to design a musical theatre blueprint that suits individual needs and talents.

Accompanist

The accompanist rules in musical theatre auditions. This is not a master or servant role, so never ask a pianist to transpose music on the spot. As part of the rehearsal routine you should make sure music is in the right key, cut to appropriate length, copied on card stock, or taped neatly together and secured in a three-ring binder. Audition music should not be so complicated that the accompanist is unable to sight-read.

Give the pianist a brief preview when you audition. Hand your music audition book to the pianist with the song page open. Identify the song and indicate where it begins and ends. Point out cuts, key changes, or repeats and indicate the tempo you prefer for the song. It will be helpful to let the accompanist know the signal you will use to begin the song. A simple "Now, please," nod of the head, or step forward is appropriate.

Do not hand the pianist a photocopy of the music from a chorus book marked in pencil, "snap fingers" to set the song's tempo, or turn in a *lead sheet,* music with only the vocal line and chord symbols, but no *piano* part! Tell the pianist what you want in specific terms — not "a little slow here" or "really fast there." It might also be helpful to quietly hum or sing a few bars to set the song. Inform the pianist how many measures are needed for the introduction, and make sure the ending of the song is clearly indicated. It's perfectly permissible, of course, to bring your own accompanist to an audition as long as they have been part of the rehearsal period and are really good.

Audition Book

Begin to collect sheet music for a portfolio of audition materials. Include the complete song, 32-bar cut, 16-bar cut, and 8-bar cut to meet audition demands. Selected songs should represent your age and vocal range as well as emphasize musical personality and versatility. A typical audition book may contain two or three Tin Pan Alley favorites, early twentieth century; two or three standard or contemporary ballads; a cabaret or story song; two Broadway pop songs; two "Golden Age" ballads, Rodgers and Hammerstein or Lerner and Loewe; two novelty songs for character actor auditions; a Sondheim special; and one "show-stopper" that knocks 'em dead each time you audition.

Standard songs are usually dated from 1950 to 1980 and are popular for stylish melodies and poetic lyrics. Contemporary songs from 1980 to the present are more complex, and require a greater vocal range to voice intricate rhythm schemes. Avoid songs with a narrative storyline or repetitive melodies that are difficult to edit. Look for songs that feature significant changes in character attitude or mood and suggest meaningful action that motivates movement during an audition. You may also wish to include one "non-theatre" song to give variety to the audition book. Like the theatre actor, you would not audition a song from the musical being cast because the director may have a vocal and physical image of that character already in mind.

Audition Songs

Most musical auditions require sixteen bars from a ballad and a show tune performed in your own singing range. Sometimes there may be a call for a novelty song to showcase your vocal range. The time limit is generally two or three minutes total, so you may need to edit songs to include only the most memorable lyrics. The sixteen-bar audition should focus attention on your musicality (phrasing), vocal range, interpretation skills, stage presence, performance style, and personality.

For a more general audition, maintain a repertoire that includes eight to sixteen measures from at least five contrasting songs. A novelty song that also serves as your personal signature is ideal for a general audition. If there is a call for chorus members, anticipate singing a maximum of sixteen bars or one solo song of two minutes. Show songs written directly for stage performance are particularly desirable to display emotional intensity at a musical audition, but avoid signature songs of well-known performers.

Coaches

Become *voice conscious* rather than *voice confused*. Always work with an experienced *voice* teacher who is familiar with open-throat exercises to free vowel sounds and a professional *vocal* coach who is skilled in both interpretation and phrasing of lyrics. A vocal coach is essential if you are not a musician. A professional vocal coach can focus attention on presentational skills, select appropriate songs, arrange music for the audition pianist, and teach "best keys" for pitch, range, and vocal quality.

If you can work with both a voice teacher *and* a vocal coach that would be the best choice. The National Association for Teachers of Singing (NATS) and the Voice and Speech Teachers Association (VASTA) are excellent sources to identify potential coaches. It is also a good idea to enroll in short courses or workshops that explore voice production, movement for actors, and musical theatre performance skills so you do not, as Shakespeare reminded us in Chapter Four, "saw the air too much with your hand, but use all gently."

Dance

Most musical auditions will include a dance component that may be an additional ingredient in final casting choices. The dance segment usually requires learning a combination of jazz, ballet, or tap in a larger group and then repeating the same combination in smaller groups to demonstrate a sense of rhythm and phrasing. A choreographer or director's primary objective in evaluating the dance segment of an audition is to determine your ability to execute a routine pattern of stylized movement set to music and to exhibit fluid and expressive dance steps. Don't layer yourself with sweats, multiple tops, leggings, and headbands. The choreographer and director will need to see shape and size to determine appropriate body types.

The body also needs to *speak* the lyrics as you move from verbal (song) to physical (dance) character expression. Your body language should have a tempo and rhythm in gesture and movement to help define the character portrait as well. In musical theatre you need to *learn* to dance in order to execute turns, jumps, and combinations with confidence and ease. Keep the body well tuned, study pilates, or enroll in a regular series of classes that focus on jazz, modern, and tap to refine your movement style. It is also crucial to include physical relaxation exercises that explore tension-free body alignment in the rehearsal period.

Song "Acting"

One of the first lessons to learn in musical theatre is that actors must *speak* character attitudes, *sing* character emotions, and *dance* character moods. This triple-threat approach to performance vividly reveals a musical character's intention or motivation and the subtext, or hidden meaning, in the lyrics. Think of song lyrics as a monologue without melody or rhythm. Interpret the lines to give the character form and shape as you voice the lyrics. Write out song lyrics as monologues and use action verbs to define character intention, motivation, and subtext.

The following lyrics from "The Impossible Dream" in *Man of La Mancha*, by Mitch Leigh and Joe Darion, provide a good model of song acting. Using just the lyrics, answer the following questions: What is Don Quixote's apparent intention or motivation suggested in the lyrics? What are his strongly held personal beliefs? What action is he prepared to take to achieve his goal? What active verbs might define the character? How will your interpretation of the lyrics give the character form and shape?

The Impossible Dream
To dream the impossible dream
To fight the unbeatable foe,
To bear with unbearable sorrow,
To run where the brave dare not go.
To right the unrightable wrong,
To love pure and chaste from afar,
To try when your arms are too weary,
To reach the unreachable star.
This is my quest,
To follow that star —
No matter how hopeless,
No matter how far.
To fight for the right
Without question or pause,
To be willing to march into hell
For a heavenly cause.
And I know if I'll only be true
To this glorious quest
That my heart will be peaceful
and calm when I'm laid to my rest.
And the world will be better for this, that
one man scorned and covered with scars
still strove with his last ounce of courage.
To reach the unreachable star.

Musical Clues

Never sing to an *empty chair!* Place musical characters in the center of the back wall at eye level, several inches above the heads of the audience. Lyrics have a poetic quality so *act* between pauses and add gestures or subtle movement between beats to place emphasis on individual words or phrases in the song. Look for musical clues in phrasing, word choice, intervals between notes, and repletion of key phrases. Long, short, held, or extended musical notes may also provide insight to a character's attitude or mood at a particular moment in time. Imagine a scene in rehearsal suggested by the lyrics and later, in the audition, try to recall the gestures or movement that surfaced in that imaginary scene as part of your audition performance. Remember not to close your eyes while singing in audition!

Wardrobe

A musical audition wardrobe is similar to the stage actor's as described earlier in Chapter Two. Dress should be simple and flatter you physically. For dance auditions, wear authentic dance attire — leotards and tights or sweats — and bring a variety of comfortable footwear like ballet slippers, tap shoes, and jazz shoes or jazz sneakers. For acting and singing auditions, wardrobe should be selected in terms of line, texture, and modest ornament to reflect *you* the person. It may also be necessary to make subtle changes in wardrobe as you move from acting to singing to dance segments of an audition.

Under no circumstances should you wear a theatrical costume to a musical audition. Men wear dress pants or pressed jeans, hard-sole shoes, casual shirt, and, occasionally, sport coat and tie. Women wear a skirt to the knees, soft-colored blouse, and high heels if the audition is for a period musical. No sneakers or flip-flops enter a musical theatre audition! Men and women avoid extreme colors like black or white, tight jeans, cut-offs, excessive jewelry, piercing, and decorative accessories that inhibit vocal or physical activity in the individual segments of an audition. Respect the audition space and do not litter the floor with gum wrappers, empty water bottles, soda cans, or snacks. Finally, no cell phones, pagers, watch alarms, or electronic and recording devices permitted in the audition space.

Wrap-Up

Do not try to choreograph your songs for a musical audition, but do stand tall, poised, and relaxed so the focus is on your voice and facial expressions. Try not to shift weight from one foot to the other or sway back and forth while singing. If the music director asks you to vocalize higher and lower or to sing a song again in a different attitude, style, or tempo, do so with energy and enthusiasm. You must be exhibiting potential if the audition is being extended.

MUSICAL NOTES

Musical auditions are an opportunity to emphasize your special skills. If you play an instrument, do comedic impressions, or perform a specialty act, don't hesitate to identify those skills to the casting director. Approach each audition in a confident and relaxed manner rather than as a competition with other equally talented actors. There may, of course, be musical auditions in which the most diligent and thoughtful preparation and rehearsal will not provide answers to explain why you may not be cast in a production. As a consequence, it is crucial to have the right attitude in an audition.

First, be *positive*. Practice audition material daily and refrain from performing monologues or songs that have not been solidly rehearsed. Solicit constructive criticism from acting teachers, dance instructors, and vocal coaches as a learning tool for other auditions that will follow. Second, be *prepared*. Double check music, markings, and notations to make sure they complement your vocal qualities. Review specific instructions with the accompanist and carefully organize audition materials. Third, be *professional*. Dress sensibly and tastefully. Treat everyone you meet at an audition with respect, and don't forget to be courteous to those who are part of the staff.

Continue to seek public performance experience in cabaret, revue, and workshop settings that generate immediate audience responses. Formal and informal venues like these will provide invaluable experiences to cultivate a polished stage presence. Always remember to place yourself in the *I* position, as the person who is living the story or singing the words of the story, at every audition and your performance will radiate with the kind of infectious spontaneity that choreographers and directors are searching for in their casting call.

MUSICAL MONOLOGUES

Musical theatre scripts often include imaginative monologues that enrich an actor's performance skills and talents in an audition. The musical monologues that follow have the look and feel of traditional theatre monologues and include colorful characters with thoughtful points of view. There are also creative opportunities here to explore personal self-portraits and *present tense* acting styles that were discussed in Chapter Six.

The Pirates of Penzance (1879)
by W. S. Gilbert

This period comic opera is one of the most frequently revived works in musical theatre. Frederic, apprenticed as a child to a band of tender-hearted pirates by his nurse — who, hard of hearing, had mistaken her master's instructions to apprentice the child to a pilot — is now twenty-one-years-old and free to return to polite society. Unfortunately, he was born on February 29 in a leap year and must remain with the pirates until his twenty-first birthday. One of Frederic's most memorable encounters is with the pompous Major General, who knows nothing about military strategy but is an expert in executing tongue-twisting song lyrics.

MAJOR GENERAL: I am the very model of a modern
    Major-General,
I've information on vegetable, animal, and mineral,
I know the kings of England, and I quote the fights
historical,
From Marathon to Waterloo, in order categorical;
I'm very well acquainted too with matters mathematical,
I understand equations, both the simple and quadratical,
About binomial theorem I'm teeming with a lot o'news —
With many cheerful facts about the square of the hypotenuse.
I'm very good at integral and differential calculus,
I know the scientific names of beings animalculous;
In short, in matters of vegetable, animal, and mineral,

I am the very model of a modern Major-General.
I know our mythic history, King Arthur's and Sir Caradoc's,
I answer hard acrostics, I've a pretty taste for paradox,
I quote in elegiacs all the crimes of Heliogabalus,
In comics I can floor peculiarities parabolous.
I can tell undoubted Raphaels from Gerard Dows and
Zoffanies,
I know the croaking chorus from the *Frogs* of Aristophanes,
Then I can hum a fugue of which I've heard the music's
dinafore,
And whistle all the airs from that infernal nonsense
Pinafore.
Then I can write a washing bill in Babylonic cuneiform,
And tell you every detail of Caractacu's uniform;
In short, in matters vegetable, animal, and mineral,
I am the very model of a modern Major-General.
In fact, when I know what is meant by "mamelon" and
"revelin,"
When I can tell at sight a chassepot rifle from a javelin,
When such affairs as sorties and surprises I'm more wary
at
And when I know precisely what is meant by "commissariat,"
When I have learnt what progress has been made in
modern gunnery,
When I know more of tactics than a novice in a nunnery:
In short, when I've a smattering of elemental strategy,
You'll say a better Major-General has never sat a gee —
For my military knowledge, though I'm plucky and
adventury,
Has only been brought down to the beginning of the century;
But still in matters vegetable, animal, and mineral,
I am the very model of a modern Major-General.

You're a Good Man, Charlie Brown

by Clark Gesner

Based on the comic script *Peanuts* by Charles M. Schultz

Charlie "Good Grief!" Brown is one of the most misunderstood and lovable characters in musical theatre. His transition from the world of newspaper cartoon anti-hero to the bright lights of the stage has lost none of its comic appeal, and he remains ageless in his eternal search for happiness. Here, Charlie Brown, alone as usual, sits on a playground bench with his sack lunch and contemplates his un-romantic life.

CHARLIE BROWN: I think lunchtime is about the worst time of the day for me. Always having to sit here alone. Of course, sometimes mornings aren't so pleasant, either — waking up and wondering if anyone would really miss me if I never got out of bed. Then there's the night, too — lying there and thinking about all the stupid things I've done during the day. And all those hours in between — when I do all those stupid things. Well, lunchtime is among the worst times of the day for me.

Well, I guess I'd better see what I've got. *(He opens the bag, unwraps a sandwich, and looks inside.)* Peanut butter. *(He bites and chews.)* Some psychiatrists say that people who eat peanut butter sandwiches are lonely. I guess they're right. And if you're really lonely, the peanut butter sticks to the roof of your mouth. *(He munches quietly, idly fingering the bench.)* Boy, the PTA sure did a good job of painting these benches. *(He looks off to one side.)* There's that cute little redhead girl eating her lunch over there. I wonder what she'd do if I went over and asked her if I could sit and have lunch with her. She'd probably laugh right in my face. It's hard on a face when it gets laughed in. There's an empty place next to her on the bench. There's no reason why I couldn't just go over and sit there. I could do that right now. All I have to do is stand up. *(He stands.)* I'm standing up. *(He sits.)* I'm sitting down. I'm a coward. I'm so much of a coward she wouldn't even think of looking at me. She hardly ever does look at me. In fact, I can't remember her ever looking at me. Why shouldn't she look at me? Is there a reason in the world why she shouldn't look at me? Is she so great and am I so small that she couldn't spare one little moment just to … *(He freezes.)*

She's looking at me. *(In terror he looks one way, then another.)* She's *looking* at me. *(His head looks all around, frantically trying to find something else to notice. His teeth clench. Tension builds. Then, with one motion, he pops the paper bag over his head.)* Lunchtime is among the worst times of the day for me. If that little redhead girl is looking at me with this stupid bag on my head she must think I'm the biggest fool alive. But if she isn't looking at me, then maybe I could take it off quickly and she'd never notice it. On the other hand, I can't tell if she's looking until I take it off. Then again, if I *never* take it off, I'll never have to know if she was looking or not. On the other hand, it's very hard to breathe in here. *(There is a moment of tense silence. Then his hand rises slowly, jerks the bag from his head and folds it quickly as he glances furtively in the direction of the little girl. He smiles.)* She's not looking at me. *(He looks concerned.)* I wonder why she never looks at me. *(The school bell jangles once again.)* Oh well, another lunch hour is over with. Only two thousand, eight hundred and sixty-three to go.

Fantasticks
by Harvey Schmidt and Tom Jones

This musical theatre classic about the pains of early adolescence revolves around two scheming fathers who decide they want their children to fall in love … and plot a faux family feud to encourage the youngsters' love even more. Luisa, the daughter, is a romantic daydreamer with a vivid imagination who glows throughout the bitter-sweet tale of intrigue, a mock abduction, and heart-rending redemption. Luisa is at her whimsical best as she captures a fleeting glimpse of her own self-identity in "Don't Let Me Be Normal."

LUISA: This morning a bird woke me up. It was a lark, or a peacock; something like that. So I said hello. And it vanished, flew away, the very moment I said hello! It was quite mysterious. So do you know what I did? I went to my mirror and brushed my hair two hundred times, without stopping. And as I was brushing it, my hair turned mauve. No, honestly! Then red. Then some sort of a deep blue when the sun hit it ... I'm sixteen-years-old, and every day something happens to me. I don't know what to make of it. When I get up in the morning and get dressed, I can tell ... something's different. I like to touch my eyelids, because they're never quite the same. Oh, oh, oh! I hug myself till my arms turn blue, then I close my eyes and cry and cry till the tears come down and I can taste them. I love to taste my tears. I am special. I am special! Please god, please, don't let me be normal!

Big River
The Adventures of Huckleberry Finn
by William Hauptman and Roger Miller
Adapted from the novel by Mark Twain

Here is a faithful and rousing retelling of Mark Twain's American classic novel of the young rascal Huck Finn and his attempt to escape civilization before his Aunt Sally has a chance to adopt and "tame" him. With his companion Jim, a runaway slave, Huck must first stage his own "death" before setting off down the Mississippi River on a raft.

Here are two monologues — the first from the musical and the second from Mark Twain's novel — that offer contrasting views of Huck Finn's spirit of reckless adventure and later genuine honesty and compassion. In the musical monologue Huck recalls his successful death escapade, and in the original novel monologue Huck shares some of his life-changing experiences with Jim on the Mississippi River.

HUCK: The sky looks ever so deep when you look up in the moonlight. Everything was dead quiet, and it looked late, and *smelt* late — you know what I mean. Just me and the drift logs and the moon. *(He drags the canoe ashore on Jackson's Island.)* When I got to Jackson's Island, I was tired and sort of lonesome. There ain't no better way to put in time when you are lonesome than sleep. You can't stay so; you soon get over it. So I slept for the better part of three days. *(When the sun rises, Huck lies in a cool green glade, filled with the sound of singing birds.)*

219

I was woke up by this deep boom. *(Thump of a cannon going off. Huck looks through his spyglass. Through a scrim upstage, we see the people board the ferry.)* Through my spyglass I seen the ferryboat crossing the river. They were firing off a cannon to make my body rise to the top — 'cause that's supposed to go right to a drowned carcass and stop. Then I knowed my plan had worked and they thought I was dead. There's Pap ... and Judge Thatcher ... and the widow and Miss Watson ... and Ben Rogers and Jo Harper, and there's Tom Sawyer! *(Laughs.)* The look on their faces! [...] But when they were gone, I felt almost lonely again. So I started exploring the island. I was the boss of it; it all belonged to me, so to say. And I was thinking: here was a place where a body didn't have to be nobody but himself.

. . . .

HUCK: I felt good and all washed clean of sin for the first time I had ever felt so in my life, and I knowed I could pray now. But I didn't do it straight off, but laid the paper down and then set there thinking — thinking how good it was all this happened so, and how near I come to being lost and going to hell. And went on thinking. And got to thinking over our trip down the river; and I see Jim before me all the time: in the day and in the nighttime, sometimes in moonlight, sometimes storms, and we a-floating along, talking and singing and laughing. But somehow I couldn't seem to strike no place to harden me against him, but only the other kind. I'd see him standing on my watch on top of his'n 'stead of calling me, so I could go on sleeping and see him how glad he was when I came back out of the fog; and when I come to him again in the swamp, up there where the feud was; and such-like times; and would always call me honey, and pet me, and do everything he could think of for me, and how good he always was; and at last I struck the time I saved him by telling the men we had smallpox aboard, and he was so grateful, and said I was the best friend old Jim ever had in the world, and the only one he's got now; and then I happened to look around and see that paper. It was a close place. I took it up, and held it in my hand. I was a-trembling, because I'd got to decide, forever; betwixt two things, and I knowed it. I studies a minute, sort of holding my breath, and then says to myself: "All right, then I'll go to hell" — and then tore it up.

Part Two:
PLAYING THE MEDIUM

"Do not invent something, but make something out of reality."
— Thomas Mann

This introduction to playing the medium is a basic review of audition approaches and the range of performance opportunities available in television. A major part of the discussion focuses on the literacy and vocabulary of the medium for beginners. The overview of principles and techniques at work in the medium simplifies the issues that may affect audition success, but there is no substitute for professional training courses or technical workshops in acting for the camera.

The medium rarely places emphasis on an actor playing a character. The primary focus is on casting men and women who *are* the character. For our purposes, the medium will include commercials, industrial films, soap operas, and popular television situation comedies. In spite of similarities in acting style, actors sometimes find the transition from *stage to page* challenging because of the medium's limited size and scope. There is also less informative description and narrative related to character building and script interpretation available in the medium.

For example, the stage actor performs a role that has been thoroughly described in the text. In front of a camera lens, however, the actor has to invent imaginary experiences to help flesh-out a brief, incomplete character outline. To give form and substance to the outline, the medium actor relies primarily on self-expression to create a believable character whose primary objective is *selling products* to a targeted market audience. Perhaps that is why stage actors sometimes appear awkward on screen portraying average, honest looking and sounding people who are simply telling an abbreviated story about a product while trying to persuade you to buy it in thirty seconds.

OVERVIEW

The medium we are exploring in this chapter is primarily film-related. Commercials are generally thought of as non-linear, and are filmed in segments that may be shot or re-shot a number of times. Industrials, soap operas, and television situation comedies are more linear, and are generally filmed sequentially from beginning to final episode using multiple cameras. These filming techniques require the actor to rely primarily on *external* techniques in character building. External techniques assume that there is a clear distinction between the actor as a person and the actor as a character.

The external technique is frequently referred to as acting from the *outside* rather than the *inside*. An external actor's approach to character building is to train the voice and body to respond to *physical* actions in a script. The external actor asks, "How would this character *act*?" rather than "How would this character *feel*?" The answer to that question allows the actor to clarify the action, objectify the character intention or motivation, and simplify the situation described in the script.

Acting style in the medium is more subtle than performing on a theatre stage. The typical television studio is arranged side-to-side rather than front-to-back, with limited and narrow depth. Given these dimensions, the camera then serves as the imaginary *fourth wall* that separates actor from audience. An actor's energy and enthusiasm are thrust forward and projected toward the camera. The medium acting style is a little more *show* than *tell,* and physical or vocal responses appear more natural given the camera's smaller frame of reference.

The storyline of medium scripts also influences acting style. Unlike the stage actor who builds character through overt action and movement indicated in the text, medium scripts reveal the storyline in simple *words* and complex facial *reactions* captured by the camera. It is the camera that gives meaning to the story and the actor's reactions — like those of a musical actor singing a song — which come *before* the dialogue. In other words, medium actors listen with the *face* and respond with the *voice* to give varied shades of meaning to an interpretation of the character.

Commercials

Actors interested in commercial auditions will need to secure an agent and gain admission to the Screen Actors Guild (SAG). Commercial producers generally employ casting agencies or independent scouts to identify potential talent. Agencies contact clients and send their headshots and résumés to the producer. Producers or a member of their staff review photographs and contact agents, who receive ten percent of a client's gross pay, to set-up preliminary auditions. If you have not yet signed with an agent, locate a reputable representative in your area and send a professional headshot, résumé, and brief letter of introduction to request a meeting to discuss representation. It might also be helpful to submit a two or three-minute video or digital reel of sample work to prospective agents.

Enroll in a commercial class or workshop before signing with an agent. You need to learn basic techniques in how to voice commercial scripts and how to execute expressive facial expressions for the camera. Attending professional classes or workshops will prepare you for the fast-paced world of commercials in which it is how you look, sound, and identify with the viewer that wins roles ... and sells products. You should also learn the "3-S's" of commercial acting: Keep it simple, short, and subtle.

Here is a sample of an original commercial to help you become familiar with some of the unique features associated with reading a cold script in an audition. After a quick initial reading, turn your attention to *vocal orchestration* of the script, interpreting the dialogue with different tones and shades of meaning to emphasize specific words that describe the product. Speak at a comfortable rate, produce vowel sounds that are crisp, and keep your breathing natural and relaxed. It may be helpful in this exercise to stand in front of a full-length mirror, holding the script at mid-chest, and direct facial expressions straight ahead as if the mirror were a camera. Try to refrain from distracting bodily actions or looking down at the script.

Extravagant! That's the only way to describe the warm, sensuous feeling you experience with *Desire,* a provocative new aroma created by the House of Alba. The first scent of the morning brings back memories of spring and rain; and the last scent of the evening brings forth dreams of forbidden love and unbridled passion. Available now in the rainbow decanter, a collection of vibrant colors designed by Henri Piaget. One of a kind! That's ETU. The perfume created exclusively for desirable women! Only $75 at your favorite boutique.

Now repeat readings of the sample script using different vocal tones to emphasize phrasing, which should help you achieve marked improvement in vocal variety and also promote an initial measure of self-confidence in commercial auditions. Continue to sharpen your ear for potential changes in pitch, rate, and volume to give the voice its emotional honesty when reading from a cold script. Remember that commercial auditions require distinctive vocal variety *and* facial expressions to direct audience response and gain listener attention.

Industrial Films

Industrials are training or promotional films for a corporate or sales company. They are similar to commercials in acting style, but the focus is essentially instructional and the script includes technical language and definitions. Industrial auditions are also arranged through casting agencies or independent scouts. In industrial films the actor's role is spokesperson or "front person" who works with charts, graphs, or projections that flash on-and-off screen as a narrative script is being read. Studio space is restricted, so acting style is more presentational and smaller in scope. Emphasis is placed on the educational nature of the script and an actor's ability to effectively communicate ideas, define technical terms, and share information in a relaxed and conversational manner.

One of the immediate challenges a stage actor faces in an industrial audition is the use of a teleprompter. The teleprompter, attached to a camera just below the lens, scrolls the script so the actor can read it and still maintain eye contact with the camera. Actors accustomed to memorizing character dialogue may find this medium technique distracting or inhibiting, and will need to gain self-confidence in reading their lines from a teleprompter without having to frequently look down as the script is being scrolled. Audit a professional workshop to get first-hand experience working with a teleprompter, and learn the technical terms used in working in front of and behind the camera.

A practical way to approach industrial film auditions is to secure a copy of the script in advance. It is more likely, however, that the script will only be made available at audition. Here is an abbreviated sample of an *infomercial,* a relatively short commercial in a television format. The goal of a product spokesperson is to have a pleasant voice, excellent vocal variety, and a relaxed posture while voicing a technical script that includes unique names and unusually detailed instructions with confidence and precision. In the exercise that follows it may be useful to tape record only the voice as you speak in a conversational tone to an imaginary audience seated directly in front of you. Don't forget to emphasize the *tag line* that concludes the infomercial and states the product slogan.

The new and improved HB LaserJet 27 X represents the new science of high volume printing and is designed to meet print quality and reliable standards of performance excellence. HB LaserJet 27 X is the latest in a series of ultra-precision toner cartridges guaranteed to increase high volume printing quality. HB LaserJet 27 X is committed to providing inventive, high-quality products and services. Simply fold the bands and insert the cartridge. LaserJet takes off from there! For toner cartridge returns please contact your authorized UPS drop-off center or call (516) 555-4102 for additional information. This special offer is not applicable to HP inkjet cartridges or non-HP cartridges. Warranty returns guaranteed. For preferred customer service please go immediately to the HB LaserJet helpdesk at www.hb.org/ret./recycle. If you are not using HB LaserJet 27 X toner, you're not getting HB high quality printing.

In rehearsing an infomercial, cultivate a resonant vocal tone to hold the attention of the listener and focus on the product or service being advertised. Play back the tape and chart any pausing, phrasing, or vocal patterns that may need adjustment to give added clarity or emphasis to the script. When confident that your vocal delivery reveals subtle nuances of thought and meaning to sell the product, videotape the infomercial in a recording studio setting to include *both* the voice and the body as an on-the-air preview audition.

Soap Operas

Soap operas, named for original television sponsor Proctor & Gamble products, are the most popular daytime dramas. The storylines are good old-fashioned melodramas and romances with lots of dream sequences, fantasies, and flashbacks to express a character's intention or motivation in an episode. Special attention is paid to the turmoil that takes place as characters struggle to express their inner anxiety or frustration. Although soap opera scripts are often superficial, serious soap actors play their roles with emotional intensity.

You will need to have an agent represent you for soap auditions. Principal roles are played by seasoned actors with formal contracts that extend over a number of years. Some soap actors may have recurring roles, and their contracts only extend the length of time the character role they are playing appears in a script. Beginning actors are more likely to audition as a *day player, under-5*, or *extra*. A day player may have more than five lines of spoken dialogue, but works only one day on a single episode of a soap opera. The under-5 actor works only one day as well, but has five lines of spoken dialogue or less. An extra, of course, has no speaking lines but may appear frequently in multiple episodes that call for crowd scenes, passersby, or background faces at social gatherings. A casting director selects day players and under-5s from headshots and résumés submitted by an actor's agent. Extras are identified as needed in open casting calls by staff assistants.

Situation Comedies

Situation comedies, or sitcoms, are a favorite family evening entertainment and feature a number of well-defined stock character roles. Each week, for about twenty-six minutes, these character types are actively engaged in a single episode objective: overcome an obstacle or resolve a problem that restores harmony and meaning to their lives. Sitcom actors have ample opportunity to invest a role with personal traits like comic flair, physique type, or peculiar vocal quality to give a distinct uniqueness to the role as it slowly emerges in weekly episodes. The sitcom has gained increased popularity in recent years with the addition of celebrity guests who appear unannounced as comic character types, or just play themselves, in individual episodes.

Sitcom actors are represented by professional agents who submit client headshots and résumés to prospective television producers or directors planning a new pilot series and request a client audition. Sitcom actors play the humor in each episode's *situation* to sustain the comic tempo of a scene. Physical movement is limited for the most part to the frame line of the camera, so character thoughts are communicated primarily through facial expressions, hand gestures, or limited physical movement. There also are numerous opportunities for actors to engage in buffoonery or even gross exaggeration in sit-coms, but moderation and restraint — rather than mayhem and mischief — are still the basic principles of a medium acting style.

AUDITION PRACTICES

Significant theatre experience alone may not be sufficient to make a distinction between your *theatrical* and *personality* persona needed to bridge the unspecified gaps in time, place, and action that characterize playing the medium. The vocal subtleties of *pausing* and *phrasing* are more important in interpreting a medium script than a traditional theatre script. The shared performance objective, however, remains the same: clarity and precision in voice and body to suggest truth and honesty.

In medium auditions you will be asked to *slate* first and then your audition will be videotaped. To slate, face the camera full-front and state your name *and* the name of the agency representing you. Standing on a floor mark, four to six feet from the camera, slowly turn in profile left and then right. The camera shot for slating is head and shoulder, and the script is held at mid-chest so eye contact is not distracting as you look down to read the audition text. For commercials, the casting director will cue you to read from a *storyboard*. The storyboard is a pictorial, scene-by-scene sequence of the script's action in a series of frames that illustrate the story of the product being advertised.

There are usually ten to twelve frames per storyboard, and each frame indicates character dialogue and stage directions. Study the storyboard and look for visual clues in the dialogue that help clarify the action and define the character. You will not be provided a copy of the script in advance, so ask your agent for information on the product's advertising scheme, character type, or age range. At some auditions you may be asked to read from cue cards rather than a storyboard.

At the end of a day's shoot, audition tapes are sent to the advertising agency representing the product and reviewed by clients as well as the director of the commercial. Callbacks follow for those who match the *look* or capture the *feel* of the commercial. If you are auditioning for a commercial or a soap, it is important to know the specific call time so consult with your agent for a schedule. The slate moment is part of the audition, so be brief but cordial in the introduction and demonstrate energy to voice the script.

It is a good rehearsal technique to videotape a practice slate of introducing yourself and then selling an imaginary product using descriptive lines of dialogue from a number of familiar commercials. The rehearsal period is also the time to practice keeping your eyes open when looking into a camera lens and exploring facial, vocal, or physical responses to subtly emphasize the nuances of a script. Finally, remember that auditions for the medium are pictorial and the performance is playing for an audience of *one* rather than many.

ADDITIONAL DIMENSIONS

Playing the medium in a distinctly personal style includes special attention to an audition wardrobe to help visualize familiar stock characters that appear in commercials, industrials, soap operas, or situation comedies. For example, auditioning for the role of an executive may require a three-piece suit, a mother figure may be dressed in a house dress or slacks and blouse, and an athlete in a jogging suit. Although the studio wardrobe staff may provide an occasional costume piece at auditions you should have at hand suggestive costume pieces that would be appropriate for these popular medium characters: lab coat for dentist or nurse, hat for cowboy, sweater for grandfather, overalls for repairman, or an apron for the waitress. In addition, do not wear white on video or you will appear ghost-like, red will bleed on tape and distort your features, and black may slim an actor down but you will *fade* into the background.

An audition wardrobe should complement rather than costume the character. The wardrobe can also target a product to a specific audience by suggesting social status, lifestyle, economic background, or occupation. You may want to copy current clothing trends in both design and detail. Medium characters often appear to have been dressed from a wholesale catalog or from a department store discount rack. The most practical approach to wardrobe is that the best way to sell a product is directly and simply, with a minimum of extravagance.

Do not neglect your physical appearance either. Exercise regularly, especially aerobics or jogging, and keep hair styled and neatly trimmed. Do not attempt to enhance your features with wigs, long sideburns, hair extensions, or a mustache. If you happen to wear glasses, use contact lenses instead; and remember that white, straight teeth is a medium trademark!

Focus attention on an explicit *visual* and *vocal* character portrait for the camera lens. The camera, like a lie detector machine, quickly registers visual deception and vocal deceit in an audition. One of the first steps to take in exploring an authentic visual and vocal character portrait for the medium is to analyze the *beats* in a character's dialogue. As you may recall from the Chapter One discussion, a beat begins when a character's intention begins and ends with its completion. Using beats as action maps should be one of the first steps in charting a character's changing attitude, mood, or point of view in a medium script.

Acting style in the medium is frequently determined by length of the camera shot. For example, in a *long shot*, ten to twelve feet from the camera, the acting style may be slightly exaggerated as the *body* does the acting; and in a *medium shot*, four to six feet from the camera, the style will be more restrained as character attitude or mood does the acting. In an intimate close-up shot, of course, reactions are more natural and *facials* do the acting. Understanding the length of a camera shot is also essential to determine the role your voice will play in a medium script. In a long shot the voice is slightly louder than polite conversation, in a medium shot the voice is more informal in tone, and in a close-up the voice is hushed or a soft whisper.

Learning to adjust body to the length of the camera shot is an invaluable insight to help reveal a character's subtext as well. Remember to direct subtle physical reactions to the camera focused on your character, and direct vocal responses to the nearest microphone positioned on the shoot by the boom operator. To highlight phrases or individual words, speed up the *pace* of dialogue rather than increase volume and don't lower your energy level while speaking in a close-up. Determine tempo by the action described in an individual episode, and only define performance adjectives or verbs after a careful analysis of the complete script.

Even if you have a non-speaking role, there is still an opportunity to sketch a meaningful character portrait. Remember that characters, even non-speaking ones, have objectives and *do* actions to achieve them. Define a non-speaking character with *ing* action words that express an immediate desire suggested in the script, and then determine the character's objective in trying to achieve that desire. Don't forget to explore sensory responses that may give a non-speaking character distinctive gestures or mannerisms.

Have a realistic understanding of your *type* — age range, physical appearance, personality — before auditioning for the medium. A character type, for example, has pronounced facial features and a flair for comedy; an urban type is clean shaven, stylish, and has a trendy look; a model type has striking good looks with high cheekbones, perfect teeth, strong jaw line, and a well-toned body; a suburban type is mainstream, casual, and has a semi-rugged outdoor look; and an off-beat type is rather average looking but a little quirky in voice or body. Once you know your type and are comfortable playing it make sure your professional photographs emphasizes that type in different poses and wardrobe.

REVIEW PRINCIPLES

Medium actors attract and hold listener attention with *sound* rather than movement. It is the sound that tells the story and it is visual images framed by the camera that create the backdrop of the story. That is why the standard medium acting style is conversational and immediate in tone to create a sense of familiarity between actor and viewer. There is also less emphasis in the medium on faithfully recording real-life experiences as accurately as the stage actor hopes to accomplish in a theatre performance. Here are some basic review principles to keep in mind that may help distinguish the medium actor from the stage actor.

- The medium actor reduces traditional theatre gestures and vocal tones to more moderately expressive gestures and more subtle vocal intonations.
- The medium actor imitates average people engaged in daily routine activities rather than heroic figures whose intention or motivation is suggested in the comprehensive analysis of a finely detailed complete script.
- The medium actor's acting style is essentially determined by the director and film editor in terms of pace and rhythm in the sequence of events and camera shots to be filmed.
- The medium actor provides character transitions through simple gestures (glance to side or a look over shoulder), limited movement (stand or sit), and facial or physical reactions (frown, raised eyebrow, shift weight, or cross legs) rather than through aggressive stage action or movement to punctuate changes in character attitude or mood.

Physical Image

Perhaps the most noticeable distinction between medium and stage actors is physical image. Unlike the stage performer, who may play a number of different character roles, the medium continues to favor performers who resemble a single physical type while projecting a camera-friendly personality that sells products. Medium actors play their age range, know their body type, and have significant vocal training. Medium actors also appear to be more aware of the physical inventory preferred in acting for the camera and can more easily identify their best feature (high cheekbones or forehead), least attractive feature (large nose or sagging chin), and most flattering feature (eyes or smile) in an audition.

The medium actor obviously places more emphasis upon facial features and has to be concerned with shape of face (oval or thin), forehead (high or low), cheeks (full or hollow), eyes (color and size), nose (flat or full), eyebrows (thick or thin), and posture (poised or stiff) to attract viewer attention. Medium actors are also more aware of personal mannerisms than stage performers and eliminate repetitive hand gestures, frequent smiling or frowning, and eyes blinking or nose twitching when speaking or reading a script from the teleprompter.

An expressive physical image for the medium actor is one that clearly highlights character posture and reveals character attitude or mood in a few selectively chosen gestures or body positions. A well executed physical image *externalizes* the action described in the storyline of a medium script and encourages the medium actor to be more spontaneous in shaping a character portrait with meaning and substance.

Vocal Image

The medium actor's vocal image also plays a significant role in successful auditions. The voice is clear, distinct, and capable of subtle shades of nuance that highlight individual words or phrases with clarity and color. It is interesting to note that vocal sounds and vibrations any performer hears when voicing dialogue or singing songs are not what an audience hears. In playing the medium, however, the way the voice sounds on professional recording equipment is the performer's vocal image.

An objective approach to determine your own vocal image is to have a professional recording tape made before an audition. The tape should include a ten to fifteen minute excerpt from a variety of speaking experiences that include an informal conversation, reading a narrative aloud, voicing a familiar commercial, and performing a brief monologue. Listen to the tape and take the following inventory — when you recover from the initial shock! — to determine if the vocal image that emerges has the quality and variety in expression needed for you to be successful in playing the medium. You may discover, however, that you need to work regularly with a voice and diction teacher or a vocal coach to achieve a more competitive vocal image for the medium.

Vocal Inventory

- Pitch — high, low, scratchy, or squeaky
- Rate — fast, medium, moderate, or slow
- Volume — soft, loud, medium, or varied
- Tone — sensual, bland, animated, or subdued
- Articulation — crisp, clipped, sloppy, or careless

- Resonance — full, flat, thin, or hollow
- Quality — weak, harsh, nasal, or husky
- Rhythm — staccato, uneven, sing-song, or fluid
- Accent — regional dialect, theatrical, or standard English
- Overall impression — pleasing, bland, soothing, or irritating

Now compare results of the vocal image with the inventory of your physical image. Do they complement each other? Is the relationship between voice and body images natural, or is there a contradiction or imbalance that may provoke confusion, distraction, or even humor in a medium audition? For example, a robust body and a thin, high-pitched voice or a thin body and a baritone voice. What adjustments, if any, will be necessary to reconcile the apparent physical and vocal imbalance?

END NOTES

Whether you are auditioning for the part of Joe the plumber or Rosie the homemaker, the basic fundamentals of character building in the medium are similar to the stage actor's approach to role-playing: your primary frame of reference is the *script*. Look for intention and motivation in the text and subtext, simplify actions and reactions, and avoid cliché approaches to characterization and interpretation. Creating a *character biography,* a theatre acting technique familiar to Stanislavsky-trained performers, may be helpful for beginning medium actors as well.

The biography approach to acting technique identifies the *givens* in a script — dialogue, exposition, background hints, or comments made by others in the text — and provides a rough outline of the character's essential qualities or traits. The actor then completes the tentative outline by incorporating more concrete details associated with the given qualities or traits to reveal an imagined life history that may have influenced character attitude or mood in the script. The actor also relies on the biography to integrate voice and body into a believable, realistic character portrait.

MEDIUM MODELS

The following samples of original medium scripts should give you a good indication of what to anticipate at an audition. Review the copy and pay particular attention to interpreting the text exclusively with the voice. You may need to transcribe each sample copy onto a sheet of paper and hold it mid-chest as you would at an audition. Remember that a pleasant and persuasive medium voice has excellent variety in pitch, rate, and volume as well as precise articulation and crisp pronunciation to give the presentation vitality and vividness. It may also be useful in voicing these sample scripts to play a different medium character type in each sample model.

Commercials

The *spokesperson* commercial format is the one most familiar to a television audience. It features a solo actor facing the camera and speaking directly to a listening audience. A commercial spokesperson communicates general information or specific facts about a product or service to engage the audience in an emotional experience and then encourages the listener to purchase the product or service. In playing the spokesperson commercial that follows, it is crucial that your voice be conversational and your facial expressions concise to suggest a real, flesh-and-blood character.

Sample Script 1

What a day! I was late getting up, late for breakfast, late for the car pool, and late for work! Well, at least I found time to put some *Cling On* in my hair! Look, I don't have a lot of time to waste with all the running around I do, so it's important that at least my hair doesn't look like a smorgasbord of knots and tangles. *Cling On* is great for a working stiff like me — no fuss and no fur. It's natural. No messy oil and no smelly gel. Just a few drops in the morning, and you're set to go. No more tire treads on your head! Take a tip from a real road runner. Slow down ... with *Cling On!*

In a commercial recording or voice-over audition for television and radio you will likely read the script in a small office or sound studio in front of a single microphone. Your audition may also be videotaped and kept on file for future reference. The *doubles* sample copy below features an off-camera announcer and an on-camera jogger. The commercial is targeted to an urban audience and the marketing scheme is to promote a new product line for potential customers who may only have time for a quick energy snack between hectic appointments or other scheduled events.

Sample Script 2

Open on medium shot of jogger
running across screen eating
bag of popcorn

	(Announcer) Excuse me.
	(Jogger) Look, I'm in a hurry here.
	(Announcer) Yes, I can tell.
Stops jogging and glances at watch	(Jogger) What do you want?
	(Announcer) You eat on the run, don't you?
	(Jogger) Yes, can't you see?
Off-camera announcer hands jogger Dingles donuts	(Announcer) Here, try some of these.
	(Jogger) What's this?
	(Announcer) Go ahead. Take a bite.
Takes a bite	(Jogger) Wow! This is really good!

	(Announcer) I thought you'd enjoy it.
	(Jogger) What are they?
	(Announcer) Dingles. Mini-donuts on the go.
	(Jogger) Mini-donuts on the go?
	(Announcer) Yes. For people on the go.
Takes another bite	(Jogger) Great idea!
	(Announcer) We thought so.
Starts jogging in place and glances at watch	(Jogger) Got to go.
	(Announcer) Don't forget your Dingles.
Takes Dingles	(Jogger) Terrific! Thanks for the treat.
	(Announcer) No. It's my pleasure.
Long shot of jogger now running across screen eating donut	(Jogger) I could run all day now. Dingles are delicious!
Off-camera	(Announcer) Dingles. Mini-donuts. The instant energy treat. Dingles. For busy people on the go. Dingles. Guaranteed to keep you running all day. Available at all Trudy's stores.

Medium shot of jogger running back toward announcer	(Jogger) Dingles are delicious!
Jogger runs across screen as announcer hands out more Dingles donuts.	
	(Announcer) Dingles. The instant energy mini-donut. Don't be left behind. Jog on over to Trudy's now!

Soap Opera

This original pilot of a soap opera segment is appropriate for both radio and television. Auditions for pilot scripts are primarily focused on casting actors who will give a solid reading of the script and play the character roles with emotional intensity. Although there is no guarantee that actors cast in a pilot episode will also play similar roles if the pilot is later optioned by a major radio or television network, it is not uncommon for agents, producers, and directors to identify talented actors in a pilot and consider them for roles in other commercials, industrials, or independent film projects.

The segment that follows is part of popular melodrama storylines fashionable in today's afternoon soap operas on both radio and television. The basic soap opera ingredients of intrigue, mystery, and suspense surround the characters at all times. There is also an abundance of anxiety, frustration, and emotional intensity to express each character's apparent intention or motivation in the episode. In playing these soap opera roles it will be important to highlight an *inner* and *outer* character to clarify the subtext of the action being described, and to cultivate a natural and conversational tone of expression, particularly in the *surprise* ending of the segment.

Midnight Madness

Opening Music
(An air of gloom and foreboding engulfs the scene as John and Mary open the door of a mysterious old abandoned house rumored to be haunted.)
JOHN: *(Knocks.)* This must be the place.
MARY: It's so dark here, John.
(Sound: Clock strikes twelve.)
JOHN: Let's go in, Mary.
MARY: What's that?
JOHN: I don't know.
(Sound: Cough. Cough.)
MARY: Someone's behind that door.
JOHN: You stay here. I'll be right back.
(Enters: Door creaks open.)
MARY: John!
(Enters: Door creaks closed.)
VOICE: Don't be frightened.
MARY: Who's that?
VOICE: Help me, please!
MARY: Where are you?
VOICE: Here, next to the fireplace.
MARY: I can't see you!
(Sound: Wind in the trees.)
VOICE: Just reach out to me.
MARY: I can't.
VOICE: Please!
MARY: Leave me alone!
(Sound: Chains rattling on stairs.)
VOICE: I'll come for you … later.
MARY: John!
JOHN: *(Suddenly appears.)* What's wrong, Mary?
MARY: I heard that voice again. It was calling me.
JOHN: It must have been the wind.
MARY: No! I heard that voice.
JOHN: Are you sure?
MARY: Yes! But I couldn't see anyone there.

JOHN: It must have been your imagination, again.

VOICE: Mary! Mary!

MARY: There! Do you hear? It's calling me!

JOHN: What? I didn't hear anything.

VOICE: Mary! Mary!

MARY: No! No! Leave me alone!

JOHN: Calm down, Mary! You're acting like a frightened child.

MARY: Can't you hear it, John?

JOHN: I didn't hear anything. But you know what the doctor said —

MARY: No, John. I swear. I swear. I heard it!

(Sound: Door creaks open. Chains rattle on stairs.)

VOICE: Mary! Mary! I'm coming for you!

MARY: No! No! Help me! Someone help me!

JOHN: Calm down, Mary! I'm going to have to call the doctor again.

MARY: Please, John. Don't call the doctor. Not again!

JOHN: Maybe it would be better.

MARY: I don't want to be locked up again! I'm not sick!

JOHN: You can't go on like this much longer.

VOICE: Mary! Mary! I'm coming for you.

MARY: No! I'm leaving! It's driving me mad!

JOHN: Wait for me, Mary! Good job, Bill! She's scared to death now.

VOICE: Did you like the voice?

JOHN: It was better this time, but still a little hollow.

VOICE: I'll work on it some more.

JOHN: The sound effects were really good.

VOICE: Did you like the chains?

JOHN: Yes, that was a nice touch.

VOICE: Same time tomorrow night?

JOHN: Same time tomorrow night.

VOICE: It shouldn't take much longer.

JOHN: No. She's scared to death right now.

VOICE: Well, I've got to pack up now.

JOHN: Thanks again, Bill.

VOICE: Adios!

JOHN: Bill! Don't forget to bring those sound effects!

VOICE: I'm on it!

JOHN: *(Smiles.)* It won't be long before she cracks up again.

LEGAL ACKNOWLEDGEMENTS

COPYRIGHT CAUTION

Copyright laws exist to protect the artistic and intellectual property rights of creators of original works. All creative works, such as theatre scripts and music lyrics, are considered copyrighted. There are, however, a number of "fair use" exceptions for educational or institutional purposes related to classroom performance. The theatre scripts and music lyrics in this collection are fully protected under the copyright laws of the United States, the British Empire, the Dominion of Canada, and all other countries of the Copyright Union. For additional information related to performance, full-scale production, or other available scripts by the contributors, please contact the author or author's representative at the address listed.

Chapter One: Audition Preview

Chapter Two: Audition Process

The League of the Unexpected, by George Sauer. Copright © 2008 by George Sauer. Reprinted by permission of the author. For additional information please contact the author at 45 Fuller Street, Dedham, Massachusetts 02026.

Chapter Five: Playing the Period

"Don Juan," by Moliere. Translation and adaptation by Dick Dotterer. Copyright © 1990 by Dick Dotterer. Reprinted by permission of Dramaline Publications. For additional information please contact the publisher at 36-851 Palm View Road, Rancho Mirage, California 92270.

Chapter Six: Playing the Contemporary

"Spell #7," by Ntozake Shange, from *Three Pieces.* Copyright © 1981 by Ntozake Shange. Reprinted by permission of St. Martin's Press. For additional information please contact the publisher at 175 Fifth Avenue, New York, New York 10010.

"Reckless," by Craig Lucas, from *Award Monologues for Women.* Copyright © 1989 by Craig Lucas. Published by Theatre Communications Group. Reprinted by permission of Theatre Communications Group. For additional information please contact the publisher at 520 8th Avenue, 24th Floor, New York, New York 10018.

"Napalm the Magnificent: Dancing with the Dark," by David S. Craig. Copyright © 2006 by David S. Craig. Published by Playwrights Canada Press, Toronto. Reprinted by permission of the author and Playwrights Canada Press. For additional information please contact the publisher at 215 Spadina Avenue, Suite 230, Toronto, ON, M5T 2C7, Canada.

"You Could Die Laughing," by Billy St. John. Copyright © 2003 by Billy St. John. Reprinted by permission of Samuel French, Inc. For additional information please contact the publisher at 45 West 25th Street, New York, New York 10010.

"Thank You for Flushing My Head in the Toilet, and other rarely used expressions," by Jonathan Dorf. Copyright © 2007 by Jonathan Dorf. All rights reserved. Reprinted by permission of the author and Playscripts, Inc. To purchase acting editions of this play, or to obtain stock and amateur performance rights, you must contact Playscripts, Inc. at one of the following: info@playscripts.com or http://www.playscripts.com. You may also phone 1-866-NEW-PLAY (639-7529).

"Sorrows and Rejoicings," by Athol Fugard. Copyright © 2001 by Athol Fugard. Published by Theatre Communications Group. Reprinted by permission of William Morris Agency on behalf of the author. For additional information please contact the author's agent at the William Morris Agency, 1325 Avenue of the Americas, New York, New York, 10019.

Chapter Seven: Playing the Musical and the Medium

ABOUT THE EDITOR

Gerald Lee Ratliff is the award-winning author of numerous articles and textbooks in classroom teaching strategies, performance studies, and theatre essays. He has served as President of the Speech and Theatre Association of New Jersey, Eastern Communication Association, Theta Alpha Phi, and the Association for Communication Administration.

He was awarded the Distinguished Service Award by the Eastern Communication Association, Theta Alpha Phi, and the Theatre Division of the National Communication Association. He has also been a Fulbright Scholar to China, served as USA delegate of the John F. Kennedy Center for the Performing Arts to Russia, and received multiple outstanding teacher awards for pioneering creative approaches to curriculum design and classroom instructional practices. Most recently, he was awarded the prestigious International da Vinci Diamond Award for his contribution to theatre.

Order Form

Meriwether Publishing Ltd.
PO Box 7710
Colorado Springs, CO 80933-7710
Phone: 800-937-5297 Fax: 719-594-9916
Website: www.meriwether.com

Please send me the following books:

_____	**The Theatre Audition Book 2 #BK-B309**	**$17.95**
	edited by Gerald Lee Ratliff	
	Playing monologues from contemporary, modern, period, Shakesperean and classical plays	
_____	**The Theatre Audition Book #BK-B224**	**$17.95**
	edited by Gerald Lee Ratliff	
	Playing monologues from contemporary, modern, period and classical plays	
_____	**Young Women's Monologs from Contemporary Plays #BK-B272**	**$15.95**
	edited by Gerald Lee Ratliff	
	Professional auditions for aspiring actresses	
_____	**Young Women's Monologs from Contemporary Plays #2 #BK-B300**	**$15.95**
	edited by Gerald Lee Ratliff	
	Professional auditions for aspiring actresses	
_____	**Millennium Monologs #BK-B256**	**$15.95**
	edited by Gerald Lee Ratliff	
	95 contemporary characterizations for young actors	
_____	**Audition Monologs for Student Actors #BK-B232**	**$15.95**
	edited by Roger Ellis	
	Selections from contemporary plays	
_____	**Audition Monologs for Student Actors II #BK-B249**	**$15.95**
	edited by Roger Ellis	
	Selections from contemporary plays	

These and other fine Meriwether Publishing books are available at your local bookstore or direct from the publisher. Prices subject to change without notice. Check our website or call for current prices.

Name: _____ e-mail: _____

Organization name: _____

Address: _____

City: _____ State: _____

Zip: _____ Phone: _____

❑ **Check enclosed**

❑ **Visa / MasterCard / Discover / Am. Express #** _____

Signature: _____   Expiration date: _____ / _____
     (required for credit card orders)

Colorado residents: Please add 3% sales tax.
Shipping: Include $3.95 for the first book and 75¢ for each additional book ordered.

❑ *Please send me a copy of your complete catalog of books and plays.*